M000081462

JEWISH LAW AS A JOURNEY
Finding Meaning in Daily Jewish Practice

David Silverstein

JEWISH LAW AS A JOURNEY

FINDING MEANING IN DAILY JEWISH PRACTICE

Yeshivat Orayta
Menorah Books

Jewish Law As A Journey
Finding Meaning in Daily Practice

First Edition 2017

Menorah Books
An imprint of Koren Publishers Jerusalem Ltd.

POB 8531, New Milford, CT 06776-8531, USA
& POB 4044, Jerusalem 9104001, Israel
www.menorah-books.com

Copyright © Rabbi David Silverstein, 2017

The publication of this book was made possible through
the generous support of *Yeshivat Orayta* and the *Fisher Family.*

All rights reserved. No part of this publication may be
reproduced, stored in a retrieval system or transmitted in any
form or by any means, electronic, mechanical, photocopying, or
otherwise, without the prior permission of the publisher, except in
the case of brief quotations embedded in critical articles or reviews.

ISBN 978-1-940516-75-2, *hardcover*

A CIP catalogue record for this title is
available from the British Library.

Printed and bound in the United States.

Contents

All biblical translations (unless otherwise noted) are adapted with modifications from the Stone Chumash.

All talmudic translations (unless otherwise noted) are adapted with modifications from the Artscroll Gemara.

Dedication

In June 2016, at the finish line of a charity triathlon for Kids in Crisis, Samuel Fisher z"l, known fondly to us as our beloved Sammy, collapsed inexplicably and could not be resuscitated. He was 24 years old and is survived by his girlfriend, brothers, parents, Holocaust survivor paternal grandparents, and Chinese maternal grandparents. Sammy was extremely close to his family, and an extraordinary bond of love ties the four brothers Jonathan, Sammy, Jeremy, and Benjamin together. While people around Sammy knew of his sincerity, empathy, and generosity, only since losing him have we more fully understood the profound imprint he left and the many lives he touched.

We remember Sammy for his exuberant passion for life—his own and those of the many people around him. Never judgmental, he embodied sensitivity and inclusiveness. We learned that, while at Harvard College, he often invited the homeless to join him for a warm meal. We remember Sammy the scholar, tirelessly searching for meaning with exceptional intellectual integrity. Emanating a quiet brilliance, he was a deep thinker. The year at Yeshivat Orayta and learning with Rav David Silverstein greatly shaped his outlook—constantly seeking to understand life, our role in the world, and how to be our best. In his weekly column "From the Heart of Jerusalem," published in *The Jewish*

Star (New York), he shared many small stories with big lessons: to live in the moment, appreciate what we have rather than covet what we do not, and seek positive change.

Despite straight As at Harvard and a rapid upward trajectory at Goldman Sachs, Sammy was humble, unassuming, and kind. A colleague explained that each year staff members with strong mentoring skills were selected to train new Goldman interns. While most staff were assigned either zero or one intern, Sammy was assigned three. He was so smart, but also giving, warm, and funny.

We are grateful for the opportunity to dedicate Rav David's book in Sammy's memory. Sammy would be inspired by this beautiful volume and share our enthusiasm for others to benefit, as he did, from the wisdom of Rav David.

Claire, David, Jonathan, Natalie, Jeremy, and Benjamin Fisher
Newton, Massachusetts

Acknowledgements

The idea for this book began about eight years ago when I started teaching a course on the philosophy of Jewish law to students at Yeshivat Orayta in Jerusalem. The process of researching these topics and discussing them with students, colleagues, family, and friends has been exceptionally rewarding.

My personal intrigue with finding meaning in Jewish observance is a direct outgrowth of the extraordinary home in which I was raised. My father, Rabbi Alan Silverstein, instilled in me a passion for Jewish learning. Our house was filled with books and articles of Jewish interest, and his own commitment to academic Jewish studies serves as a continued source of inspiration for my own Torah learning.

My father taught me that the study of Jewish texts cannot remain simply a matter of theoretical discourse. Through his work in his synagogue and world Jewry at large, he modelled for me the need to bring Jewish wisdom into the homes and hearts of Jews across the globe.

While my father—by his own example—kindled my love for study, my mother, Rita Silverstein, nurtured my Jewish heart and soul. It was her example that gave me my emotional bond with the Torah and the Jewish people. A child of Holocaust survivors, my mother truly felt the beauty and majesty of Jewish living. She passed those feelings on to me, as well as a deep sense of responsibility to keep our Jewish familial legacy alive. This book is a testament to my parents' exceptional ability to engender in the next generation the primacy of Jewish living and learning.

I am also blessed to have two exceptional grandmothers. My maternal grandmother, Cili Neufled, as well my grandmother-in-law, Anne Hiltzik, both serve as the matriarchs of our family. According to the Talmud, grandparents play a unique role in transmitting Judaism as a lived tradition. Nanny and Granny, each in their own unique way, remind my family of our own ancestral roots and continue to serve as our link to the great drama of Jewish history.

For the past nine years, I have been privileged to spend my days teaching Torah at Yeshivat Orayta in Jerusalem. Yeshivat Orayta is a truly unique Torah institution and is guided by exceptional educational and administrative staffs. In particular, I would like to thank Rabbi Binny Freedman, Rabbi Moish Kornblum, and Scott Apfelbaum, who believed in this project from its inception and worked tirelessly in helping bring this book to fruition.

Many close friends and students read parts of the book and offered critical and insightful observations. I would like to thank Rabbis Myles Brody, Dan Katz, Yakov Nagen, Yitzchak Blau, Judah Dardik, Dr. Benjy Bekritsky, Yaakov Landman, Adam Lavi, Corey Gold, as well as Eitan and Sophie Melamed, for all their sharp insights and critiques. Endless thanks as well to Shira Shreier and Meira Mintz for their exceptional editing of the early drafts of this book.

Working with the talented staff at Menorah Books, an imprint of Koren Publishers Jerusalem Ltd., has been a real privilege. Ashirah Yosefah guided the editing of this book with clarity and precision. The insights of the Menorah team really sharpened and enhanced the structure and style of the book. Special thanks as well to Tani Bayer for her extraordinary work on designing the book cover.

Lastly, I would like to thank my wife Lisa and our children Noa, Ezra, Elisheva and Michal. Lisa is my best friend and continues to inspire me every day with her endless dedication and passion for life. She carefully read and edited many of the chapters in this book and offered critical observations and insights about the book's style and substance. Without her love and support, the publication of this book would never have happened.

My children are an endless source of joy. They each bring so much color to my life and being able to spend time with them is the greatest gift.

This book is dedicated to the memory of Sam Fisher z"l. Sam was a student at Yeshivat Orayta in 2010-2011 and part of the inaugural group of students in my Philosophy of Jewish Law class. Sam was a brilliant student, constantly offering challenging and thoughtful observations both inside and outside the classroom.

Beyond his brilliance, however, Sam will always be remembered for his exceptional curiosity. His passion for the world of ideas was contagious. He simply loved to question. I remember so fondly the conversations we had together about many of the topics covered in this book.

Sam came to Yeshivat Orayta will lots of questions and spent his entire year looking to develop a worldview shaped and inspired by the wisdom of the Jewish tradition. Sam's tragic death sent shockwaves throughout the Yeshivat Orayta community. It is my hope that the publication of this book helps continue the legacy of Sam Fisher z"l and will inspire others to follow Sam's example in seeking to live a life dedicated to meaning and purpose.

I would like to thank the Fisher family for their extraordinary generosity in dedicating this book. I am privileged to have had both Sam z"l and his very special brother Jeremy in my *shiur* at Yeshivat Orayta, and it is a tremendous *zechut* to be able to partner with such an exceptional family. Both Sam z"l and Jeremy epitomize the *middot* of humility and curiosity, always asking challenging questions with respect and genuine intrigue. Clearly these unique attributes exemplified by Sam z"l and Jeremy are a reflection of the wonderful home in which they were raised.

I would also like to thank Sam's close friends Ariel and Aviva Menche for their tremendous efforts in making this dedication happen. Ariel and Aviva's care for others is truly inspiring, both modelling the biblical ethic of עולם של חסד יבנה.

David Silverstein
Modiin, Israel

Introduction

Jewish Law and the Delicate Balance Between Meaning and Authority

FRAMING THE CONVERSATION

One of the most dramatic episodes in the Torah describes the Israelites in a state of panic when their leader, Moshe, doesn't return from Mount Sinai as early as they expected him. In their haste to fill the void in leadership, the Israelites embark on the theologically disastrous venture of building a golden calf to serve as Moshe's replacement.

Using this story as a philosophical springboard, Ibn Ezra[1] notes that some "empty-minded" people wondered why it took so long for Moshe to descend from the mountain.[2] What could he possibly have been doing for forty days and forty nights? Should it really take that long to receive a list of 613 commandments?

In Ibn Ezra's view, the people who asked such questions were "empty-minded" because their wonderment was based on a faulty premise. They erroneously assumed that God's mitzvot (commandments) are

---

1. R. Avraham b. Meir Ibn Ezra, twelfth century, Spain.
2. Ibn Ezra, Ex. 31:18.

simply a list of rules to be observed solely out of a commitment to divine obedience. As a result, it should not have taken Moshe so long to receive a list of arbitrary statutes. They failed to realize, of course, that mitzvot are *not* a random list of actions that the Jewish people are intended to follow simply by virtue of God's authority. On the contrary, mitzvot are complex regulations that represent the physical actualization of a divine set of values and ideals.[3] In theory, Moshe could have spent a lifetime on Mount Sinai learning the secrets of divine providence, as well as the philosophical and theological meanings that underlie God's commandments.

In the view that Ibn Ezra criticizes, observance of the law is an end in itself. Obedience and compliance are God's ultimate goals for humankind. The spiritual meanings of the mitzvot are at best secondary, or at worst irrelevant. Ibn Ezra, on the other hand, argues passionately that the primary concern of halakha (Jewish law), is that our hearts are affected by the physical performance of mitzvot. Performance of mitzvot without an awareness of the larger philosophical vision of the commandments may be legally effective, at least *ex post facto*. However, in its ideal vision, Jewish law demands that a person understand the rationale behind the mitzvot, and therefore be spiritually transformed by the divine messages imbedded in mitzva observance.

THE PREFERENCE FOR AN OBEDIENCE-BASED MODEL

The tension that Ibn Ezra highlights is not new. The question of whether Jewish law should be observed primarily from a place of obedience, or from a vision of halakha that is rooted in deeper meaning and understanding, has been debated since the talmudic period. In the medieval era, for example, rabbinic scholars engaged in vigorous debates about the religious appropriateness of searching for rationales behind divine

---

3. For additional perspectives on this topic see, Rabbi Ethan Tucker, "Halakhah and Values," available at http://mechonhadar.s3.amazonaws.com/mh_torah_source_sheets/ CJLVHalakhahandValues.pdf?utm_source=CJLV+Ha%27azinu+5777&utm_campaign= CJLV+Ha%27azinu+5776&utm_medium=email; as well Rabbi Yuval Cherlow (in Hebrew), "The Image of a Prophetic Halakhah," available at http://www.bmj.org.il/ userfiles/akdamot/12/serlo.pdf. See also, Rabbi Cherlow's essay (in Hebrew), "The Thought of Nachmanides and its Influence on Halakhic Decision Making," at http://asif. co.il/download/kitvey-et/zor/zhr%2033/zhr%2033%20(11).pdf

legislation. Some rabbinic voices expressed strong condemnation of this quest, while others conveyed enthusiastic support. Rabbi Avraham Yitzhak HaKohen Kook,[4] however, notes that although many rabbinic scholars have strongly encouraged the search for *ta'amei hamitzvot* (reasons for the commandments), throughout Jewish history, there has been an asymmetry between the small number of books devoted to the meaning behind the law, and the amount of published scholarship devoted to outlining the legal and practical contours of the law itself.[5] This trend has continued into the twenty-first century, which has seen a literary explosion of books dedicated to detailed discussion of practical areas of Jewish law that were rarely given such extensive treatment in earlier eras in Jewish history.[6]

THE DISADVANTAGES OF EXCESSIVE FOCUS ON OBEDIENCE

While the increased focus on practical halakha certainly helps to make halakhic observance more accessible and facilitates greater commitment to halakhic detail, it generates its own set of challenges as well. After all, a commitment to Jewish law without a parallel commitment to the meaning behind Jewish ritual runs the risk of turning halakha into a formulaic set of laws without any larger spiritual vision. Moreover, overemphasis on authority without a corresponding focus on meaning creates a fundamental disconnect between the practitioner of the law and the law itself. How can we truly feel a sense of pride in our observance of God's commandments if we cannot articulate and appreciate the underlying messages of the halakha?

This attitude can also have serious effects on the way in which people observe Jewish law. After all, blind obedience can feel burdensome, and there is a natural tendency to look for ways to lighten the burden. When the focus of halakha is heavily tilted in the direction of

---

4. Rabbi Avraham Yitzhak HaKohen Kook, twentieth century, Latvia/Pre-War Israel.
5. Rabbi Avraham Yitzhak HaKohen Kook, *Talelei Orot with Commentary from Haggai London* (Eli: Machon Binyan Hatorah, 2011), 23-24.
6. For an important sociological discussion of this trend, see Dr. Chayim Soloveitchik's essay, "Rupture and Reconstruction," available at http://www.lookstein.org/links/orthodoxy.htm.

obedience, practitioners of Jewish law will naturally seek out ways to avoid the technical violation of halakhic mandates while neglecting to keep in mind the law's spiritual purpose. One example of this is the current effort to create gadgets that circumvent Shabbat laws. Certain trends in contemporary synagogue life, such as talking throughout services or leaving early for "kiddush clubs," may also be reflections of this disconnect.

Increased focus on the spiritual substance of halakha will hopefully help to address some of these challenges. If we were to truly understand the religiously transcendent messages that prayer and the Torah reading convey, would we be tempted to talk during the service or leave early in order to gain an additional few minutes of socializing with friends? If we had clarity about the spiritual goals of the details of Shabbat observance, would the possibility of an iPhone app that claims to permit the use of a smartphone on Shabbat sound religiously appealing? Readjusting the delicate balance between meaning and authority, with an added focus on understanding the religious messages of halakha, will not only facilitate a more mindful and meaningful observance of Jewish law, but will also promote a more intense commitment to the details of halakha.

TA'AMEI HAMITZVOT AS THE SOURCE OF JEWISH PRIDE

Maimonides (the Rambam),[7] one of the most important thinkers of his time, affirmed the need to understand the reasons for God's commandments (*ta'amei hamitzvot*). He argues forcefully that all mitzvot have some rational basis and serve some ethical, societal, or personal religious function.[8] To substantiate his view, he cites the verse from Deuteronomy that tells of the gentile nations when they "hear all those statutes (*chukkim*)," they will respond by saying, "Surely this great nation is a wise and understanding people!" (Deut. 4:6). The Rambam notes

---

7. Rabbi Moshe b. Maimon, twelfth century, Spain/Egypt.
8. *Guide of the Perplexed* 3:31. Cf. *Hilkhot Temura* 4:13, where the Rambam writes that the majority of the mitzvot are intended to "improve one's character and make one's conduct upright." Translation from: https://yaakovbieler.wordpress. com/2016/02/14/a-possible-explanation-for-rambams-curious-turn-of-phrase/

that if a significant number of the 613 mitzvot have no rational basis, what would compel the gentile world to find beauty in a life dedicated to God's commandments?

The Maharal[9] goes one step further, utilizing the same proof-text cited by the Rambam to argue that not only do the general categories of mitzvot have some clearly explicable inherent meaning, but even the seemingly arbitrary details of Jewish practice are rooted in divine ideals.[10] According to the Maharal, just as God has a specific reason for instituting the laws of sacrifices, for example, there must similarly be some religious message inherent in the obligation to use certain animals for specific sacrifices.

According to this model, the quest to find the rationale behind the laws facilitates a greater identification with the divine messages that the laws attempt to convey. The Torah imagines that the gentile world will look at the laws of the Torah and marvel at its wisdom. Understanding the transcendent values that the law embodies affirms this vision of the Torah's self-identity and allows the Jewish people to similarly understand how their God-given set of laws transforms them into a "great nation."

TAAMEI HAMITZVOT AS THE VEHICLE FOR ACCESSING THE SPIRITUAL MESSAGES OF THE LAW

Articulating a sophisticated vision of *ta'amei hamitzvot* affirms the spiritual significance of Jewish law and the critical function of mitzvot in actualizing these values in the real world. This position is eloquently expressed by the Shela.[11]

In order to fully understand the position of the Shela, let's imagine what Jewish law would look like if certain physical objects simply never came into existence. For example, Jewish civil law deals with injury cases involving pits, animals, and fire. Imagine for a moment that these things were never created. What would happen to their accompanying halakhot? The Shela answers that the spiritual messages of the halakha exist *independently* of their physical manifestations. In such a scenario,

9. Rabbi Yehudah Loew b. Betzalel, sixteenth century, Prague.
10. *Tiferet Yisrael* ch. 7.
11. Rabbi Yeshaya Horowitz, sixteenth/seventeenth centuries, Prague.

therefore, these divine ideals would simply find expression through some other physical medium.[12]

The Shela takes this idea even further, arguing that the spiritual substance of the law existed even during the time of Adam and Eve. Since they lived in the spiritual bliss of the Garden of Eden, halakha expressed itself at that time exclusively in spiritual terms. However, as humanity moved away from the intense spirituality of that time towards a more physically-oriented existence, the expression of Jewish law shifted and the practical performance of mitzvot became the most effective medium to experience divine values in a physical space. The laws themselves thus serve as "spiritual entry points" to experience God. Since halakha is rooted in transcendental divine virtues, each time we observe Jewish law, we also act as a conduit for bringing divine energy into the world.

Interestingly, Rabbi Yehuda Amital[13] argues that the requirement to experience the eternal values of the law through the physical medium of practical halakha is the result of a historical shift that occurred after the Jewish people received the Torah at Sinai. Because of the spiritual greatness of our forefathers, they were able to tap into the religious messages of the Torah even without observing the practical halakha itself.[14] Rabbi Amital notes that "the *avot* did not observe the mitzvot in the sense in which we observe them. They did not put on tefillin or shake the lulav. But they understood and appreciated the underlying messages of the mitzvot."[15] After the giving of the Torah, by contrast, God insisted that the spiritual messages underlying the law could be accessed only through firm commitment to halakhic detail.

Thus, Rabbi Amital writes:

> Avraham, Yitzhak, and Yaakov were able to intuit these basic notions, which *Chazal* understand as being comparable to

---

12. *Shaar HaOtiot, Shaar Aleph, Emet VeEmuna,* pp. 48b, 70a.
13. Rabbi Yehuda Amital, twentieth/twenty-first centuries, Israel.
14. See also the comments of the *Nefesh HaChayim* 1:21, cited in *Minchat Asher Bereishit* (Jerusalem: Machon Minchat Asher, 2007), 273.
15. Rabbi Yehudah Amital, *Yaakov Was Reciting the Shema,* a Sicha for Shabbat from the Roshei Yeshiva Yeshivat Har Etzion, adapted by Dov Karoll, http://etzion.org.il/en/yaakov-was-reciting-shema.

performing the mitzvot in the time before the Torah was given. In the time after the giving of the Torah, these underlying ideas need to be integrated with practice.[16]

Beyond connecting us to the ideals rooted in God Himself, searching for the profound messages that the mitzvot convey also ensures our connection to the world of the patriarchs and matriarchs and affirms our commitment to seeing our own halakhic identity as a natural outgrowth of their spiritual worldview.

TA'AMEI HAMITZVOT AND THE LEGAL FRAMEWORK OF HALAKHA

In addition to expressing the themes and messages that underlie observance of the law, analyzing the rationale behind the commandments also helps us to grasp the unique legal framework of Jewish law. For example, in multiple instances, the Torah refers to the requirement for the Jewish people to "be holy." What is the legal force of this directive? Is this simply a biblical homily, or is there some halakhic consequence associated with this command? The Rambam writes that some codifiers erroneously counted the imperative to "be holy" as its own positive mitzva.[17] In reality, the Rambam claims, "*kedoshim tehiyu*" is not an independent commandment, but is rather the meta-value that drives the entire system. The goal of halakhic living is to be holy, and the quest for holiness requires us to perform mitzvot as if they are meant to be transformative.

Similarly, Rav Kook notes that one of the most distinct features of Mosaic legislation is its ability to link specific commandments to a larger spiritual vision that motivates the legal conversation.[18] According to Rav Kook, the prophets, by contrast, focused nearly exclusively on the overarching vision of the halakha, while neglecting to place a parallel emphasis on the mechanics of the law and how the details serve as an application of the larger vision. Reacting to the failure of the pro-

---

16. Ibid.
17. *Book of Mitzvot, shoresh* 4.
18. Rabbi Avraham Yitzchak Hakohen Kook, "*Chakham Adif MiNavi*," cited in *Orot* (Jerusalem: Mossad HaRav Kook, 2005), 120–121.

phetic model of the law, the rabbis of the Talmud placed extraordinary emphasis on the details of halakha in order to ensure the preservation of Jewish identity and society. It is for this reason that the Talmud states, "A sage is preferable to a prophet."[19] After all, while the prophet can clearly articulate the vision and message that governs the law, it is the sage who is able to guide the people and safeguard the observance of the law itself.

According to Rav Kook's conception, the ideal model of adjudication is the Mosaic one. This paradigm places the details of the law in context and, as a result, presents a holistic vision of what the law is meant to facilitate. Nahmanides (the Ramban)[20] offers a powerful example of this model, noting that after listing details of biblical monetary law, the Torah concludes by stating that the overarching principle is "to be good and just in the eyes of God."[21] Similarly, after delineating many of the details of the laws of Shabbat, the Torah articulates the larger directive of Shabbat as "a day of rest."[22]

What these examples indicate is that the search for the larger religious messages inherent in traditional Jewish observance is not some external exercise imposed on the law itself. Rather, Jewish law is predicated on viewing the mitzvot as the medium for religious transformation. Therefore, the search for additional clarity regarding the spiritual substance of halakha furthers the Torah's self-declared goals.

TA'AMEI HAMITZVOT AND THE BALANCE OF MEANING AND AUTHORITY

While this book attempts to shift the contemporary conversation of halakha back towards an increased focus on the search for meaning in halakhic detail, this reorientation still validates the critical role of obedience and submission in forming a holistic commitment to halakha. Viewing halakha from a place of *both* meaning and authority is crucial in order to facilitate commitment to Jewish law in its entirety. On a

---

19. *Bava Batra* 12a.
20. Rabbi Moshe b. Nachman, twelfth/thirteenth centuries, Spain/Israel.
21. Deut. 6:18.
22. Ex. 34:21; Ramban, Lev. 19:2.

pragmatic level, exclusive focus on the world of meaning can create challenges regarding mitzvot whose rationale is simply not known. In a model devoted solely to the transformative messages of halakha, how are we supposed to be religiously moved by rules whose meaning we do not understand? It is precisely in these moments that our broader commitment to obedience becomes critical.

Understanding the rationale behind the commandments is crucial to ensure that Jewish law facilitates its goal of religious transformation. Nonetheless, the reasons themselves are not *why* we observe the law. In fact, despite being one of the greatest proponents of *ta'amei hamitzvot*, the Rambam declares, "If [one] cannot find a reason or a motivating rationale for a practice, he should not regard it lightly."[23]

Beyond the pragmatic problem, a halakhic approach that is exclusively committed to meaning is fundamentally compromised from a philosophical perspective. While excessive focus on obedience can create an observance paradigm that is formulaic and dry, overemphasis on meaning can generate a halakhic model that is self-centered and ultimately rooted in the ego. If we were to observe *only* those rituals that we fully understand and find personally meaningful, we would effectively be engaging in a commitment to ritual in which the self is the primary object of worship. Embracing the need for periodic submission by observing even those commandments that we do not understand ensures that our observance of halakha is truly a self-transcendent exercise.[24] As Rabbi Joseph B. Soloveitchik[25] ("the Rav") notes, "The

---

23. Laws of Me'ila 8:8, translation at http://www.chabad.org/library/article_cdo/aid/1062936/jewish/Meilah-Perek-8.htm.
24. For alternative suggestions regarding the role of submission in halakhic discourse, see Rabbi Hertzl Hefter, "Surrender or Struggle: The Akeidah Reconsidered," at http://www.thelehrhaus.com/timely-thoughts/surrender-or-struggle-akeidah. See also the response of Rabbi Tzvi Sinetsky, "There's No Need to Sacrifice Sacrifice: A Response to Rabbi Hertzl Hefter," at http://www.thelehrhaus.com/timely-thoughts/2016/12/18/theres-no-need-to-sacrifice-sacrifice-a-response-to-rabbi-herzl-hefter. See also Rabbi Ethan Tucker, "Halakhah and Values," at http://mechonhadar.s3.amazonaws.com/mh_torah_source_sheets/CJLVHalakhahandValues.pdf?utm_source=CJLV+Ha%27azinu+5777&utm_campaign=CJLV+Ha%27azinu+5776&utm_medium=email.
25. Rabbi Joseph B. Soloveitchik, twentieth century, United States.

religious act begins with the sacrifice of one's self, and ends with the finding of that self. But man cannot find himself without sacrificing himself prior to the finding."[26]

The quest to understand the rationale that underlies the mitzvot assumes that we should strive to articulate the spiritual messages of the halakha. Ideally, we attempt to minimize the number of times that we need to invoke the submission model. Nonetheless, the presence of some laws whose meaning remains mysterious serves an important religious purpose. Such laws provide a periodic opportunity for us to surrender our intellectual capacities before the divine command and remind ourselves that halakha allows us to find our true selves by connecting to values that transcend our own egos. Moreover, by affirming our commitment to those laws whose reasons we may find personally or ethically challenging, we ensure that the Torah is, in fact, the source of our value system, and not simply an ancient text that validates the contemporary *zeitgeist*.

Additionally, a commitment to halakha that is exclusively rooted in meaning fails to affirm the central roles of trust and confidence in developing a meaningful relationship to God. It is possible to articulate the meaning and rationale behind the overwhelming majority of mitzvot. The awareness of these ideals should ensure that a practitioner of Jewish law feels confident and proud of the divine values that the halakhic system represents. It is against this philosophical background that we approach those mitzvot whose rationale is still a mystery. Here, a commitment to an ethic of submission and the observance of these currently inexplicable laws affirm our trust and confidence in God's benevolence. After all, the same God who is the source of those mitzvot that we understand is also the source of the mitzvot that we do not yet fully comprehend. Refocusing our efforts on understanding the transcendent messages of the law, while ensuring that our commitments are not contingent on understanding these values, most authentically captures the spiritual vision of halakha.

---

26. *Divrei Hashkafa*, 254-255, cited in *Lecture #24: The Akeida* by Rabbi Chayim Navon, http://etzion.org.il/en/akeida.

ABOUT THIS BOOK: A SPIRITUAL JOURNEY

As indicated above, this book is an attempt to reorient the contemporary conversation of halakha towards an increased focus on meaning in halakhic observance, while simultaneously validating the need to periodically submit to those statutes whose rationale is not yet clear. The title of the book is *Jewish Law as a Journey*. Like a journey, Jewish law is designed to move us from one spiritual place to another. An awareness of the ideals that underlie the halakha will foster a commitment to view the practice of Jewish living as a spiritual system intended to enable religious movement.

I have attempted to outline the spiritual messages of many of the central mitzvot that we encounter in the course of a given day. In theory, each chapter is self-contained; however, in order to fully appreciate the overarching vision and the profound values likely to be encountered in a twenty-four-hour period of halakhic commitment, I encourage you to first read the book in its entirety, and only afterwards, review specific chapters of interest.

I used three basic criteria to determine which daily mitzvot to analyze in this book. First, I chose mitzvot that are most familiar to large segments of the Jewish world. The chapters discussing kippa, tzitzit, tefillin, *talmud Torah,* prayer, *shema,* mezuza, and washing before meals are representative of this category. Some of these rituals are traditionally performed only by men, but I decided to include them nonetheless since the values they underscore are relevant to all Jews irrespective of gender. Moreover, it is these expressions of Jewish observance that are often the most well-known and therefore serve as a familiar starting point for a discussion of Jewish law that is rooted in meaning and virtue.

The second category I included are mitzvot that provide religious and spiritual context to halakhic life as a whole. Following in God's ways and loving God are examples of this type of mitzva. The last category includes those rituals that provide daily opportunities for divine encounters, but tend to get overlooked when discussing Jewish Law and the quest for meaning. *Birkat HaTorah,* washing one's hands in the morning, and the bedtime shema are mitzvot that fall into this category.

I have consciously avoided any contentious and controversial topics. While these issues are of great significance and dominate much of the public dialogue about halakha, they unfortunately tend to overshadow the spiritual opportunities provided by the overwhelming majority of mitzvot, which are agreed upon by Jews irrespective of ideological orientation.

Last, I have tried to cite a broad spectrum of source material, referencing both traditional as well as academic works, thus providing a maximally holistic vision of halakhic ideals and allowing the reader access to an ever-expanding Jewish library.

In the final chapter of the book, I include meditative reflections, based on the traditional sources discussed in the book, that can be utilized to facilitate a more mindful observance of halakha. My hope is that this book will serve as a daily guide to help facilitate a more passionate and meaningful commitment to the beauty and wonder that a life dedicated to Jewish law seeks to embody.

Chapter 1

Modeh Ani

Giving Thanks and Living in the Moment

Aday committed to the observance of Jewish law is a spiritual journey. From the moment we get up in the morning until we lie down at night, Jewish law offers endless opportunities for meaningful divine encounters. The journey begins with the ever-difficult task of getting out of bed.

A poem by the Native American leader, Tecumseh, offers a powerful insight in guiding our first thoughts as we slowly open our eyes to begin a new day. According to Tecumseh, "When you arise in the morning, give thanks for the food and for the joy of living. If you see no reason for giving thanks, the fault lies only in yourself."[1] Tecumseh challenges us to see our initial encounter with conscious reality as an opportunity to give thanks. If we are unable to express gratitude, then we should immediately begin a reflection on what exactly is preventing us from appreciating what we have.

The Jewish version of Tecumseh's poem is a short piece of liturgy known as *Modeh Ani.*

---

1. https://www.goodreads.com/author/quotes/8340698.Tecumseh.

According to Jewish law, immediately upon waking up, we are required to declare, "I thank You, living and eternal King, for giving back my soul in mercy. Great is your faithfulness." Rabbi Jonathan Sacks[2] notes that, according to the Talmud, sleep is considered one-sixtieth of death. Therefore, waking "is a miniature rebirth." According to Rabbi Sacks, "by expressing gratitude at the fact of being alive, we prepare ourselves to celebrate and sanctify the new day."[3]

Despite the widespread acceptance of this prayer by codifiers of Jewish law, the text of the *Modeh Ani* prayer is unique for a variety of reasons. First, it contains no mention of God's name. Second, it is said prior to the required morning handwashing, and is thus in conflict with the halakhic insistence on avoiding reciting supplications with ritually impure hands. Finally, *Modeh Ani* seems unnecessary, since the more elaborate and detailed prayer of *Elokai Neshama*, which expands on the themes of *Modeh Ani*, is recited daily as part of the morning service. Given these perplexities, what is the theological value of reciting *Modeh Ani*?

THE TALMUDIC STORY: A STORY OF REDEMPTION

While the exact text of *Modeh Ani* is not found in the Talmud, there are talmudic passages that provide precedent for the requirement to acknowledge God immediately upon rising. For example, we are taught:

> When one wakes, he says: My God, the soul You placed within me is pure, You fashioned it within me, You breathed it into me, You safeguard it within me, and eventually, You will take it from me and restore it to me in the time to come. As long as the soul is within me, I thank You Hashem, my God, and the God of my forefathers, Master of all worlds, Lord of all souls. Blessed are You, Hashem, Who restores souls to dead bodies.[4]

2. Rabbi Jonathan Sacks, twenty-first century, England.
3. Rabbi Jonathan Sacks, *The Koren Siddur with Introduction, Translation, and Commentary by Rabbi Jonathan Sacks* (Jerusalem: Koren, 2009), 5.
4. Berakhot 60b.

One of the central themes in this blessing is the relationship between waking up in the morning and the resurrection of the dead. This is highlighted by the Talmud Yerushalmi, which quotes the view of R. Yanai, stating that when we wake up in the morning, we should recite the blessing of "He who resurrects the dead."[5] Similarly, Lamentations Rabba notes that through the daily experience of waking up, we solidify our belief in God, who will ultimately "wake up" the dead from their sleep.[6] Appreciating the miracle of life allows an individual to use this daily moment of wonder to tap into Judaism's broader theological tenets. In particular, the amazement of our first breaths each morning enables us to fortify our belief in the ultimate redemption and resurrection of the dead.

It seems particularly appropriate to reflect upon this theme of resurrection when we wake up in the morning. For many Jews, the belief in an ultimate resurrection may be difficult to grasp. Waking up from sleep, by contrast, is an experience to which everyone can relate. Think about all the millions of potential health challenges that could prevent a person from indeed waking up anew each day. By acknowledging God's hand in the act of waking, we affirm that what we perceive to be ordinary is actually extraordinary.

Moreover, by heightening our sensitivity to the miraculous, we assert our commitment to belief in the ultimate resurrection. Just as God allows the living to wake up anew each day, He will ultimately awaken the dead as well.

THE *MISHNA BERURA:* LIFE AS A GIFT

The need to formally acknowledge God's involvement in the miracle of waking up in the morning is codified in the *Shulchan Arukh.*[7] Referring to the talmudic blessing cited above, the *Shulchan Arukh* states that when we wake up, we must recite the blessing of "My God, the soul You placed within me is pure (*Elokai Neshama*)."[8]

---

5. Y. Berakhot 4:2.
6. Lamentations Rabba (Buber Edition) 3.
7. Rabbi Yosef Karo, sixteenth century, Sefad.
8. *Shulchan Arukh*, Orach Chayim 46:1.

After the requirement to recite the *Elokai Neshama* prayer, the Shulchan Arukh contains a long list of blessings that we are required to recite each day. For example, when we get dressed, we bless God as "He who clothes the naked." Similarly, upon standing up straight, we affirm that God "straightens the bent."

The *Mishna Berura*[9] makes a fascinating observation articulating the exact nature of this list of blessings. According to the *Mishna Berura*, the requirement to recite these benedictions is rooted in the talmudic prohibition against experiencing any type of physical benefit without first thanking God.[10] This formulation of the *Mishna Berura* explains why, for example, we must recite a blessing before getting dressed; wearing clothes is physically beneficial, and we must therefore thank God before deriving benefit from our clothing.

The blessing of *Elokai Neshama*, by contrast, seems more difficult to categorize. What physical benefit does this blessing relate to? The answer is that the simple act of being alive provides physical benefit, and the blessing is therefore actually an expression of gratitude for the gift of life itself! The blessing of *Elokai Neshama* thus not only helps us utilize our experience of waking up in order to reaffirm our connection to the belief in an ultimate resurrection, but the initial moments of one's day offer the opportunity to thank God and express our appreciation for the gift of life.

RABBEINU YONAH OF GERONDI: THANKING GOD IN COMPROMISED SITUATIONS

So far, our discussion has centered on the blessing of *Elokai Neshama*. While this blessing has its roots in the Talmud and thematically mirrors much of *Modeh Ani*, the question of the history and philosophy of the *Modeh Ani* blessing still remains.

Both the *Shulchan Arukh* and the Rambam rule that when arising in the morning, we should recite the *Elokai Neshama* prayer.[11]

---

9. Rabbi Yisrael Meir Kagan, twentieth century, Radin.
10. *Mishna Berura,* Orach Chayim 46:1:1.
11. *Shulchan Arukh,* Orach Chayim 46:1; Rambam, *Laws of Prayer and the Priestly Blessing* 7:3.

However, the *Kesef Mishneh*[12] cites the view of Rabbeinu Yonah,[13] who significantly qualifies the ruling of the Rambam. According to Rabbeinu Yonah, the requirement to recite *Elokai Neshama* without delay upon waking applied only in talmudic times, when Jews were particularly pious and scrupulous in their observance of purity rituals. Jews living in the post-talmudic era are not on the same level of piety, and they therefore should recite *Elokai Neshama* only after washing their hands in the morning.[14]

This ruling of Rabbeinu Yonah created a theological vacuum. On the one hand, there is significant religious value in dedicating the first moments of every day to thanking God. The Rambam highlights this ethic, explaining that *Elokai Neshama* should be recited while "still [on one's] bed."[15] Rabbeinu Yonah's ruling means, however, that we cannot acknowledge the divine gift immediately upon waking, since we must *first* ritually wash our hands and, only then, recite the *Elokai Neshama* prayer. The challenge became how to fill these few crucial moments of the day with meaningful reflection, while abiding by Rabbeinu Yonah's requirement of washing hands before reciting God's name.

The *Modeh Ani* prayer, in which the actual name of God is not mentioned, was instituted as a solution to this problem. Because God's name is not explicitly invoked in the text, the *Mishna Berura* notes that there is no halakhic problem with reciting *Modeh Ani* even before washing hands. The practice of reciting *Modeh Ani* is codified by both the *Magen Avraham*[16] and the *Mishna Berura*.[17] Citing tannaitic material, the *Mishna Berura* notes that the *Modeh Ani* text affirms our faith in God, who returns the souls we "deposit" with Him before going to bed.

---

12. Rabbi Yosef Karo (author of *Shulchan Arukh*), sixteenth century, Sefad/Israel.
13. Rabbi Yonah b. R. Avraham Gerondi, thirteenth century, Barcelona.
14. *Kesef Mishneh, Laws of Prayer and the Priestly Blessing* 7:3.
15. Rambam, *Laws of Prayer and the Priestly Blessing* 7:3.
16. Rabbi Avraham Gombiner, seventeenth century, Poland; *Orach Chayim* 4:28.
17. *Mishna Berura, Orach Chayim* 1:8.

RABBI YAKOV NAGEN: *MODEH ANI* AND
THE POWER OF THE MOMENT

Besides the talmudic themes found in the *Elokai Neshama* prayer, *Modeh Ani* provides additional theological messages. Rabbi Dr. Yakov Nagen[18] offers an important insight into the unique theology of the *Modeh Ani* prayer.[19] Citing Rabbi Nahman of Breslov (Rebbe Nachman),[20] Rabbi Nagen argues that being asleep as opposed to being awake is not exclusively a physiological status. More broadly, Rebbe Nachman defines sleep as "the removal of consciousness." According to Rabbi Nagen, it is possible to be in a non-conscious state even while physically awake. This state of "sleep" most likely occurs when we are heavily invested in thoughts of past mistakes or anxieties about the future. Even though we might be physically awake, we closely resemble someone who is asleep, since focus and consciousness are completely disconnected from our present reality. When we are totally focused on the present, by contrast, we are considered fully awake, since our mental energies are completely committed to the present moment. Rabbi Nagen explains:

> The *Modeh Ani* prayer is a prayer thanking God for returning to me my soul and my life. [By reciting *Modeh Ani*,] I affirm the fact that I do not assume my life to be a given. Rather, I see life as a gift from God. [I declare] that I received *this day* as a gift from God, but have not yet received [any days in the future]. When I receive these [future] days, I will thank God as well. In the interim, I am going to live *this day* [to its fullest]. Today is not simply a means towards tomorrow or just a consequence of yesterday. Rather, [living today fully] is a goal in and of itself.[21]

In support of his view, Rabbi Nagen cites a fascinating passage in the Talmud, a debate between Hillel and Shammai about the appropriate

---

18. Rabbi Yakov Nagen, twenty-first century, Israel.
19. Rabbi Yakov Nagen, "תודה על התודה" https://yakovn.wordpress.com/tag /.
20. Rabbi Nachman of Breslov, eighteenth century, Ukraine.
21. Rabbi Yakov Nagen, "תודה על התודה" https://yakovn.wordpress.com/tag/.

way to prepare for Shabbat.[22] Shammai's practice was to eat the entire week with the Shabbat meals in mind. For example, whenever he would find a nice animal for consumption, he would put it aside and declare, "This is for Shabbat." As soon as he would find a better animal, he would eat the first one, while designating the second animal for the Shabbat meal. Hillel, by contrast, would eat whatever food he had available on a given day. This practice ensured that each day he was acting for the sake of Heaven in the firm belief that he would find food for Shabbat, as it says in the verse, "Blessed is God each and every day."[23] According to Hillel's approach, every day was lived for itself, not as a step toward something else. Living each day for the sake of Heaven ensures the sanctity of every day.

Rabbi Nagen's insight adds another layer to our understanding of the *Modeh Ani* prayer. In addition to reflecting on the resurrection of the dead and the miraculous nature of daily living, *Modeh Ani* reminds us of the opportunities that *each* day provides. When we wake up in the morning, we immediately reflect on what we hope to accomplish on that specific day. This reflection should not be viewed as a task to cross off a list. Rather, as Rabbi Joseph B. Soloveitchik[24] emphasizes, each of us is divinely invested with a unique purpose and mission that we are obligated to maximize during our short time on this earth.[25] Every day offers a powerful opportunity to further this crucial religious goal.

RABBI MENAHEM MENDEL SCHNEERSON: ORGANIC GODLINESS

An additional perspective is beautifully articulated by Rabbi Menachem Mendel Schneerson, the Lubavitcher Rebbe.[26] According to Rabbi Schneerson, it is not coincidental that *Modeh Ani* is recited specifically *before* one washes hands in the morning. Reciting *Modeh Ani* in

22. Beitza 16a.
23. Ps. 68:20.
24. Rabbi Joseph B. Soloveitchik, twentieth century, United States.
25. Rabbi Joseph B. Soloveitchik, *Yemei Zikaron*, ed. Moshe Krone (Jerusalem: World Zionist Organization, 1986) 9-29.
26. Rabbi Menachem Mendel Schneerson (the Lubavitcher Rebbe), twentieth century, United States.

an impure state highlights the fact that "all the impurities of the world cannot contaminate the *Modeh Ani* of a Jew. It is possible that a person may be lacking in one respect or another, but his *Modeh Ani* always remains perfect."[27]

What exactly is the "*Modeh Ani* of a Jew," and how does it remain eternally perfect? Rabbi Schneerson explains that, based on mystical Jewish texts, there are five levels to the Jewish soul:

> While the first four levels have the potential to become impure, the fifth level, *Yechida*, is constantly united with the essence of God; there is no connection to or possibility whatsoever for defects and impurities… It always remains perfect and whole. This also explains why there is no mention of God's name in the *Modeh Ani* prayer. Since *Modeh Ani* comes from the level of *Yechida*, the essence of the soul, the thanksgiving expressed by the essence of the soul, is directed to the essence of God, which is not contained in any name.[28]

In other words, the recitation of *Modeh Ani* specifically at a time when we are somewhat groggy captures the more organic and intrinsic connection that we have with God. We often think of our relationship with God from the philosophical perspective, but philosophical inquiry requires focus and attention. Moreover, philosophical proofs can easily be refuted, leading us to search for an alternative model to substantiate our faith commitments. The *Modeh Ani* aspect of Jewish identity, by contrast, is not linked to any philosophical construct. It transcends formal logic and relates to a metaphysical connection that a soul has with its Source. It is precisely when we have just awakened that this aspect of our identity is most clearly manifest. We are tired and certainly not in an intellectual space to engage in intense dialogue. Nonetheless, we recite *Modeh Ani* precisely at this moment in order to acknowledge that our connection to God is not dependent on philosophical proofs of His

27. Rabbi Menachem Mendel Schneerson, *On the Essence of Chassidus* (Brooklyn: Kehot Publication Society, 1986), 45.
28. Ibid., 46.

existence. Before going about our day with a more philosophically developed God-consciousness, we take a few moments to thank God from a religious space that speaks to our inner awareness of the Divine. This profound connection is uniquely apparent during our initial moments of being awake each morning.

SUMMARY

The historical development of this short but powerful prayer highlights the fact that even the smallest details of Jewish law contain profound and inspiring theological messages. Every morning when we wake up, we have a powerful choice. We can view the recitation of *Modeh Ani* simply as a formal requirement and the fulfillment of a religious duty, or alternatively, we can reflect on the values that *Modeh Ani* highlights and view this religious requirement as a medium to confront transcendent religious messages. In particular, reciting *Modeh Ani* while considering the powerful concepts it contains enables us to:

- Reflect on central themes of Jewish theology, such as God's ultimate redemption and resurrection of the dead (Talmud, Lamentations Rabba)
- Appreciate God's hand in the miracle of waking up each morning (Rabbi Jonathan Sacks, *Mishna Berura*)
- Cultivate an appreciation for each day as its own unit of time (Rabbi Nagen)
- View each day as an opportunity to actualize our personal religious mission (Rav Soloveitchik)
- Develop a heightened consciousness to live in the moment (Rabbi Nagen)
- Appreciate our innate connection to the Divine that transcends philosophical inquiry (Rabbi Schneerson)

Chapter 2

Washing Hands in the Morning

The Spiritual Power of the Hands

I mmediately after reciting *Modeh Ani,* the spiritual journey of Jewish law continues with the requirement to ritually wash our hands upon getting out of bed.

What is the spiritual significance of this obligatory ritual washing? Is there a hygienic reason for this obligation, or is the washing ritual exclusively a religious exercise? Moreover, what is the significance of our obligation to wash our hands specifically three times, and why must it be performed only after an extended period of sleep?

This topic is particularly fascinating because much of the discussion includes overlap between traditional halakhic sources and classical mystical texts. By highlighting the various approaches to this ritual, we can begin to understand the spiritual opportunities implicit in this daily religious obligation.

THE BIBLICAL STORY: HOW THE
PRIEST PREPARES FOR WORK

The Torah itself does not contain any explicit command for a non-priest to wash hands daily; but in the context of the command to construct the Tabernacle, God instructs Moshe to make "a copper laver and its base of copper, for washing (*lerachtza*); place it between the Tent of Meeting and the altar, and put water there."[1] Addressing the purpose of this utensil, God states that:

> From it, Aaron and his sons shall wash their hands together with their feet. Whenever they come to the Tent of Meeting, they shall wash with water and not die, or when they approach the altar to serve, to raise up in smoke a fire offering to the Lord. They shall wash their hands and feet and not die. It shall be for them an eternal decree, for him and his offspring for their generations.[2]

The significance of this ritual washing is highlighted by the ruling of the Rambam:

> It is a positive commandment for a priest who serves [in the Temple] to sanctify his hands and feet and afterwards perform the service, as it states: "And Aaron and his sons will wash their hands and their feet from it" (Ex. 30:19). A priest who serves without having sanctified his hands and feet in the morning is liable for death at the hand of heaven, as it states: "They shall wash with water and not die" (30:20). Their service – whether that of a high priest or an ordinary priest – is invalid if they do not perform the ritual washing.[3]

Interestingly, the Targum[4] translates the word *lerachtza* (to wash) as "to sanctify."[5] Similarly, the Mishna describes the priestly ritual as "the

---

1. Ex. 30:17-18.
2. Ibid. 19-21.
3. Laws of the Temple 5:1, translation from: http://www.chabad.org/library/article_cdo/aid/1008246/jewish/Biat-Hamikdash-Chapter-5.htm.
4. Targum Onkelos, second century.
5. Ex. 30:18.

sanctification of the hands and feet."[6] Rabbi Yakov Nagen notes that the linguistic switch from the word "washing" to "sanctifying" is intentional.[7] *Washing* implies that the priests are simply getting rid of dirt, while *sanctifying* highlights the spiritual component of this priestly ritual.

Rabbi Samson Raphael Hirsch[8] notes that the hands and feet are the only parts of the body that the priestly garments do not cover. All other bodily parts are sanctified by virtue of the priestly garb. The hands and feet – which are the parts of the body that facilitate all of the priest's sacred work – acquire their sanctity through this ritual washing.[9]

Rabbi Nagen makes another important observation. The sanctification ritual of the priest consists of four elements: the priest immerses himself in water; dresses in the sacred garments; anoints himself with special oils; and finally washes his hands and feet. Three of the four elements (immersion, dressing, and washing of the hands and feet) must be repeated daily. As Rabbi Nagen notes, the spiritual posture of the priest has to be re-evaluated every day. It is not sufficient for him to rely on his ritual preparations from the day before.

The priest who washes his hands and feet daily is an individual who understands that sacred acts require preparatory rituals. It is not sufficient to assume that the special priestly garments worn by the priest will provide the proper spiritual context for his work. Rather, the hands and feet must be *sanctified* daily to ensure that the priest is aware of the spiritual power of his holy duties. Moreover, by insisting on the daily repetition of the sanctification routine, the Torah ensures that the priest understands that each day stands alone as a spiritual unit and that yesterday's preparations have no bearing on today's service.

THE TALMUD: WASHING AS PREPARATION FOR PRAYER

In the Talmud, which was compiled after the destruction of the Temple, many ideas connected with the priestly service were transferred to the act of daily prayer performed by all Jews. Thus, beginning with the

---

6. Mishna Tamid 1:4.
7. Yakov Nagen, נטילת ידיים של בוקר-"יעוד מחדש" https://yakovn.wordpress.com/2006/11/10.
8. Rabbi Samson Raphael Hirsch, nineteenth century, Germany.
9. Ibid., Commentary on Exodus 30:18.

Talmud, the washing, which was originally a preparation for priestly service, becomes a preparation for prayer.

The Talmud states, "When one washes his hands [upon rising], he should say, 'Blessed are You, Lord our God, King of the Universe who has made us holy through His commandments and has commanded us about washing hands.'"[10] And in another passage, citing R. Yohanan, the Gemara states:

> One who wishes to accept upon himself the yoke of Heaven's sovereignty in a complete manner should relieve himself, wash his hands, don tefillin, [and then] recite *keriat shema* and pray... R. Hiyya bar Abba said in the name of R. Yohanan... [Anyone who does this,] Scripture regards it is as if he has built an altar and offered upon it a sacrifice, as it says, "I wash my hands in cleanliness and circle around Your altar, Lord." (Ps. 26:6).[11]

Rabbi David Brofsky notes that beyond simply linking ritual washing to prayer, this source clearly connects the washing of our hands to the larger religious goal of accepting divine sovereignty during prayer.[12]

The Rosh,[13] writing in the thirteenth and fourteenth centuries, acknowledges the link between handwashing and prayer and makes a few important observations.[14] First, according to the Rosh, morning handwashing is not primarily linked to the removal of the "negative spirits" (see further on). Rather, we wash our hands daily in order to purify them after they inevitably come in contact with normally covered parts of the body during sleep. Moreover, the rabbis legislated daily washing in order to prepare properly for an encounter with God through prayer. As a proof-text for his position, the Rosh quotes Psalms 26:6: "I wash my hands in cleanliness and circle around Your altar, Lord."

---

10. Berakhot 6ob.
11. Berakhot 14b-15a.
12. Rabbi David Brofsky, "Washing Hands Upon Waking and Before Prayer," http://etzion.org.il/en/washing-hands-upon-waking-and-prayer.
13. Rabbi Asher b. Yechiel, thirteenth/fourteenth centuries, Germany/Spain.
14. Rosh, Berakhot 9:23 and Responsum 4:1.

And the Malbim,[15] writing in the nineteenth century, adds that while Psalm 26:6 describes the physical act of handwashing, at least symbolically this ritual serves as a cleansing of the soul, separating ourselves from sin before engaging in worship of God.[16]

These passages from the Talmud, along with the comments of the Rosh, link our daily washing in the morning with the larger imperative to prepare properly for the act of prayer. Just as the priests wash their hands in order to prepare for their sacred work in the Temple, we wash our hands every day to highlight the fact that we cannot transition into the sacred world of prayer without proper preparation.

THE MYSTICAL TRADITION: NEGATIVE SPIRITS AND ELEVATED CONSCIOUSNESS

In traditional sources rooted in mystical concepts, the requirement for all Jews to wash their hands each morning became associated with the need to remove spiritual impurity. This begins in the Talmud; for example, the Talmud quotes a *beraita* that states:

> He [R. Mona] would say: A hand [that is put] to the eye should be cut off. A hand [that is put] to the nose should be cut off. A hand [that is put] to the mouth should be cut off. A hand [that is put] to the ear should be cut off… [The] hand causes blindness [if it touches the eye], [the] hand causes deafness [if it touches the ear].[17]

Rashi[18] explains that the *beraita* is cautioning against contact between certain body parts and unwashed hands. Rashi further notes that during sleep, "negative spirits" enter the body, and these spirits can be harmful.[19] The Talmud itself refers to this "negative spirit" and states that it

---

15. Rabbi Meir Leibush b. Yechiel Michel Wisser, nineteenth century, Ukraine.
16. Ps. 26:6.
17. Shabbat 108b–109a.
18. Rabbi Shlomo Yitzchaki, eleventh century, France/Germany; Berachot 108b, s.v. *yad laayin*.
19. Rashi, Shabbat 108b, s.v. *tiktzatz*.

is uniquely powerful and can be removed only by washing the hands three times.[20]

The danger of these spirits is discussed elsewhere in the Talmud as well. For example, in Tractate Yoma, we are told that although there is a general prohibition against washing oneself on Yom Kippur, "a woman may wash one hand with water [before giving bread] to a child... because of *shivta* (negative spirits)."[21] Rashi comments that this talmudic requirement assumes that unwashed hands can transfer the "negative spirits" onto food itself.[22]

What exactly is the nature of these "negative spirits?" Can they actually cause physical damage to a person's body? The nineteenth and twentieth-century *Kaf HaChayim*[23] quotes from an earlier work, *Solet Belula*, which explains that unwashed hands cannot cause physical damage. Rather, touching parts of the body without washing the hands three times can cause *spiritual* blindness or deafness, since the "negative spirit" has the potential to compromise one's ability to properly study and internalize the Torah.[24]

A fascinating passage in the classical work of Jewish mysticism, the Zohar, helps clarify the idea of "negative spirits," and explains the reason that the body is susceptible to these spirits specifically during sleep. As cited by the *Beit Yosef*,[25] the Zohar states:

> There is no human who does not taste the taste of death at night, and consequently an impure spirit (*rucha mesaava*) descends upon him. Why does this happen? When the holy soul leaves the human body... an impure spirit descends upon the body. When the soul is returned to the body and the impurity is removed, it remains upon his hands, and it cannot be removed until the human washes them, thereby being sanctified.[26]

---

20. Shabbat 108b-109a.
21. Yoma 77b.
22. Rashi, Yoma 77b, s.v. *medicha*.
23. Rabbi Yosef Chayim Sofer, nineteenth/twentieth centuries, Iraq.
24. *Kaf HaChayim* 4:19.
25. Rabbi Yosef Karo, sixteenth century, Spain/Sefad
26. Zohar 1:184:2, translated by Rabbi David Brofsky at http://etzion.org.il/en/ washing-hands-upon-waking-and-prayer.

Referring to this passage, Rabbi Eliezer Melamed[27] explains that when a person sleeps, he experiences a taste of death. While sleeping, we are passive and not fully cognizant of our feelings and thoughts. It is at this stage that the "negative spirit" of impurity rests upon his body. When we fall asleep and lose full control of our intellectual capacities, we are susceptible to forms of impurity that are associated with death. When we wake up and regain full consciousness, the impurity is immediately removed. However, even in our state of full awareness, the "negative spirit" of impurity still lingers on our hands. Therefore, we wash three times in the morning to remove these remnants of impurity.[28]

The Zohar reminds us of the responsibilities generated by a state of full awareness. We cannot transition from being asleep to being awake without engaging in a purification ritual that creates a clear distinction between the passive state of sleeping and the opportunities provided by a more proactive state of consciousness. When we wash our hands in the morning, we thereby remove any lingering impurities that are associated with the act of sleeping and positively affirm the opportunities provided by another day of total awareness.

THE RAMBAN: WASHING AS AFFIRMATION OF THE COVENANT

The Ramban broadens the conversation beyond issues of consciousness and ritual preparation to include a discussion about God's covenant with Avraham. Referring to mystical concepts, the Ramban states:

> By way of the Truth [the mystical teachings of the Kabbala], these parts of the body had to be washed because the extremities of the person's body are his hands and feet, for when the hands are upraised, they are higher than the rest of the body, and the feet are the lowest point. They allude in the human form to the Ten Emanations, with the whole body between them, just as the rabbis have said in *Sefer Yetzira*: "He made a covenant with him [i.e.,

---

27. Rabbi Eliezer Melamed, twenty-first century, Israel.
28. Rabbi Eliezer Melamed, "הלכות נטילת ידים של שחרית" http://www.yeshiva.org.il/midrash/1946.

Avraham] between the ten fingers of his hands and the ten fingers of his feet, with the protrusive part of the tongue and with the protrusive part of the nakedness." Therefore, the ministers of the One on High were commanded to wash their hands and feet, this washing for the sake of holiness.[29]

According to the Ramban (citing *Sefer Yetzira*), while the washing of the hands sanctifies the priest ritually, it also involves a covenantal component. By sanctifying his hands (and by extension his whole body), the priest reaffirms his bond with the Abrahamic covenant.

Rabbi Yakov Nagen also cites *Sefer Yetzira* and elaborates on the significance of washing the hands. According to *Sefer Yetzira*, there exists a parallel between the ten *Sefirot* of the cosmos and the ten fingers of the human body. Just as God uses the *Sefirot* to cosmically affect daily affairs, so, too, human beings are called upon to use their hands, or "human *Sefirot*," to affect their daily lives.[30]

This model highlights the role of the hands in positively affecting the world and furthering the values of the divine covenant. Having functioning hands provides wonderful opportunities, but also implies a great responsibility. We wash our hands in the morning, sanctify them, and thus reflect upon how we are going to use our hands in positive ways throughout the day. Moreover, by associating this daily washing with the covenant of Avraham, we connect with the historical mission of the Jewish people and remind ourselves that our daily actions are intended to further God's covenantal ideal.

THE RASHBA: WASHING AS AN ACT OF THANKS

The Rashba[31] offers additional insight, reflecting upon the act of washing and its relationship to God's kindness.[32] After reviewing the relevant source material, the Rashba wonders why we insist on washing our

---

29. Ramban, Ex. 30:19, translation based on R. Chavel edition at: http://www.chabad.org/kabbalah/article_cdo/aid/380255/jewish/Cleansing-the-Spiritual-Worlds.htm.
30. Rabbi Yakov Nagen,. "נטילת ידים של בקר: ייעוד מחדש" https://yakovn.wordpress.com/2006/11/10/נטילת-ידיים-שך-בוקר-מחדש.
31. Rabbi Shlomo b. Aderet, thirteenth century, Barcelona.
32. Responsa Rashba 1:191.

hands in the morning but not in preparation for prayer services such as Mincha or Maariv. He answers that each morning we are created anew, and we must therefore thank God each day for giving us another opportunity for life. This, he explains, is the reason that the rabbis instituted a blessing for the morning washing. To substantiate his view, the Rashba cites the verse from Lamentations 3:23, which affirms that God's kindness never ceases: "They are new every morning, great is Your faithfulness." Rashi understands this verse to mean that by acknowledging God's endless kindness, we increase our trust in God's commitment to fulfilling His promises.[33] Thus, according to the Rashba, by washing our hands, we symbolically acknowledge the opportunity that each day provides and we thank God for allowing us to serve Him.

The Rashba notes the parallels between the ritual washing performed by the priests in the Tabernacle and our daily washing. For example, just as the priest washes his hands specifically from a vessel, we are similarly required to wash our hands from a ritual cup. For the Rashba, handwashing is a preparation not only for prayer but for all our daily activities. While the priest performs his daily "work" in the Tabernacle, non-priests perform their daily tasks in their homes and at their places of work. While the priest must sanctify himself before engaging in holy activities, ordinary Jews need to be purified before beginning their day.

This model, therefore, reminds us of traditional Judaism's insistence that holiness can be found even in the most mundane environments. When we wash our hands, we affirm the fact that our homes, our workplaces, and everywhere in between contain profound opportunities for divine encounters. The one requirement is that we always approach life through the lens of the Torah and view our hands as instruments for the actualization of God's ideals.

This position is summarized well by Rabbi Shneur Zalman of Liadi:[34]

> Man entrusts his soul [to God at night] tired and exhausted, and God restores it to him rejuvenated and refreshed so that he may serve his Creator with all his capacity, this being the purpose of

---

33. Rashi, Lamentations 3:23.
34. Rabbi Shneur Zalman of Liadi, eighteenth/nineteenth centuries, Belarus.

man. Therefore, we should sanctify ourselves with His holiness, and wash our hands with water from a vessel before serving Him and ministering to Him, like the priest who would wash his hands from the basin each day before beginning his service [in the Holy Temple in Jerusalem].[35]

SUMMARY

The morning handwashing is a mitzva with profound and complex meanings that are rooted in a very special interplay among philosophy, mysticism, and law. After the recitation of *Modeh Ani*, washing hands represents the next stage provided by the halakha to confront the eternal values that underlie Jewish law. In particular, reflecting upon the spiritual messages of this mitzva allows us to acknowledge:

- The importance of proper preparation before engaging in sacred acts (biblical reference to the daily handwashing by the priest)
- The need to spiritually reflect every day and not be content with yesterday's spiritual accomplishments (Rabbi Nagen)
- The religious and spiritual challenges of compromised consciousness (the Zohar as explained by Rabbi Melamed)
- Our daily affirmation of our commitment to the Abrahamic covenant (Ramban)
- The power of our ten fingers to transform the world, paralleling the ten *Sefirot,* through which God engages the world of the cosmos (*Sefer Yetzira*)
- Our need to fully prepare to accept divine sovereignty through daily prayer (Rosh)
- The importance of spiritual cleansing before encountering the Divine (Malbim)
- The central role of thanking God for awakening anew (Rashba)
- Our responsibilities as a nation of priests (Rashba)

---

35. *Shulchan Arukh HaRav* 4:1, translated at http://www.chabad.org/library/article_cdo/aid/1452816/jewish/Whats-Up-with-the-Hand-Washing.htm.

Chapter 3

The Kippa

Piety and Belonging

F ew external symbols identify the modern Jew to the outside world more than the kippa *(yarmulke,* skullcap). The extent to which the kippa has become a badge of Jewish identity is highlighted by the fact that different ideological groups within Orthodox Judaism wear different types of *kippot.* In Israel, for example, the black velvet kippa is a defining feature of ultra-Orthodoxy, while the knitted kippa is typically associated with Religious Zionism.

Beyond its cultural and social significance, the kippa is a profoundly religious symbol with a rich history starting with the Bible itself. In fact, the story of the kippa is a complex one encompassing issues of piety, assimilation, identity, and belonging. The goal of this chapter is to trace the development of the kippa from its biblical roots to its contemporary applications. In particular, the aim is to provide a theological framework that demonstrates the values of the kippa, thus allowing a Jew to proudly wear his kippa in a modern setting.

THE BIBLICAL STORY

The Bible does not mention any requirement for an ordinary Jew to cover his head. However, God does instruct Moshe to make special priestly garments, including a turban to be worn on the head of the high priest:

> Make vestments of sanctity for Aaron your brother, for glory and splendor. And you shall speak to all the wise-hearted people whom I have invested with a spirit of wisdom, and they shall make the vestments of Aaron, to sanctify him to minister to Me. These are the vestments that they shall make: a breastplate, an ephod, a robe, a turban [*mitznefet*], and a sash.[1]

While this turban is worn exclusively by the high priest, the Torah elsewhere requires ordinary priests to wear "headdresses of linen."[2] The Rambam codifies the requirement for both the high priest and ordinary priest to cover their heads:

> The turban [the Torah] mentioned with regard to Aaron corresponds to the hat mentioned with regard to his sons. [The difference is that] the turban of the high priest is worn like fabric swathed around an object. The hat of the ordinary priest, by contrast, is worn like an ordinary hat; hence, its name.[3]

The Malbim argues that the head covering is intended to create a sense of humility by symbolically reminding the priest that God's presence rests above him.[4] While the priesthood has the potential to lead to feelings of entitlement and arrogance, the turban worn during the priestly service provides a religious framework for the thoughts of the priest, ensuring a proper mental state during his holy work.

Applying this model to the contemporary experience, the *kippa* is intended to facilitate a posture of humility, reminding the wearer that

1. Ex. 28:2-5.
2. Ex. 39:28.
3. Laws of the Temple Vessels 8:2, translation from http://www.chabad.org/dailystudy/rambam.asp?tdate=4/18/2016&lang=hebtamar&rambamChapters=3.
4. Malbim, Exodus, "Ramzei Bigdei HaKodesh."

God rests above him. When we place a *kippa* on our heads in the morning, we affirm that our lives are not exclusively about the fulfillment of our own selfish needs; rather, our actions are intended to serve a larger divine ideal. By wearing the *kippa,* we affirm our commitment to a life devoted to the fulfillment of God's will.

THE TALMUDIC STORY

While the Bible focuses exclusively on the obligation for priests to cover their heads, the Talmud expands the conversation and discusses the requirement of non-priests to cover their heads as well. For example, the Talmud notes that the mother of R. Nahman bar Yitzchak advised her son to always cover his head so that the "fear of heaven" would always be above him.[5] Similarly, the Talmud states that Rav Huna would never walk four handbreadths (*amot*) with his head uncovered, claiming that the Divine Presence always hovered over his head.[6] Highlighting the fact that a head covering was associated with the fear of God, the Talmud notes that the turban worn by talmudic scholars was called a *sudra.* This term was understood as a pun on the verse, "*Sod Hashem leyere'av* (The secret of the Lord is revealed to those who fear him)." (Ps. 25:14).[7]

The talmudic texts cited thus far all discuss the head coverings that were worn by various rabbinic personalities. What about non-rabbinic figures? Are there any talmudic texts that address head coverings worn by ordinary Jews?

The Talmud cites a remarkable story about R. Nahman bar Yitzchak. As an illustration of the fact that celestial signs hold no sway over Jews, the Talmud recounts:

> The astrologers once told R. Nahman bar Yitzchak's mother: Your son will be a thief. [As a result of this], she never allowed him to uncover his head, and she told him, "Cover your head so that the fear of Heaven should be upon you, and pray for mercy [that you

---

5. Shabbat 156b.
6. Kiddushin 31a.
7. Shabbat 77b.

should be protected from the evil inclination.]" He never knew why she told him this, [until one day] he sat studying under a palm tree and the cloak fell off his head. He lifted his eyes and saw a palm [that was not his], his evil inclination overpowered him, and he went up and chopped off a cluster of dates with his teeth.[8]

Commenting on this passage, the Maharsha[9] states that while it was standard practice for Jews to cover their heads to show reverence for God, R. Nahman bar Yitzchak's mother demanded that he wear a more elaborate head covering to counteract any natural thieving tendencies of her son.[10]

While we could certainly debate whether these talmudic texts require, or simply advise, the wearing of a head covering at all times, it is clear from the talmudic sources that the rabbis associated covering the head with added reverence and fear of God. Additionally, the story of R. Nahman highlights the power of the head covering to protect one from the evil inclination.

THE MEDIEVAL STORY: A SHIFT FROM PIETY TO IDENTITY

The extent to which head coverings became a distinct feature of Jewish life in the medieval period is attested by an interesting observation of the *Terumat HaDeshen*.[11] The background of the *Terumat HaDeshen's* statement is a discussion of whether or not a Jew is permitted to go bareheaded in order to disguise himself as a Christian when traveling through areas forbidden to Jews. Commenting on gentile attitudes towards Jews who go out in public bareheaded, the *Terumat HaDeshen* writes that "the gentiles in Germany assume that it is absolutely prohibited for a Jew [to go out bareheaded in public]… . He who does so is assumed to be a heretic."[12] This statement of the *Terumat HaDeshen* highlights the role that head coverings play in forging a distinct Jewish identity.

8. Shabbat 156b.
9. Rabbi Shmuel Eliezer b. Rabbi Yehuda HaLevi Edels, sixteenth century, Poland.
10. Maharsha, *Ḥiddushei Aggadot*, s.v. *gilui*.
11. Rabbi Israel Isserlin, fifteenth century, Germany.
12. *Responsa Terumat HaDeshen* 196. Translated by Eric Zimmer. "Men's Headcovering: The Metamorphisis of the Practice," in *Reverence, Righteousness and Rahmanut: Essays*

The most striking example of this medieval trend is found in a remarkable responsum of Rabbi Israel of Bruna.[13] Rabbi Israel was asked to rule on the permissibility of excommunicating someone who refused to cover his head after being reminded by his peers to do so. Rabbi Israel responded:

> I replied that excommunication is a valid [response to this transgression]. Even though the Talmud (Kiddushin 8a) refers to R. Kahana as a great man [and this is why he did not go out bareheaded] ... which implies that for ordinary people this act [going bareheaded] would be permissible ... this ruling [allowing ordinary people to keep their heads uncovered] only applies in Israel [where Jews are the majority]. However, since we live amongst gentiles who walk around with their heads uncovered, it [going bareheaded] is considered a gentile practice. Moreover, since we are only visibly distinguished [from our gentile neighbors] by virtue of our head covering, one who goes outside with his head uncovered violates the talmudic precept of ignoring time-honored Jewish customs ... and since this person was warned [to cover his head] and refused to acquiesce, this person is considered a heretic.[14]

According to Dr. Eric Zimmer, "this responsum is significant because it is the first association of bareheadedness with an absolute normative violation."[15] Besides the historical uniqueness of this responsum, it is fascinating because it expands the discussion of head covering beyond issues of piety and reverence to issues of identity and distinctiveness. Any Jew living in a gentile setting must cover his head as a distinguishing trademark of his Jewishness. By linking this requirement to the general halakhic obligation to observe customs unique to Jews, any Jew failing

---

in Memory of Dr. Leo Jung, ed. R. Jacob J. Schachter (Northvale New Jersey: Jason Aronson, 1992), 334.

13. Mahari Bruna, fifteenth century, Germany.

14. *Responsa Mahari Bruna* 34.

15. Eric Zimmer, "Men's Headcovering: The Metamorphisis of the Practice," in *Reverence, Righteousness and Rahmanut: Essays in Memory of Dr. Leo Jung*, ed. R. Jacob J. Schachter (Northvale New Jersey: Jason Aronson, 1992), 334.

to observe this practice removes himself from the community and violates the prohibition of imitating gentile norms.

Moreover, since the primary issue being addressed is one of identity, the ruling of Rabbi Israel sets the stage for theoretically discouraging certain head coverings that are not sufficiently distinctive. For example, wearing a baseball hat in New York City would not fulfill Rabbi Israel's requirement, since the baseball hat does not clearly identify the man with the Jewish people. Rabbi Israel's responsum leaves open the question of how we would apply his construct to modern Israel. Is the issue of identity relevant where Jews are the majority, although there is still a significant Arab minority?

This important historical shift highlights the critical role that the kippa plays in fostering a sense of pride that allows us to comfortably express our Jewish observance in a public manner. Beyond the religious virtues of humility and fearing God, wearing a kippa publicly affirms our belief in the transcendent messages of the Torah, serving as a type of Jewish uniform. The challenge becomes to wear this badge of identity with confidence and pride.

While Rabbi Israel's responsum highlights the role that identity plays in the development of Jewish attitudes to head coverings, the seventeenth-century sage Rabbi David HaLevi Segal (the *Taz*)[16] explains head covering as a ritual that distances Jews from gentile practices. According to the Taz, there is a formal prohibition for a Jew to go out bareheaded:

> It seems to me that it is completely forbidden for a Jew [to go out without a head covering] … . Since it is a gentile statute to remove the hat immediately upon sitting, this practice [going bareheaded] is included [in the biblical prohibition] against imitating gentile norms. Moreover, [this practice is critically important], since covering the head [facilitates an increased] fear of Heaven.[17]

Since the Taz's focus is on distancing Jews from the problematic practice of uncovering their heads, he would make no distinction as to what type of head covering a Jew decides to wear. While Rabbi Israel of Bruna

---

16. Rabbi David HaLevi Segal, seventeenth century, Poland.
17. *Taz, Orach Chayim* 8:3.

would frown upon wearing a head covering that is not distinctly Jewish, the Taz would accept *any* covering, since the very act of covering the head solves the problem of imitating gentile norms.

This important position affirms the kippa's power as a symbol that can neutralize the risks associated with religious and cultural assimilation. Covering the head reminds us that, while we can be fully immersed in worldly endeavors, we must also be cautious about the potential influences of behavior patterns that are contrary to Jewish tradition.

RABBI MOSHE FEINSTEIN: THE KIPPA
AND AMERICAN JEWISH IDENTITY

The great decisor, Rabbi Moshe Feinstein,[18] wrote multiple responsa discussing the requirement for a Jew to cover his head. In one fascinating responsum, Rabbi Feinstein discusses whether it is permissible to wear a kippa in religiously compromised settings. Rabbi Feinstein begins by noting that attending these places at all is halakhicly problematic. However, he continues to write that, despite the problematic nature of the places in question, Jews would still not be permitted to uncover their heads there. Rabbi Feinstein asserts that permitting a Jew to uncover his head when he is in a place where he shouldn't be in the first place would add an extra sin to his already problematic behavior. However, Rabbi Moshe qualifies this by suggesting that if the Jew entered a religiously compromised area, despite being warned, perhaps it would be better if he did remove his *kippa* to avoid desecrating God's name by associating observant people with problematic social venues.[19]

For many Jews in the Diaspora, the question of whether to wear a kippa becomes especially critical in the workplace. For a variety of reasons, many observant Jews refrain from wearing their kippot to work, justifying this practice by noting the kippa's status as more of a custom than a formal halakhic requirement. A responsum by Rabbi Feinstein discusses the permissibility of going bareheaded to work in an establishment that does not hire people who cover their heads.[20]

---

18. Rabbi Moshe Feinstein, twentieth century, New York.
19. *Iggerot Moshe*, Orach Chayim 2:95.
20. Ibid., Orach Chayim 4:2.

While Rabbi Feinstein permits not wearing a head covering in this case, in a different responsum, he adds an important qualification, writing that his permissive ruling applies only in the office itself, while a head covering is required while travelling to and from work. Moreover, Rabbi Feinstein reiterates that he permits Jews to go to work with their heads uncovered only if they would otherwise lose their jobs. If he would be mocked by co-workers but still be able to maintain his work, he would not be allowed to go bareheaded.[21]

Beyond the requirement to cover the head, there is also the question of the required size of the covering. The first responsum in Rabbi Feinstein's eight-volume work, *Iggerot Moshe*, deals with the question of whether it is permissible to wear a very small kippa.[22] The starting point for the responsum is an analysis of the position of Rabbi Shlomo Kluger,[23] who maintains that a Jew should be careful to cover the majority of his head. Rejecting Rabbi Kluger's position, Rabbi Feinstein argues that in principle, there is no problem with wearing a small kippa. In fact, he notes that in his time, this was in fact the practice of many observant Jews.

These responsa of Rabbi Feinstein emphasize both the pietistic as well as identity elements related to the practice of covering the head. Rabbi Feinstein notes that wearing a head covering has become a "quasi-prohibition" in recent times, and should thus be taken very seriously. Nonetheless, as Dr. Eric Zimmer notes, Rabbi Feinstein recognized that the social behavior of the contemporary Jew in America differs significantly from that of his predecessors, so that Jews can now be found in places where they never would have been found before.[24] The result of these social challenges compelled Rabbi Feinstein to evaluate the role of the kippa in fostering a more complex modern identity. In his brilliant juridical style, Rabbi Feinstein ensured that the kippa retained its status

---

21. Ibid., Choshen Mishpat 1:93.
22. Ibid., Orach Chayim 1:1.
23. Rabbi Shlomo Kluger, nineteenth century, Poland.
24. Eric Zimmer, "Men's Headcovering: The Metamorphisis of the Practice," in *Reverence, Righteousness and Rahmanut: Essays in Memory of Dr. Leo Jung*, ed. R. Jacob J. Schachter (Northvale New Jersey: Jason Aronson, 1992), 347.

as a social marker defining the Jew to the outside world and protecting him from cultural assimilation.

RABBI OVADIA YOSEF: THE KIPPA AND MODERN ISRAEL

Much of our discussion thus far has focused on Jews wearing head coverings in non-Jewish surroundings. Rabbi Ovadia Yosef[25] discusses the significance of a head covering in modern Israel. After discussing the views of earlier scholars, Rabbi Yosef states:

> It seems as though, nowadays, covering one's head is more than a pietistic practice. After all, it is well known that secular Jews walk around bareheaded, [and therefore the head covering] serves as a symbol distinguishing an observant Jew from his secular brethren … . [In fact,] it serves as a sign that one is committed to a life of observance and that the fear of God is upon him. Moreover, if one goes out in public with his head uncovered, there is a problem of *"mar'it ayin,"* lest someone think he has removed the yoke of heaven.[26]

Commenting on the required size for a proper kippa, Rabbi Yosef rules that a small *kippa* is permissible as long as it is visible from all sides of the head. However, during prayer and the recitation of the Grace after Meals, he advises wearing a hat, or at least a *kippa* that covers the majority of the head.

What is remarkable about this responsum is how Rabbi Yosef is able to apply the identity constructs first documented in the responsum of Rabbi Israel of Bruna to a modern Israeli setting. While Rabbi Israel viewed the head covering as creating a distinctly Jewish identity in a non-Jewish setting, Rabbi Yosef understands the kippa as a ritual that ensured an *observant* Jewish identity in a secular Jewish environment.

---

25. Rabbi Ovadia Yosef, twentieth/twenty-first centuries, Israel.
26. *Yechaveh Da'at* 4:1.

Rabbi Eliezer Melamed expands on Rabbi Yosef's position and advocates wearing a large *kippa*.[27] He concurs with Rabbi Yosef that the kippa has become a symbol of Jewish identity. As a result, he argues, wearing a large kippa, which is visible from all sides, sanctifies God's name by making a statement that we are proud of our Jewish identity and not embarrassed to wear external signs that display this commitment.

SUMMARY

Wearing a kippa is a powerful religious means to refine our character and connect to God. Beyond neutralizing problematic character traits such as arrogance, the kippa offers an important measure of the extent to which we feel proud to outwardly express our Judaism and connect with the larger story of the Jewish people. Understanding the values that underlie the Jewish head covering enables us to don the kippa with confidence and pride.

In particular, wearing a kippa each day allows the modern Jew to:

- Reflect on the ethic of humility by being reminded that God rests "above" him (Malbim, Shabbat 156b, Kiddushin 31a)
- Meditate on what it means to fear God (Shabbat 77b)
- Avoid issues of arrogance and entitlement (Malbim)
- Safeguard his identity against the evil inclination (Shabbat 156b)
- Assert his distinct Jewish identity (Mahari Bruna)
- Ensure that he maintains his religious uniqueness and avoids imitating gentile norms (Taz)
- Avoid the desecration of God's name by ensuring that his behavior is consistent with the values associated with the *kippa* (Rabbi Moshe Feinstein)
- Assert with pride his commitment to a life of observance (Rabbi Ovadia Yosef, Rabbi Eliezer Melamed)

---

27. Rabbi Eliezer Melamed, *Peninei Halakha Likutim* 1 (Israel: Machon Har Beracha, 2006), 169.

Chapter 4

The Tzitzit (1)

The Jewish Uniform and the Power of Will

Observant Jews traditionally wear a four-cornered garment known as the *tallit katan* (small tallit), commonly referred to as "tzitzit" (ritual fringes).

Why is this ritual so central to Jewish living? What is the symbolic significance of the strings and the knots of tzitzit? Analyzing the primary sources dealing with the spiritual significance of tzitzit will help provide a more meaningful framework for a modern Jew to proudly wear this ancient Jewish uniform.

TZITZIT IN THE BOOK OF NUMBERS: A STORY OF WILL

The first biblical source for the mitzva of tzitzit is found in a collection of verses at the end of *Parashat Shelach*:

> Speak to the children of Israel and say to them that they shall make themselves tzitzit on the corners of their garments throughout the generations. And they shall place upon the tzitzit of each corner a thread of turqoise wool. It shall constitute tzitzit for you, that you may see it and remember all of the commandments of

the Lord and perform them; and not explore after your heart and after your eyes after which you stray. So that you may remember and perform all my commandments and be holy to your God. I am the Lord, your God, who has removed you from the land of Egypt to be a God unto you; I am the Lord, your God.[1]

According to these verses, the tzitzit serve as a visible reminder that we are to keep God's commandments, thereby protecting us from potential sin. Ibn Ezra highlights this aspect of the mitzvah, insisting that it is more important to wear tzitzit outside the prayer setting than during morning services. While, ideally, we should wear tzitzit both inside and outside of the synagogue, he argues that outside of the synagogue environment we are more likely to be tempted by sin, and therefore should always be zealous in wearing tzitzit.[2]

The Talmud illustrates this theme with a story[3] about a man who was particularly strict in observing the mitzva of tzitzit, though he was lax in his observance in other areas of Jewish law. Overcome by his evil inclination, this man decided to visit a famous harlot. Arriving at her house, he waited by the doorway to be called in. However, immediately before engaging in the act of sexual impropriety, his "four tzitzit pelted him on his face." Humiliated by the fact that he was about to engage in a sinful sexual encounter, the man removed himself from the harlot's bed and sat on the ground. The story continues:

> [After seeing this man remove himself from her bed], the harlot responded by stating… "I will not leave you until you tell me what flaw you saw in me." The man replied, "[I swear] that I have never seen a woman as beautiful as you. However, there is one mitzva that Hashem, our God, has commanded us, and tzitzit is its name. [And] regarding this mitzva the phrase, 'I am Hashem, your God' is written twice [in the Torah]; [one time] to inform us that 'I am He who will ultimately exact punishment [from the corrupt]',

---

1. Num. 15:37-41.
2. Ibn Ezra, Numbers 15:39.
3. Menachot 44a.

and [one time] to inform us that 'I am He who will ultimately give reward [to the righteous]'. At that moment, [these tzitzit] appeared to me like four witnesses [that would attest to the sin that I was about to commit]." She said to him, "I will not leave until you tell me what your name is, what the name of your city is…and what the name of the academy where you study Torah is." He wrote the information down and put it in her hand.

[After he left], she arose and divided all her possessions [into three parts]: She gave one third to government officials [as a bribe to allow her to convert],[4] one third to the poor, and one third she took in her hand. [She divided all her property this way] except for her linens, [which she brought with her]. She came to R. Chiyya's house of study and said to him, "Rabbi, give instructions on my behalf that they should make me a convert." He said to her, "My daughter, [do you truly wish to convert for the sake of Heaven]? Perhaps you have set your eyes upon one of the students [in order to marry him]?" She took out the written note from her hand, gave it to him [and related the entire incident, persuading him that she wanted to convert for the sake of Heaven]. [After she converted], R. Chiyya told her, "Go [and marry the student that you encountered in your home]." [She did so] and those [same] linens that she had arranged for him illicitly, she now arranged for him permissibly.

This fascinating story demonstrates how tzitzit can be an effective safeguard against sinful behavior. As the verse in Numbers notes, tzitzit allow us to "remember all of the commandments" and not explore "after [our] hearts and after [our] eyes, which lead us astray."

Rabbi Yakov Nagen offers an additional explanation, noting that this talmudic account not only focuses on the power of the tzitzit to neutralize our desire to sin, but also highlights the fact that the evil inclination is a negative force only when we allow it to take control of our decisions.[5] If, however, we channel our desires properly, then even the evil inclination can be transformed into a tool for success. Rabbi

---

4. Rashi, ibid., s.v. *shlish*.
5. Rabbi Yakov Nagen, *Waking Up to A New Day* (Jerualem: Koren, 2013), 263-271.

Nagen notes that perhaps the most fascinating aspect of the story is the harlot's desire to keep her bed linens, though she gave away the majority of her possessions. In an extraordinary turn of events, at the end of the story, we are told that "those same linens that [the harlot] arranged for him illicitly, [were now] arranged for him permissibly."

Rabbi Nagen believes that the power of the tzitzit to turn uncontrolled desires into something religiously positive is alluded to in the verses of Numbers themselves. In verse 15:39, we are told that after looking at the tzitzit, we are to "remember the commandments of the Lord and perform them." Then, in an apparent redundancy, in the next verse, we are told to "remember and perform all of [God's] commandments and be holy to your God." Rabbi Nagen thinks that these verses are not repetitive, but actually refer to two distinct functions of the mitzva of tzitzit. Verse 39 refers to the tzitzit as an aid in prevention of wrongdoing, while verse 40 describes a more elevated phase, wherein the impulse to sin is transformed into something positive that enables an individual to "be holy" before God.

This biblical model, expanded upon by Rabbi Nagen, highlights the role of tzitzit in preventing us from engaging in problematic activities. On the most basic level, tzitzit serve as a reminder of God and His commandments. We would be less likely to eat non-kosher food, for example, when wearing tzitzit. By looking at the tzitzit before engaging in sinful activity, we are reminded to behave in accordance with transcendent Torah values, and not fall prey to instinctive bodily desires.

On a more positive level, the tzitzit highlight the fact that the Torah does not fundamentally frown upon engagement with the physical world. Instead of completely neutralizing our physical needs, the Torah calls upon us to elevate the physical world by engaging in positive and religiously valuable activities.

TZITZIT IN THE BOOK OF DEUTERONOMY: THE STORY OF THE JEWISH UNIFORM

While the verses in *Parashat Shelach* focus on the role of tzitzit as a means of neutralizing sin, the book of Deuteronomy shifts the discussion to another critical element associated with this mitzva.

Chapter 22 of Deuteronomy begins with a detailed description of a variety of ritual commandments, including, "You shall not wear combined fibers, wool and linen together" (verse 11). Immediately afterwards, the Torah commands: "Make for yourselves twisted threads on the four corners of your garments with which you cover yourselves" (verse 12). Noting the juxtaposition of the mitzva of tzitzit and the prohibition against wearing wool and linen (*shatnez*), Rashi cites the talmudic view that tzitzit can, in fact, be made from this forbidden combination.[6]

Prof. Jacob Milgrom suggests that the permission to mix wool and linen while preparing the tzitzit garment reflects the Bible's emphasis on the connection between tzitzit and the priesthood.[7] The garments of the priests were made of a mixture of wool and linen; the similar exception to the prohibition of *shatnez* in the case of tzitzit is meant to emphasize the parallel between the two. As Prof. Milgrom writes:

> Israelites not of the seed of Aaron may not serve as priests, but they may – indeed, must – strive for a life of holiness by obeying God's commandments...The fact that the cord is woolen and violet marks it as a symbol of both priesthood and royalty, thereby epitomizing the divine imperative that Israel become "a kingdom of priests and a holy nation."

Prof. Milgrom's suggestion adds an important layer to our understanding of the mitzva of tzitzit. Beyond helping to neutralize sin, tzitzit serve as the national uniform of the Jews, highlighting their status as a nation of priests. Donning tzitzit in the morning connects us with the larger Jewish collective and reminds us that our personal mission is directly linked to the larger religious mission of the Jewish people.

Similarly, Rabbi Eliezer Melamed[8] notes that Rabbi Tzvi Yehuda Kook[9] encouraged his students to wear their tzitzit *outside* of their clothing to ensure that they are always visible. Rabbi Melamed says it

---

6. Rashi, Deuteronomy 22:12.
7. Jacob Milgrom, *The JPS Torah Commentary Numbers* (Philadelphia/New York: Jewish Publications Society, 1990), 413.
8. Rabbi Eliezer Melamed, *Peninei Halakha, Likkutim* 1, (Israel: Machon Har Beracha, 2006), 178.
9. Rabbi Tzvi Yehuda Kook, twentieth century, Israel.

is praiseworthy for us to be sure our tzitzit are visible when we are in a work setting or in the Israeli army, because walking around with clearly visible tzitzit demonstrates pride both in the Jewish "team uniform" as well as the ideals that it represents.

TEKHELET: PRIESTHOOD, HUMILITY, AND MAJESTY

So far, our discussion has focused on two models presented by the Bible: the approach of *Parashat Shelach* addresses the role of tzitzit in neutralizing sin, while Deuteronomy focuses on tzitzit as the uniform of the Jewish people, highlighting our national mission as a nation of priests.

While both interpretations provide compelling rationale for the mitzva of tzitzit, the Torah does not clearly delineate how glancing at an arbitrary set of strings will automatically cause an individual to reflect on the messages in the various biblical verses.

Sensitive to this question, Rashi argues that the numerical equivalent of the word "tzitzit" (combined with the number of knots formed by the white and blue strings) equals the number 613, thus creating an immediate association between tzitzit and a life committed to the 613 mitzvot of the Torah.[10] According to Rashi, when we look at the tzitzit with an awareness of their numerological significance, we are immediately reminded of the tzitzit's power to direct our behavior towards a life committed to mitzvot.

The Ramban rejects Rashi's interpretation and understands the symbolism of tzitzit to be centered in the blue string, known as the tekhelet.[11] The Ramban's perspective is based on a talmudic passage quoting R. Meir, who wonders:

> What distinguished tekhelet from all other types of dyes [so that it was selected for coloring tzitzit]? It is because the color of tekhelet is similar to that of the sea, and that of the sea is similar [to the color] of the sky, and [the color of the sky] is similar [to

---

10. Rashi, Numbers 15:39.
11. Ramban, Numbers 15:38. Contemporary halachic authorities debate whether or not we should attach a techelet string to our tzitzit nowadays. For a variety of articles on this topic see: http://tekhelet.com/library-search/.

the color] of the throne of glory, for it is stated "and under His feet was like sapphire brickwork, and like the essence of heaven in purity."[12] And it is written, "Like the appearance of sapphire stone is the likeness of the throne."[13]

On the surface, this passage is difficult to understand. As the Ritva[14] comments, the Talmud unnecessarily creates extended visual associations beginning with tekhelet, continuing to the sea and the sky (*rakia*), and only then arriving at the throne of glory.[15] Why not simply say that the tekhelet resembles the "throne of glory?" The Ritva explains that the added visual reminders are essential to understanding the mitzva of tzitzit. The sea, according to the Ritva, is symbolic of bodies of water in which miracles were performed for the Jewish people (such as the splitting of the sea). The sky (*rakia*), on the other hand, reminds us of God "descending" through seven firmaments (*riki'in*) to give the Jewish people the Torah.

According to this perspective, when we glance at our tzitzit (with the tekhelet), we embark on a journey through Jewish history, highlighting God's involvement in the world (Exodus from Egypt) and His covenant with the Jewish people (Mount Sinai).

Here, the Ramban offers us an interesting observation about the spiritual significance of the mitzva of tzitzit. After all, as Prof. Milgrom explains, the tzitzit serve as the national uniform of the Jewish People, reminding us of the collective mission of the Jews. The Ramban's interpretation highlights the fact that the Jewish people's destiny is governed by divine providence. By reminding us of both the Exodus from Egypt and the Revelation of the Torah at Mount Sinai, the tzitzit affirm that the history of the Jewish people is guided by the hand of God. Glancing at our tzitzit, therefore, reminds us of the interconnectedness between God and the fate of His people.

---

12. This verse implies that the color of the sky is like sapphire.
13. Menaḥot 43b.
14. Rabbi Yom Tov b. Avraham Ashvili, thirteenth/fourteenth centuries, Spain.
15. Ḥullin 89a.

The *Kli Yakar*[16] offers an alternative understanding of this tal-mudic passage, adding another layer of meaning to the mitzva of tzitzit.[17] According to the *Kli Yakar*, the sea and the sky capture two different dimensions of mitzva observance. The sea, with its uncompromising precision and power, symbolizes halakhic observance performed from a place of fear. The sky, by contrast, highlights the beauty associated with a life of commitment to halakha and signifies divine worship from a place of love. In this philosophical paradigm, tzitzit symbolize the ladder that every Jew must climb to achieve religious intimacy. Fear of God is the baseline of observance, while a more elevated religious identity is based on a love of God. It is this approach that facilitates ultimate access to the divine throne of glory.

The presence of the tekhelet thus provides an important context for the daily observance of Jewish law. On the one hand, tzitzit remind us to behave according to the ideals of the Torah; on the other hand, the tekhelet highlights the fact that the ideal form of Jewish observance should stem from a place of profound connection to the values that the mitzvot represent. When we follow this paradigm, we shift the conversa-tion about observance away from an exclusive focus on obedience and impel us towards a broader dialogue incorporating the ethics of mean-ing and love.

While the Ramban and the *Kli Yakar* articulate two important models for reflection about the significance of the tekhelet, Prof. Milgrom provides significant historical data that emphasizes the unique theological vision of the ancient Israelites. He notes that it is not accidental that the Torah insisted that the Jewish people's national uniform contain a string of tekhelet. In antiquity, "Roman emperors retained for themselves the exclusive privilege of wearing purple mantles, thus giving rise to the color names still used today, "royal blue," and "royal purple." While in other soci-eties, the tekhelet was reserved for royalty, the Torah bestows this ancient privilege on every Jew, since every Jew must attach this royal color to his daily attire. This legislation therefore "enhances its symbolism as a mark of nobility... since all Jews are required to wear it, a sign that Jews are a people

---

16. Rabbi Shlomo Ephraim b. Aaron Luntschitz, sixteenth century, Poland.
17. *Kli Yakar*, Numbers 15:38.

of nobility."[18] By insisting that everyone wear a garment with tekhelet, the Torah reminds us that all Jews are equal in the eyes of God and are not distinguished by wealth or profession. In the biblical worldview, a person is defined by his actions. By glancing at the tzitzit, we are reminded that in order to become godly, our behavior must reflect the values of the Torah.

SUMMARY

If we synthesize all of these explanations, we can better appreciate the richness and meaning inherent in the mitzva of tzitzit. Before putting on his tzitzit in the morning, a Jew can reflect upon:

- Tzitzit as a means of preventing wrongdoing. By glancing at the tzitzit and remembering the 613 mitzvot, we are perpetually reminded of the choice between compliance and non-compliance with God's commandments (Rashi)
- The property of tzitzit that transforms the evil inclination into a tool for positive religious growth (Rabbi Nagen)
- Tzitzit as the uniform of the "kingdom of priests" (Prof. Milgrom)
- Tzitzit as affirmation of pride in our religious identity (Rabbi Melamed)
- Tzitzit as a vehicle for reflecting on Jewish theology, in particular our relationship to God's role in history (the Exodus from Egypt) and our unique covenantal bond with Him (the covenant at Sinai) (Ritva)
- The dual imperative to worship God both from fear (symbolized by sea) and from the more elevated place of love (symbolized by sky) (*Kli Yakar*)
- Tzitzit as the uniform of nobility (Prof. Milgrom)

---

18. Jacob Milgrom, *The JPS Torah Commentary Numbers* (New York: Jewish Publication Society, 1990), 412.

Chapter 5

The Tzitzit (2)

The Obligation to Wear Tzitzit: Opting-In

In the previous chapter, we discussed the broader religious ideals and messages that underlie the mitzva of tzitzit. Unfortunately, many observant Jews question the necessity of wearing tzitzit daily. After all, they note, strictly speaking, we are required to attach tzitzit only to a four-cornered garment. Since four-cornered garments are rarely worn anymore, they contend that the mitzva of tzitzit is no longer legally required.

On the surface, this argument does have some merit. In fact, the *Shulchan Arukh* rules that we are obligated in the mitzva of tzitzit only if we are wearing a [minimum] four-cornered garment.[1] Theoretically, one could go his entire life without wearing a four-cornered garment, thereby effectively circumventing the entire mitzva without violating any formal prohibition.

It is unfortunate that the model of halakhic discourse that views halakhic living exclusively from the perspective of what is strictly required tends to permeate much of the modern discussion of halakha. There is often a sense that halakhic observance means following the strict

---

1. *Shulchan Arukh*, Orach Chayim 24:1.

letter of the law without reflecting and asking ourselves what our attitude should be to those actions that are religiously praiseworthy, even if not formally required. Using tzitzit as a case study, this chapter attempts to shift the halakhic conversation to a deeper understanding of the transcendent values that the law seeks to facilitate. Once we recognize that halakha provides spiritual opportunities that should ideally be embraced and not circumvented, we will be more open to observing even those religious rituals that may not be formally required.

THE ABRABANEL: A MORE NUANCED OBLIGATION

The biblical source for the notion that we are obligated to place tzitzit on a four-cornered garment only is a verse from the book of Numbers commanding Jews to "make themselves tzitzit on the corners of their garments for all generations."[2] Since the Torah describes the tzitzit as being placed on the "corners" of our garments, the majority of rabbinic authorities rule that only a four-cornered garment is formally obligated in the mitzva of tzitzit.

However, while this position does represent the majority view, it does not represent a rabbinic consensus. For example, Abrabanel[3] makes an interesting observation about the second half of the verse, in which the Torah states that this commandment is relevant for "all generations."[4] Abrabanel argues that this apparent redundency teaches that the mitzva of tzitzit is relevant *even* in those generations in which Jews no longer wear four-cornered garments as their default mode of dress. According to Abrabanel, even if, in subsequent generations, people stop wearing clothes with four-corners, they are still obligated to acquire a four-cornered garment in order to fulfill the mitzva of tzitzit.[5]

THE RAMBAM AND *TOSAFOT*: DESIRED OBLIGATION

While the Abrabanel affirms the minority position that one is obligated to purchase a four-cornered garment in order to fulfull the mitzva of

2. Num. 15:38.
3. Rabbi Yitzhak b. R. Yehuda Abrabanel, fifteenth century, Spain.
4. Num. 15, s.v *v'amru*.
5. Cf. Or Zarua, Laws of Hamotzi 1:140.

tzitzit, the Rambam articulates the majority view that there exists no formal obligation to wear tzitzit if we are not wearing a four-cornered garment.[6] Nonetheless, according to the Rambam, despite the lack of any formal obligation, "it is not proper for a pious person to release himself from this commandment. Instead, he should always try to be wrapped in a garment that requires tzitzit so that he will fulfill this mitzva."

This is also the view of *Tosafot*.[7] The Talmud, in Tractate Pesachim, lists different types of people who are "excommunicated" in the eyes of Heaven, and this includes someone who does not have tzitzit attached to his garment.[8] Commenting on this passage, *Tosafot* provide two alternative explanations of the harsh language used by the Talmud, despite the lack of a formal obligation to wear tzitzit.[9] *Tosafot's* first answer is that the excommunication applies to one who wears four-cornered garments but refrains from attaching tzitzit. The second answer given by *Tosafot* is that the punishment referred to in the Talmud applies even to one who does not have a four-cornered garment. The reason this person is deserving of excommunication is that he should have purchased a four-cornered garment in order to "opt-in" to the obligation.

This view of the Rambam and *Tosafot* significantly shifts the dialogue and prompts us to think about our halakhic identity beyond the formal categories of permissible and forbidden. According to both of these positions, there exists no formal requirement to wear tzitzit if we are not wearing a four-cornered garment. Nonetheless, there is a larger religious – albeit non- mandatory – imperative to actively seek out ways to obligate oneself in the mitzva.

What is the source for this philosophical model? Is this a virtue reserved for the exceptionally pious, or is this religious ethic something that all Jews should strive to incorporate into their spiritual lives? Sensitive to this question, *Tosafot* cite a passage in Tractate Sota that asks:

---

6. Rambam, Laws of Tzitzit 3:11, translated at http://www.chabad.org/library/article_cdo/aid/936343/jewish/Tzitzit-Chapter-Three.htm.
7. *Tosafists*, twelfth-fourteenth centuries, Germany/France.
8. Pesachim 113b.
9. Ibid., s.v *ve'ein*.

> Why did Moshe our teacher desire to enter the Land of Israel?
> Did he need to eat its fruits? Or did he need to sate himself
> with its bounty? [Obviously not!] Rather, here is what Moshe
> said [to himself]: "There are so many mitzvot that the Jewish
> people have been commanded that cannot be fulfilled except
> in the Land of Israel. [Therefore,] I will enter the land so that
> all [the mitzvot] will be fulfilled through me." [God] replied
> to him, "Do you seek anything other than to gain reward?
> [Even though you will not enter the Land of Israel to have
> those mitzvot performed], I will reckon it for you as if you
> have performed them."[10]

The Rosh understands this passage as a larger directive highlighting the
message that all Jews should actively yearn to fulfill God's command.[11]
Moshe serves as the exemplar for this model since, according to this
talmudic account, Moshe desired to enter the Land of Israel in order to
gain the opportunity to fulfill additional mitzvot. However, as the *Geon
Yaakov* notes, since God's decree forbidding Moshe from entering the
land was already issued, it is surprising that Moshe would beseech God
to fulfill a request that contradicts the divine command itself.[12] Rather,
the *Geon Yaakov* contends that Moshe wanted to enter the Land of Israel
briefly in order to teach the Israelites the agricultural laws of the land,
and thus facilitate observance of these statutes.

Moshe could easily have been content with his own personal
development. He had no obligation to ask God to grant him this request.
However, he understood the spiritual opportunities provided by mitzvot and was not content with absolving himself of care for the religious
welfare of the nation based on a technical exemption.

This approach, which views halakhic observance as a system that
provides endless access to spirituality, is also substantiated by a statement
of Ben Azzai. According to Ben Azzai, we should "run to do even a minor

---

10. *Tosafot*, ibid., citing Sota 14a.
11. Moed Katan 3:80.
12. Cited in Talmud Bavli Tractate Sota 14a, *The Shottenstein Daf Yomi Edition Volume 1*
(Brooklyn: Artscroll Mesorah Publications, 2000), footnote 22.

mitzva and flee from sin."[13] Explaining the logic behind Ben Azzai's view, the Rambam states that this passion for mitzva observance is one of the most powerful aspects of the Torah's religious vision. To substantiate his theory, the Rambam points to a passage in Deuteronomy that describes how Moshe set aside the cities of refuge.[14] The Rambam explains that Moshe was well aware that these three cities would not attain their legal status as "cities of refuge" until after his death when three other cities were designated in the Land of Israel. Nonetheless, he was filled with so much love and passion for mitzva observance that he desired to fulfill as many of God's commandments as possible despite their limited practical significance.[15]

This model reorients the halakhic conversation to remind us that we should yearn for opportunities to connect to God via His laws and not look for ways to circumvent His dictums. halakha presents us with entry points that facilitate divine encounters. Failure to appreciate and make use of these opportunities, even when they are not obligatory, neutralizes the opportunity to be genuinely transformed by the the Torah's precepts.

SHA'AREI TESHUVA: PUNISHMENT FOR NOT EMBRACING MITZVOT AS VALUES

The Rambam and *Tosafot* urge us to view mitzvot as opportunities to "opt-in," as opposed to rituals that we attempt to avoid. What remains unclear is whether or not there are any religious penalties for avoiding mitzvot that may not be required according to the strict letter of the law. In general, violations of religious norms require us to offer sacrifices and atonement for the sin. However, what if a person successfully avoids the law, thus technically not violating a specific divine command? For example, let's imagine a person who does not wear tzizit his entire life since he neglected to purchase a four-cornered garment. Is it fair to suggest that he will be punished for not observing a command that was never actually required of him?

---

13. *Pirkei Avot* 4:2, translated in *The Koren Siddur with Introduction, Translation, and Commentary by Rabbi Jonathan Sacks* (Jerusalem: Koren, 2009), 660.
14. Deut. 4:41.
15. Rambam, Commentary to Avot 4:2.

An interesting talmudic passage addresses this question:

> An angel [once] encountered R. Ketina while he was wearing a linen wrap. [The angel] said to him, "Ketina, Ketina, [since you wear] a linen wrap in the summer and [woolen] cloak [with rounded corners] in the winter, what will become of [the mitzva of tzitzit on your garments]?" [R. Ketina] said to him, "[Does the heavenly court] punish for the failure to fulfill a positive commandment?" [The angel] replied, "At a time when there is [an arousal of heavenly] wrath, we do punish those who neglect positive commandments."[16]

The Gemara further delineates the problematic behavior of R. Ketina, noting that he seemed to be using evasive tactics "to exempt [himself]" from mitzvot and was therefore susceptible to divine wrath. What remains unclear, however, is why R. Ketina should be punished at all. We can readily understand why someone would be punished for neglecting obligatory mitzvot, such as lulav or tefillin.[17] However, the case of tzitzit is unique; by rounding the corners of his garment, R. Ketina effectively circumvented the law and therefore, in theory, should not be punished for his behavior.

Rabbeinu Yonah addresses this question and explains that someone who tries to escape the contours of the law through loopholes is punished because he fails to imprint on his heart the "beauty of mitzvot."[18] Can we honestly say that we are engaged in a behavior that authentically captures the will of the Torah when we are consciously attempting to circumvent the law?[19]

This approach of Rabbeinu Yonah challenges us to reflect upon our actions and ensure that, beyond compliance with the letter of the law, we also relate seriously to the religious messages that are manifest in the spirit of the law.

---

16. Menachot 41a.
17. See Tosafot, ibid., s.v. *anishato.* Cf. Tosafot Arachin 2b, s.v. hakol.
18. *Shaarei Teshuva* 3:22.
19. Cf. the important comments of Rabbi Asher Weiss, "Circumventing Mitzvos," at http://www.torahbase.org/5774-6/.

RABBI ASHER WEISS: A UNIFORM OF LOVE

The working assumption of both the Rambam and the Tosafot is that, strictly speaking, we are not obligated to wear tzitzit unless we are wearing a four-cornered garment. While they both agree that wearing tzitzit is religiously optimal and represents an authentic fulfillment of the Torah's ideals, they nevertheless acknowledge that, according to the letter of law, there is no obligation. On the surface, it is difficult to understand the logic of this position. If the Torah views tzitzit as such a significant religious ritual, why not obligate everyone to purchase a four-cornered garment in order to fulfill the mitzva?

Rabbi Asher Weiss acknowledges this tension and offers a model for reflection about the underlying religious message inherent in the Torah command that only four-cornered garments are obligated in the mitzva of tzitzit.[20]

He begins by noting that in the Talmud, the mitzva of tzitzit is described using terminology associated with servitude.[21] Just as a master places a stamp on his servant that displays his status as servant, the tzitzit similarly symbolize the Jewish people's status as servants of God. However, Rabbi Weiss asserts, the subservience of the Jewish people to God is qualitatively unique. While we ordinarily associate servitude with coercion, the Jewish people *chose* divine servitude as an *a priori* ideal based on a sense of love and joy in fulfilling the divine will. Since the Jewish people understand the spiritual value of worshiping God, they do not see the divine command as a burden to be circumvented. Rather, they recognize that mitzvot provide extraordinary opportunities to engage the ideals that connect man with his Creator. The mitzva of tzitzit is *intentionally* legislated in a non-obligatory way because if we were formally required to wear tzitzit, that would imply that our uniform of servitude represents a classical form of slavery, wherein the slave serves his master based on fear of consequences. Our servitude, by contrast, is based on our belief that mitzvot are opportunities to connect with God. By ensuring that the "uniform" of the Jewish people is legally optional, the Torah facilitates a model wherein those who "opt-in" and

---

20. Rabbi Asher Weiss, "Tzitzith and Techelet," http://www.torahbase.org/733/.
21. Shabbat 57b.

47

choose to wear the uniform are clearly proclaiming that their servitude is performed out of devotion and love.

RABBI MOSHE FEINSTEIN: TZITZIT AND COMMUNITY

There is another dimension to the question of whether or not to wear tzitzit without a legal requirement.

It is undeniable that the custom of wearing tzitzit daily has become a universal practice of observant Jewry. In fact, Rabbi Moshe Feinstein notes that the practice of buying a four-cornered garment in order to consciously "opt-in" to the mitzva has become the norm. Therefore, he argues, we are obligated to purchase the four-cornered garment, based on a verse in Proverbs that requires us to follow established Jewish customs.[22] According to Rabbi Feinstein, the source of the obligatory status of tzitzit in a contemporary setting is the fact that it has become the customary uniform of the Jewish people. All observant Jews wear tzitzit despite the absence of obligation, and this communal acceptance has transformed an optional act of piety into an obligation.[23]

Rabbi Feinstein's argument is particularly significant because the claim that we can decide not to wear tzitzit (since we are not required to wear them) assumes that we are entitled to behave in a way that fundamentally detaches us from the larger Jewish collective. Rabbi Feinstein reminds us that we do not observe halakha in a vacuum. Indeed, much of our contemporary observance of Jewish law is intended to connect each individual to the greater community of Israel. "Opting-in" to the mitzva of tzitzit, therefore, acknowledges that part of the purpose of halakha is to enable both personal meaning and connection with the larger community.

SUMMARY

Wearing tzitzit daily provides an opportunity to reflect on the multifaceted nature of our personal religious obligations. In particular, the mitzva of tzitzit serves as an ideal case study to test the extent to which we view mitzvot as profound entry points to the encounter with eternal

---

22. Prov. 1:8.
23. *Iggerot Moshe*, Orach Chayim 4:4.

divine ideals, and not simply as arbitrary rules that we are obligated to observe based on fear of consequences. Beyond the inherent meaning in the mitzvah itself, reflecting upon the values that underlie tzitzit's questionable obligatory status enables an individual to focus upon:

- The complex legal question of whether or not we are obligated to purchase a garment in order to obligate ourselves in the mitzva of tzitzit (Abrabanel versus the *Shulchan Arukh*)
- The value of "opting-in" to mitzvot that are not formally required (Rambam, Rosh, Tosafot)
- Viewing mitzvot as opportunities for connection, as opposed to obligations we may try to circumvent (Rambam, Rabbi Yonah)
- Appreciating tzitzit as signifying subservience to God based on love and devotion, rather than fear and coercion (Rabbi Asher Weiss)
- Appreciating the status of tzitzit as the collective uniform of those who have chosen a life of commitment (Rabbi Moshe Feinstein)

Chapter 6

Jewish Modes of Dress

Modesty and Cultural Identity

Beyond the mitzvot of head covering and tzitzit, halakha has other implications for our general mode of dress.

Many people believe that Jewish law does not have anything in particular to say about what type of clothing to wear, aside from the overall injunction to dress modestly. However, in addition to the question of modesty, traditional sources also discuss the question of distinctiveness – whether a Jew is required to dress in a distinctly Jewish manner.

In analyzing traditional source material on these questions, we shall reflect on the interplay between Jewish law and culture, and the ways in which halakha can serve as the medium to affirm Judaism's unique cultural vision.

TZEFANYA: DRESS AND THE
CHALLENGES OF ASSIMILATION

The Torah provides limited explicit guidance about whether there is any requirement to dress in distinctly Jewish garb.[1] However, the prophet

---

1. Cf. Lev. 18:3.

Tzefanya harshly indicts those Jews who wear gentile clothing: "It will happen on the days of Hashem's slaughter that I will deal with the officials and the king's sons and all who wear foreign garments."[2]

One possible interpretation is that the prophet is admonishing those who imitate idolaters by wearing some type of religious clothing associated with foreign worship.[3] However, the *Daat Mikra* offers a different explanation, which assumes that the problem of wearing gentile clothing is not specifically an issue of religious attire. Rather, according to the *Daat Mikra*, Tzefanya admonishes those who wear *any* form of gentile garb that is visibly distinct from the clothing worn by the Jews in Judea.[4] According to this approach, the Jewish people are required to wear distinctly Jewish clothing, and failing to do so can invoke the wrath of God. While it is unclear what "Jewish clothing" actually looked like, it is evident that this text requires Jews to wear clothing that affirms their affiliation with the Jewish community.

In a similar vein, the Midrash notes that the ancient Israelites were able to maintain their cultural identity during their slavery in Egypt by preserving their own "clothing, food, and language." According to this *midrash*, these cultural affirmations allowed the Jews to remain a "separate nation, distinct from the Egyptians."[5] The *Meshekh Chokhma*[6] argues that this insistence on cultural distinction was based on a directive given by our forefather, Yaakov, as a preparatory measure to protect against assimilation during the Egyptian exile. Yaakov was aware that without a firm commitment to distinctly Jewish culture, the Jews would lose any sense of uniqueness during their sojourn in Egypt. Therefore, he directed his children to preserve their Jewish names and Jewish clothing.[7]

This approach highlights the role that clothing plays in preserving identity. While clothing styles have no intrinsic value in themselves, wearing distinctively Jewish garments affirms the power of externals and portrays our group affiliation.

---

2. Zephaniah 1:8.
3. See Rashi, ibid.
4. *Daat Mikra*, ibid., s.v *ve'al kol.*
5. *Pesikta Zutra, Ki Tavo* 45a.
6. Rabbi Meir Simha HaKohen, nineteenth/twentieth centuries, Dvinsk (Latvia).
7. *Meshekh Chokhma*, Leviticus 26:44.

RABBI AKIVA YOSEF SCHLESINGER: CLOTHING
AS AN AFFIRMATION OF JEWISH CULTURE

While the *Meshekh Hokhma* places the role of Jewish clothing in the context of fighting assimilation, nineteenth-century Orthodox rabbis expanded the conversation, emphasizing the independent value of a commitment to wearing distinctively Jewish clothing. This position is documented in detail in an article by Dr. Michael Silber, who notes that the ultra-Orthodox rabbis were insistent in their belief that "precisely these seemingly non-confessional elements [such as dress] were invested with supreme religious valence."[8] One of the leaders of ultra-Orthodoxy, Rabbi Akiva Yosef Schlesinger, wrote the following about the significance of preserving distinctly Jewish names, language, and clothing, claiming:

> If, God forbid, you remove these from Israel, then all the commandments are only an empty garment without a body, for these things are the very body of the Israelite that make him a Jew. Because of them we became a people, as Scriptures states, "I am a Hebrew; I worship the Lord, the God of Heaven" (Yona 1:9).[9]

Dr. Silber explains that Rabbi Schlesinger's reference to the verse from Yona is essential to his argument, as "the order of events is intimated in the verse: 'First came Hebrew nationhood and then followed the worship of the Lord, Judaism.'"[10]

According to this paradigm, Jewish clothing is important beyond the role it plays in protecting the Jewish people from the threat of assimilation. The Jewish people are a nation, and the nationalist spirit of Jewish identity requires Jews to wear uniquely Jewish garb. By wearing Jewish clothing, we Jews affirm our Judaism as a national calling as well as a religious vision.

---

8. Dr. Michael Silber, "The Emergence of Ultra-Orthodoxy: The Invention of a Tradition," in *The Uses of Tradition: Jewish Continuity Since Emancipation*, ed. Jack Wertheimer (New York: JTS, distributed by Harvard University Press, 1992), 68.
9. Ibid. 71.
10. Ibid.

MAHARIK: DRESS AND THE WORLD OF VALUES

While the sources cited so far affirm a requirement to dress in a way that looks particularly Jewish, other sources present a different perspective, shifting the dialogue from external appearance towards a discussion about the values that should highlight the Jewish wardrobe. The primary advocate for this view is the Maharik.[11]

According to the Maharik, clothing worn by gentiles is problematic only if it falls into one of two categories: clothing that is immodest, since it is assumed that wearing this clothing affirms the underlying assumptions associated with idolatry; and clothing that does not seem to have a rational purpose and whose source might be idolatrous, associated with a worldview that is antithetical to Torah.[12] This position is codified by Rabbi Moshe Isserles,[13] who permits a doctor to wear a white coat because this entails no breach of modesty and serves a clearly rational purpose of identifying him as a medical practitioner.[14]

In this model, there is no formal requirement for a Jew to dress in a way that is externally unique. If gentiles adopt the ideals of the Torah and dress accordingly, a Jew would not be obligated to change his clothing at all. Rather, clothing represents an opportunity to engage the world of virtues and affirm our connection to the Torah's unique spiritual worldview.

MIDRASH: THE ROLE OF INTENT

An interesting midrashic observation pinpoints the question of Jewish clothing as a question of intent. According to the Midrash, one is not allowed to say, "Just like they [gentiles wear clothing X], so too I am going to wear [the same type of clothing]."[15]

This view is expanded upon by Rabbi Menashe Klein,[16] who addresses the halakhic permissibility of wearing modern garb. While noting that it is technically permissible, Rabbi Klein encourages those who wear modern attire to make some minor change in order to demonstrate

---

11. Rabbi Yosef b. Shlomo Colon, fifteenth century, France/Italy.
12. Maharik, responsum 88. Cf. Sanhedrin 52b and Avodah Zarah 11a.
13. "The Rema," sixteenth century, Poland.
14. *Yoreh De'ah* 178:1.
15. *Sifrei*, Deuteronomy 81, s.v. *pen tidrosh*.
16. Rabbi Menashe Klein, twentieth/twenty-first centuries, New York.

that their intent is not to imitate the practices of gentiles. For example, he suggests that when wearing a suit, it should be buttoned with the right flap placed over the left, rather than with the left flat over the right, as is the modern custom.[17]

This approach compels us to reflect on the motives behind our desire to choose one form of clothing over another. One person may prefer wearing modern dress because of an attraction to the style or fashion. Another person may choose modern clothing specifically in order to culturally assimilate and blend in more smoothly to a non-Jewish environment. Focusing on intent allows us to reflect on our motives and determine the extent to which we are proud of the values that the Torah represents. Just as a Mets fan would affirm his "Mets-pride" by wearing a Mets baseball jersey at a baseball game, a Jew should similarly always dress in a manner affirming pride in the ideals that his clothing signifies.

RABBI MOSHE FEINSTEIN: CLOTHING IN A CHANGING WORLD

Rabbi Moshe Feinstein wrote an important responsum about the permissibility of wearing modern attire.[18] Citing the aforementioned view of the Maharik, Rabbi Feinstein concludes that as long as there is no breach of modesty, there is no halakhic problem with wearing contemporary clothing. Rabbi Feinstein also provides a fascinating rationale for the lenient approach to this question.

Rabbi Feinstein begins by noting that many Jews wear clothing fashioned in modern style, and it is therefore extremely difficult to determine which types of clothing are considered "non-Jewish." After all, it is possible that some of the clothing worn by non-Jews originated within the Jewish community! The *Minchat Chinukh*[19] makes a similar observation, noting that the halakhic issues associated with wearing non-Jewish clothing are contextual and can evolve over time.[20] Clothing

---

17. *Mishneh Halakhot* 4:115.
18. *Iggerot Moshe*, Yoreh Deah 1:81.
19. Rabbi Yosef b. R. Moshe Babad, nineteenth century, Galicia.
20. *Minhat Hinukh* 251:1.

styles and associations change; a person is certainly permitted to wear clothing that at one point in Jewish history was assumed to be the garb of a non-Jew but over time has become associated with traditional Jewish communities.

Due to the difficulty of distinguishing between traditional and modern clothing, decisors such as Rabbi Feinstein discuss this topic through the lens of modesty. Since modest attire is an eternal ethic, it can be observed without difficulty and without the challenges of determining which clothing is culturally Jewish.

As opposed to those ultra-Orthodox rabbis who urge maintaining distinctive dress and other non-ritual markers of Jewishess, Rabbi Feinstein offers a theoretical suggestion.[21] He posits that cultural forms of Jewish expression were critical only in the time before the giving of the Torah on Mount Sinai, when the Jewish people did not yet have a ritual framework to establish their identity. During their experience of Egyptian servitude, non-ritual markers such as distinct names and language, preserved their singularity and affirmed a uniquely Jewish culture. However, after the covenant at Sinai, this was no longer necessary. The mitzvot themselves became the way in which Jews retained their ethnic identity and separateness. Instead of eating food that was culturally Jewish, *kashrut* became the Jewish food ethic. Similarly, wearing distinctly Jewish clothing was no longer critical; dressing in a modest manner became the way in which Jews distinguished themselves, thus affirming the values of the Torah.

Rabbi Bachya[22] similarly argues that the need for Jews to dress distinctively is addressed by the mitzvot themselves. The background of his comment is a verse in Leviticus in which God states, "You shall be holy for Me, for I Hashem am holy, and have separated you from the nations to be mine."[23] Rabbi Bachya comments that the "wisdom of the Torah obligates us to be distinct in our dress, drink, and clothing."[24] In other words, the Torah itself recognizes the need to legislate in a way

21. *Iggerot Moshe,* Orach Chayim 4:66.
22. Rabbi Bachya b. Asher, thirteenth century, Spain
23. Lev. 20:26.
24. Rabbi Bachya, ibid.

that definitively created distinction between Jew and gentile. The Torah accomplishes this goal by providing biblical regulations that spiritually contextualize cultural aspects of identity, such as language and food. The emphasis, for Rabbi Bachya, is on the substance of mitzvot. The mitzvot themselves facilitate separation and provide our cultural distinction.

TALMUD: CLOTHING AND SANCTIFYING GOD'S NAME

A passage in Tractate Sanhedrin adds another perspective. In attempting to provide an example of a "minor" mitzva for which we would be obligated to give up our lives (under certain circumstances),[25] the Gemara cites the view of Rav, who says that this category refers even to a case in which a Jew is asked to "change his shoelaces."[26] Rashi explains that the Jewish manner of tying shoelaces was more modest than that of their gentile neighbors. As a result, this custom had to be preserved even at the risk of death, since publicly tying shoes in the manner of the non-Jews represents an affirmation of an ethic of immodesty and would constitute a desecration of God's name.[27] Rashi's explanation assumes that wearing Jewish clothing is not simply a matter of affirming distinction. Rather, even the way in which Jews tie their shoes represents profound Jewish ideals.

The Rif[28] maintains that the distinctive feature of Jewish shoelaces was their color: non-Jews wore red laces, while Jews insisted on wearing black in order to distinguish themselves from their non-Jewish neighbors.[29] According to one interpretation of the Rif's ruling, his underlying view is similar to that of Rashi. Red is a brighter, flashier color, and the insistence on wearing black laces was thus an attempt to affirm a more modest form of attire. However, it would be possible to read the Rif as suggesting that the goal of wearing black was simply to provide cultural distinction and establish a clear, visible contrast between Jew and gentile. According to this broader reading, under certain circumstances,

---

25. In public, or even in private during times of oppression.
26. Sanhedrin 74b.
27. Rashi, ibid., s.v *arkata*.
28. Rabbi Yitzchak Alfasi, eleventh century, Spain.
29. Rif, Sanhedrin 17b.

a Jew could be called upon to give up his life simply to avoid affirming cultural affiliation with a foreign group. Wearing the black shoelaces, thus, sanctifies God's name by affirming a Jew's commitment to the Jewish people.[30]

Whichever interpretation of this talmudic passage we adopt, it clearly highlights the sense of Jewish pride that we should have, ideally, in the clothes we wear each day. Our clothing serves an important function by delineating group affiliation, but it also presents an opportunity to publicly affirm the values of that group.

SUMMARY

The question of whether or not there is an obligation for a Jew to dress in a distinct manner demonstrates the complex interplay between Jewish law and culture. Moreover, this discussion highlights the expansive vision of Jewish law. Beyond specific mitzvot, such as ritualized handwashing and tzitzit, Jewish law provides profound opportunities to transform ordinary activities, such as getting dressed, into vehicles to connect to divine ideals. In particular, waking up in the morning and deciding to wear clothing that reflect Torah principles allows a Jew to reflect daily upon:

- The power of clothing to help prevent cultural assimilation (Midrash, *Meshekh Chokhma*)
- The way in which clothing helps affirm the nationalist component of Judaism, committed to a uniquely Jewish cultural ideal (Rabbi Akiva Yosef Schlesinger)
- The Torah's modesty ethic and how clothing affirms a commitment to this value (Maharik, Rabbi Moshe Isserles)
- The extent to which we choose clothing based on a desire to culturally assimilate (Midrash)
- Jewish identity as expressed before and after the giving of the Torah (Rabbi Moshe Feinstein)
- The power of Jewish customs to affirm Torah values and serve as a medium for sanctifying God's name (Tractate Sanhedrin)

---

30. Cf. *Haggahot Maimoniyyot*, Laws of the Foundations of the Torah 5:3.

Chapter 7

Birkat HaTorah

Torah, Community, and Individual Uniqueness

After completing the first set of morning rituals and dressing in a way that reflects Torah ideals, a Jew is then called upon to recite a blessing known as *Birkat HaTorah*. This blessing must be recited before engaging in any form of Torah study. The spiritual significance of this blessing is attested to by a talmudic statement that Jerusalem was destroyed because the Jewish people failed to recite this prayer.[1] The sentiment highlighting the religious importance of this blessing is also expressed by Rabbi Yosef Karo, who begins his discussion of the laws of *Birkat HaTorah* with an emphatic declarative that "one must be especially cautious to recite this daily blessing."[2]

These dramatic rabbinic statements raise interesting questions about the nature of the requirement to recite *Birkat HaTorah*. What is so significant about this blessing that prompted the sages to so vigorously

---

1. Nedarim 81a.
2. *Shulchan Arukh*, Orach Chayim 47:1.

emphasize its importance? Reflecting on sources that address these questions will allow us to better understand the spiritual significance of *Birkat HaTorah*, as well as the means through which this blessing provides the proper religious framework for authentic Torah study.

TALMUD AND RABBI YONASON SACKS: TORAH STUDY AND GOD'S NAME

The story of *Birkat HaTorah* and its religious relevance begins with an interesting talmudic discussion. Seeking biblical support for the requirement to recite *Birkat HaTorah*, the Gemara in Tractate Berakhot cites the position of R. Yehuda, who quotes the verse, "When I call out the name of Hashem, ascribe greatness to our God."[3] Explaining the significance of the proof text and its application to *Birkat HaTorah*, Rashi cites a passage in Tractate Yoma.[4] In the background of the talmudic debate, there is a discussion about the requirement of the people gathered in the Temple to recite a special blessing upon hearing the high priest pronounce the divine name. Interpreting the aforementioned Torah verse, the Talmud understands the verse to be a Mosaic directive, telling the Jewish people that "at the moment that I mention the name of the Holy One, blessed be He, you shall accord Him greatness." According to this discussion, the Torah legislates that upon hearing the divine name, we are required to respond with formal words of praise.

Rashi's reference to the discussion in Yoma raises an apparent inconsistency between two Talmud passages. The discussion in Berakhot cites Deuteronomy 32:3 as the source for the requirement to recite *Birkat HaTorah* before Torah study. However, Tractate Yoma cites the same verse as the source for the idea that one must bless God upon hearing an utterance of the divine name!

In order to reconcile these two passages, Rabbi Yonason Sacks[5] posits that they actually reflect the same theme.[6] Whenever a Jew

---

3. Berakhot 21a, citing Deuteronomy 32:3.
4. Rashi, Berakhot 21a, s.v. *ki*, citing Yoma 37a.
5. Twenty-first century, New Jersey. R. Yonason Sacks, *Orchot Yamim: Insights into the Laws of Keriyat Shema and Prayer*, (Passaic: Rabbi Yonason Sacks, 2007), 260.
6. See Maharsha, *Hiddushei Aggadot, Berakhot* 21a, s.v. *minayin*.

confronts the name of God, he must respond with words of praise. The text in Yoma applies this theme to the case of people who hear God's name in the Temple. The text in Berakhot assumes that the Torah itself is an expression of God's name, and therefore before Torah study – the encounter with the divine name – one must recite the appropriate blessing.

Aside from providing textual support for the requirement to recite blessings before Torah study, this approach highlights the profoundly religious nature of Torah study. Lest we view Torah study as simply an impressive intellectual exercise, the recitation of *Birkat HaTorah* reminds us that Torah study is actually a direct encounter with God Himself. Since the Torah is an expression of God's name, Torah study offers an opportunity to connect to the Divine.

This model explains the rabbinic statements emphasizing the significance of the recitation of *Birkat HaTorah*. Forgetting to recite *Birkat HaTorah* is not simply a missed opportunity to recite an additional blessing. Rather, studying Torah without the accompanying blessings implies a misguided sense of what Torah study is all about.

SHMUEL: FORMALIZING A PERSONAL REQUIREMENT

While the perspective of Rabbi Sacks gives us the source and reasoning behind the requirement for a Jew to recite words of praise prior to studying Torah, the precise language and formulation of the blessing remains vague in the discussion at Berakhot 21a. An additional discussion in Tractate Berakhot cites the view of Shmuel, who argues that before studying Torah we should recite the blessing "Who has sanctified us with His commandments and has commanded us to involve ourselves with words of Torah."[7]

Dr. Moshe Benovitz notes that this formal blessing required by Shmuel stands in contrast to earlier tannaitic prayers recited before Torah study, which were much more fluid and personal.[8] For example, the Mishna in Berakhot cites the prayer that R. Nechunya ben Hakana would recite upon entering and leaving the study hall: "When I enter, I

---

7. Berakhot 11b.
8. Moshe Benovitz, *Talmud HaIggud Meaimatay Korein at* Shema (Jerusalem: *HaIggud LeParshanut HaTalmud*, 2006), 532.

pray that a mishap not come about through me, and when I exit, I give thanks for my portion."[9]

While these personal prayers acknowledge the individual nature of Torah study and help us to connect to the experience of Torah study, they could also give the mistaken impression that Torah study is an optional exercise to be engaged in when we feel personally inspired. By introducing a blessing that uses the standard formula for ritual obligations, Shmuel reminds us that Torah study is a halakhic obligation, a daily requirement regardless of whether or not we feel motivated to study.

R. YOCHANAN: RESTORING THE PERSONAL DIMENSION OF TORAH STUDY

After citing the position of Shmuel, the Talmud goes on to cite the view of R. Yochanan, who presents an alternative text for *Birkat HaTorah*:

> Now, sweeten, Hashem, our God, the words of Your Torah in our mouths, and in the mouths of Your nation, the house of Israel. And may we be – we and our grandchildren and the grandchildren of Your nation, and the House of Israel – [may] we all [be] of those who know Your name and who occupy themselves with Your Torah. Blessed are You, Hashem, who teaches Torah to his nation, Israel.[10]

R. Yochanan's suggested blessing appears to stand independent of Shmuel's blessing, and it reflects a fundamentally different thematic approach. As Dr. Benovitz notes, the model proposed by R. Yochanan resembles the more personally-oriented supplications that were recited by the *Tanna'im* before they engaged in Torah study.[11] While Shmuel focuses on the obligatory status of Torah study, R. Yochanan reminds us that Torah study is a deeply personal experience and that the blessing recited beforehand should reflect our own personal relationship to Torah.

---

10. Berakhot 11b.
11. Moshe Benovitz, *Talmud HaIggud Meaimatay Korein at* Shema (Jerusalem: *HaIggud LeParshanut HaTalmud*, 2006), 534.

R. HAMNUNA: THE NATIONAL
SIGNIFICANCE OF TORAH STUDY

In addition to the views of Shmuel and R. Yochanan, the Talmud cites a third view quoted in the name of R. Hamnuna. According to this perspective, before engaging in Torah study, we should recite a blessing praising God: "Who chose us from all the nations and gave us His Torah. Blessed are You, Hashem, who gives the Torah." R. Hamnuna maintains that this is the ideal terminology since it incorporates thanks to Hashem along with praise of the Torah and the Jewish people.[12]

While Shmuel's suggested blessing points out the obligatory status of Torah study and R. Yochanan's model addresses the personal dimension of Torah learning, R. Hamnuna focuses on the national dimension of Torah study. In fact, the Tur[13] argues that when reciting this blessing, we should have in mind the collective experience of the Jewish people receiving the Torah at Sinai.[14] R. Hamnuna reminds us that beyond our individual experiences with Torah study, engaging Jewish texts is a national responsibility, connecting us to our shared moment of collective revelation at Mount Sinai.

R. PAPPA: SYNTHESIS

After citing the view of R. Hamnuna, the Talmud issues a final ruling: one must recite *all three* blessings daily. In our texts of the Talmud, this ruling is cited unanimously, but other talmudic manuscripts quote this view in the name of R. Pappa.[15] Dr. Benovitz notes that the citation of R. Pappa as the author of this ruling is significant.[16] In other talmudic disputes regarding the proper text of specific blessings, R. Pappa advocates combining the various formulas into one long blessing.[17] In the case of *Birkat HaTorah*, by contrast, he rules that all three blessings should be recited separately!

This ruling by R. Pappa reflects the complex dynamic of Torah study. Torah study is a deeply personal experience (second blessing)

---

12. See Rashi, Berakhot 11b, s.v. *zo*.
13. Rabbi Yaakov b. Asher, thirteenth/fourteenth centuries, Spain.
14. *Tur*, Orach Chayim 47.
15. See Rif, Berakhot 5b.
16. Moshe Benovitz, *Talmud HaIggud Meaimatay Korein at* Shema (Jerusalem: HaIggud LeParshanut HaTalmud, 2006), 544.
17. See, for example, Berakhot 59a.

that is rooted in a profound sense of obligation and responsibility (first blessing). However, these two components of Torah study address Torah study only from the vantagepoint of the individual. Beyond the personal element, Torah is the national treasure of the Jewish people. When Jews engage in Torah study, they affirm their intense connection to their larger collective self (third blessing). The requirement to recite all three blessing thus affirms the multi-dimensional dynamic of Torah study.

TOSAFOT: AWARENESS

Tosafot raise an interesting question about a unique legal feature of the laws of *Birkat HaTorah*.[18] *Tosafot* note that most mitzvot require the recitation of a new blessing each time the mitzva is performed. For example, every time we eat in the sukka, we are required by Jewish law to recite an additional blessing. However, with regard to Torah study, the recitation of *Birkat HaTorah* one time daily suffices; no additional blessings are required for any subsequent Torah study.

Explaining this halakhic oddity, *Tosafot* argue that since the obligation to study Torah is continuous, we are mentally aware of this obligation throughout the day, and therefore no added blessing is required for any further learning. The completion of other mitzvot, by contrast, creates what Rabbi Joseph B. Soloveitchik (the Rav) terms a "discontinuity of awareness," which necessitates the recitation of a new blessing.

While *Tosafot's* explanation clarifies the distinction between Torah study and other mitzvot, it fails to address the scenario in which we study Torah for a certain amount of time and then break off with the intention of studying no further Torah that day. Does this not create a "discontinuity of awareness"? Why would we not be required to recite another blessing if we subsequently change our minds and do decide to study Torah again that day?

Addressing this question, the Rav argues that according to *Tosafot*, there are, in fact, two kinds of awareness. The first "is an acute awareness, [and] clearly this is lacking when we think about other matters." The second, according to the Rav, "is latent awareness, and this awareness is still present even though we are engaged in other matters."

---

18. *Tosafot*, Berakhot 11b, s.v. *shekvar*.

In order to clarify this distinction, R. Soloveitchik compares it to the love that a mother has for her child. When a mother plays with her child, she experiences "acute awareness," since she is actively focused and attentive to her child's well-being. However, even when a mother is at work and therefore distracted, there is still a "latent awareness of her child's existence." This latent awareness remains with the mother for her entire life and "cannot be extinguished." Similarly, while a Jew may not experience "acute awareness" of Torah during every minute of a twenty-four hour period, his "latent awareness [of Torah] never ceases."[19]

In this view, *Birkat HaTorah* highlights the intrinsic connection between the Jewish people and the Torah. A Jew relates to the Torah with the same love as parents relate to their own children. The law requiring the recitation of *Birkat HaTorah* only once a day acknowledges this personal bond and allows us to continuously reflect on our passion and commitment to Torah study.

SHIBBOLEI HALEKET: TORAH STUDY AS AN EXERCISE IN JEWISH LIVING

The *Shibbolei HaLeket*[20] adds another perspective, raising the same issue discussed by *Tosafot*, yet providing a very different answer.[21] The *Shibbolei HaLeket* begins by noting that even outside the framework of formal Torah study, there are endless opportunities throughout the day to reflect upon the laws of the Torah in order to properly live a life guided by the dictates of halakha. Even when we enter the bathroom, there are detailed regulations that place the experience of relieving ourselves within a religious framework.

The all-encompassing nature of Jewish law thus explains why *Birkat HaTorah* is recited only once daily. Most mitzvot have a clear beginning and end point. As a result, any subsequent re-engagement with the mitzva requires an additional blessing. Torah study, by contrast, has no definite end point because sitting in a study hall over a tractate of Talmud is not

---

19. Rabbi Joseph B. Soloveitchik, "On the Love of Torah: Impromptu Remarks at a Siyyum," prepared by M. Kasdan, in *Shiurei HaRav: A Conspectus of the Public Lectures of Joseph D. Soloveitchik* (Hoboken: Ktav, 1974), 184.
20. Rabbi Tzedakiah b. R. Avraham HaRofeh, thirteenth century, Italy.
21. *Shibbolei HaLeket, Inyanei Tefilla* 5.

the only way to engage in the mitzva of Torah study. Simply meditating and thinking about the proper method of actualizing a halakhic practice also falls within the definition of Torah study. Since Torah study is actually a state of consciousness that we actively reflect upon throughout the day, the *Birkat HaTorah* recited in the morning is sufficient for the entire day.

While *Tosafot* focus on the intrinsic love that a Jew feels towards Torah study, the *Shibbolei HaLeket* reorients us to think about the opportunities to reflect on Torah ideas throughout the day. This approach reminds us that a halakhic life requires a contemplative posture. Beyond performing specific rituals, we should meditate on the proper mechanism for observance of the law, as well as on the underlying values of the law itself.

SUMMARY

Despite the fact that *Birkat HaTorah* is recited only once daily, the ideals behind its recitation reflect profound insights about our relationship to Torah study that continue to have an impact on our daily routines. Understanding the significance of *Birkat HaTorah* and reflecting upon its messages allow us to:

- Understand Torah study as an entry point to developing a relationship with God and understanding His essence (Talmud, Rabbi Sacks)
- Reflect upon our obligation to study Torah daily (Shmuel)
- Highlight our own unique, personal relationship with Torah (Rabbi Yochanan)
- Engage with the Torah as the national treasure of the Jewish people (R. Hamnuna)
- Appreciate how Torah study is a multifaceted mitzva containing a fixed obligation, a strong individual component, and a communal/national element (R. Papa)
- Understand our intrinsic and profound connection to Torah study and the "latent awareness" it creates (*Tosafot*, Rav Soloveitchik)
- See Torah study as a religious posture contextualizing our entire religious life (*Shibbolei HaLeket*)
- Recognize the daily opportunities to reflect and engage in conversation about Torah (*Shibbolei HaLeket*)

Chapter 8

Tefillin

Theology, Torah Study, and the Challenges of Sanctity

Traditional Jewish law assumes that after completing halakhic commitments upon waking in the morning, an observant Jew then makes his way to the synagogue for morning prayers. Before entering the synagogue, we embark on a spiritual journey introducing us to profound concepts inspired by the details of halakha. Upon arrival at the synagogue, the formal journey of Jewish law continues with the obligation to place tefillin on the forehead and arm.

On the surface, this ritual seems arbitrary. What possible spiritual message can be conveyed by placing these strange black boxes on our bodies? Moreover, what new religious lesson does one learn from fulfilling the mitzva of tefillin that could not be experienced through the other rituals we have already performed in the morning? Reflecting on sources that explain the underlying logic of this mitzva will help provide a meaningful framework to better appreciate the daily religious opportunities facilitated by the mitzva of tefillin.

HISTORICAL CONTEXT: EDUCATION

The mitzva of tefillin has its source in the Torah, which commands us four times to put the tefillin on our arms and between our eyes.[1] The precise details are spelled out by the Talmud.

The black, square boxes of the tefillin contain certain Torah passages written on pieces of parchment. Providing a historical background, Dr. Jeffrey Tigay notes that "such capsules, in the form of amulets, were a common device [in antiquity] for attaching inscriptions to the body." In fact, the "physical similarity of tefillin to amulets was clear to the ancients...talmudic sources frequently mention tefillin and amulets together and speak of the possibility of confusing them with each other." However, while tefillin and amulets may have a similar exterior, their contents are radically different. According to Dr. Tigay, "amulets typically contain magical inscriptions or materials, and aim to protect the wearer." Tefillin, by contrast, contain "biblical passages about the Exodus from Egypt and God's instructions, and thus serve an educational purpose."[2]

RABBI ELIEZER MELAMED: TEFILLIN AND JEWISH THEOLOGY

The contrast between tefillin and ancient amulets typifies the unique theological vision of the Torah. Whereas a magical amulet is supposed to mysteriously affect the cosmos, the tefillin contain theological messages and serve to remind us of our obligations to God. The passages to be placed within the boxes of the tefillin reflect this purpose.

Both the tefillin worn on the forehead and on the arm contain four separate sets of biblical verses. However, while the citations located in the tefillin of the arm are written on one piece of parchment, those in the tefillin of the head are written on four separate pieces of parchment.

Rabbi Eliezer Melamed notes that the first two passages found in the tefillin[3] describe the sanctity of the Jewish firstborn and the holiday of Pesach. By referencing these specific themes, the tefillin affirm basic

---

1. Ex. 13:9, 16; Deut. 6:8; 11:28.
2. Jefferey Tigay, *The JPS Torah Commentary: Deuteronomy* (Philadelphia/New York: The Jewish Publication Society, 1996), 441.
3. Ex. 13:1-10; 11-16.

Jewish concepts, such as the singularity of the Jewish people, God's providential role, and the centrality of the Land of Israel. The second set of passages,[4] according to Rabbi Melamed, highlight God's oneness, the requirement to love God, transmit His Torah, and the Jewish concep of reward and punishment. The tefillin are educationally effective because they provide a constant reminder of the core theological beliefs of traditional Judaism. Wearing the tefillin on both the head and the arm reminds us that we need to be both intellectually and practically committed to the ideas and laws of the Torah.[5]

KAVANA AND TEFILLIN: AWARENESS

The role that tefillin play in cultivating a more developed awareness of, and commitment to, traditional Judaism is highlighted by the level of *kavana* (intent) required in the performance of the mitzva. Generally speaking, when performing a religious ritual, the simple intention to perform a divinely mandated act is sufficient.[6] However, the Bach[7] notes that, for some mitzvot, an additional level of intent is demanded.[8] Tefillin falls into this latter category because Exodus 13:9 explicitly states that tefillin are to be worn "so that Hashem's Torah may be in your mouth."[9] Thus it is not sufficent simply to know that the wearing of tefillin is divinely ordained. Rather, when wearing tefillin, we must have the intent to understand the essence and purpose of the mitzva.

The significance of *kavana* while wearing tefillin is codified by Rabbi Yosef Karo in the *Shulhan Arukh*:

> [When wearing tefillin], one should be mindful of the four biblical passages [contained in the tefillin that reference] the oneness of God and the Exodus from Egypt on the arm next to the heart and on the head next to the brain. [The tefillin

---

4. Deut. 6:4-9; 11:13-21.
5. Rabbi Eliezer Melamed, *Peninei Halakha, Likkutin 1* (Israel: Machon Har Beracha, 2006), 191.
6. *Shulchan Arukh*, Orach Chayim 60:4.
7. Rabbi Yoel Sirkus, fifteenth/sixteenth centuries, Poland.
8. Bach, Orach Chayim 8:7.
9. Ex. 13:9.

help us]... remember the miracles and wonders that God performed for us because they teach us about His oneness. [Moreover, they testify to the fact] that He has the power and dominion in the highest places and the lowest places to do in them as He wishes.[10]

The added requirement of special intent further substantiates the educational significance of the mitzva of tefillin. Since the mitzva is intended to help us affirm central aspects of Jewish theology, and thus to inspire a more passionate commitment to mitzvot, it is essential that we understand the ideals that underlie this mitzva.

The placement of the tefillin on the the head and on the arm (next to the heart) helps further this educational goal. The *Shulchan Arukh* notes that the head represents the more elevated aspects of our identity, while the heart symbolizes our desires, which sometimes tempt us to avoid listening to the divine call.[11] Wearing the tefillin on both of these parts of the body reminds us that our actions – as directed by the heart – are to be motivated and guided by the virtues that exist in our minds. Becoming cognizant of the messages inherent in the mitzva of tefillin ensures that our actions properly reflect these ideals.

TEFILLIN AND TORAH STUDY: A PERPETUAL LEARNING OPPORTUNITY

The sources that we have seen so far emphasize tefillin's educational purpose, which is accomplished by internalizing the lessons intrinsic in the mitzva. A midrashic source elaborates on this theme, asserting that wearing tefillin is actually a fulfillment of the obligation to study Torah. The Midrash quotes R. Eliezer, who states:

God told the Jewish people that they are to learn Torah day and night. The Jewish people [replied]: Are we really capable of learning Torah all day and all night? God replied: My children, place tefillin on your heads and your arms! [By wearing

---

10. *Shulchan Arukh*, Orach Chayim 25:5.
11. Ibid.

the tefillin, it will be as if] you are learning Torah day and night, as the verse states: "It shall be for you a sign on your arm and reminder between your eyes, so that Hashem's Torah may be in your mouth."[12]

The connection between tefillin and Torah study is noted by another midrashic source, which states that "when someone wears tefillin, it is as if he is reading from the Torah, and [therefore] anyone who reads from the Torah is exempt from [the mitzva of tefillin]."[13]

On the surface, it is difficult to understand the connection between tefillin and *talmud Torah*. After all, one is an intellectual experience, while the other involves a physical act of placing black boxes on one's head and arm, an act that could be done without thinking at all. But the added intent required to fulfill the mitzva of tefillin compels us to reflect on the ideals expressed by this mitzvah, and this is in itself a form of Torah study. The goal of wearing tefillin, as Rabbi Yakov Nagen notes, is to internalize the lessons of the mitzva and make them a fixed part of our consciousness.[14]

Rabbi Nagen also cites the view of the *Tanya* that knowledge (*yeda*) comes from the biblical verse "Now that man had known (*yada*) his wife and she conceived."[15] This linkage is not coincidental. It underscores the fact that Torah study in the Jewish tradition requires an intimate internalization of Torah knowledge. This explains why wearing tefillin is an effective way of accomplishing the mitzva of Torah study. Wearing tefillin requires us to constantly reflect on the messages of the mitzva, thus intellectually internalizing the lesson and values of the Torah.

This function of internalization is underscored by the fact that ideally, tefillin are worn all day! While *talmud Torah* forces us to take a break from our ordinary activities and engage the world of the study hall, tefillin (when worn all day) provide an opportunity for us to occupy

---

12. Tractate Tefillin 1:20.
13. *Mekhilta DeRebbe Yishmael, Parashat Bo*, s.v. *lema'an*.
14. Yakov Nagen, *Waking Up to a New Day* (Israel: Maggid, 2013), 321-322.
15. *Tanya*, ch. 3, citing Genesis 4:1.

ourselves with Torah learning even in our regular environment. By wearing the tefillin and reflecting on their messages, we ensure that the day
is constantly infused with Torah study.

HESECH HADAAT: THE CHALLENGE OF
PERPETUAL INTIMACY WITH GOD

Although the wearing of tefillin all day provides an opportunity to connect with God and His Torah, it presents its own set of challenges. The
Talmud cites the view of Rabba bar R. Huna, who states that "a person is
obligated to touch his tefillin constantly [in order to be constantly aware
of their presence]."[16] To substantiate his claim, Rabba bar R. Huna
appeals to an *a fortiori* argument based on the obligation of the high
priest to maintain constant awareness of his golden headplate (*tzitz*):

> Since [concerning the] *tzitz*, which has only one mention [of
> God's name], the Torah said "and it shall be on his [the high
> priest's] forehead constantly," [which teaches] that he should not
> divert his attention from it, [then concerning] tefillin, in which
> there are many mentions of [God's name], how much more so
> [should a person not divert his attention from them]!

This requirement is codified by the *Shulchan Arukh.*[17] Rabbi Eliezer
Melamed notes that the strict letter of the law follows the view of those
authorities who maintain that Rabba bar R. Huna's dictum prohibits inappropriate thoughts only while wearing tefillin.[18] Nonetheless, traditional
halakhists encourage us to avoid any secular thoughts while wearing tefillin.

This requirement is exceptionally challenging. Is it really possible
to expect someone to neutralize any non-sacred thoughts while wearing tefillin? This is especially difficult when the tefillin are worn all day!
Can one go his entire day immersed in the world of sacred thinking?
Sensitive to these issues, the *Shulchan Arukh* explains that the challenge

---

16. Menachot 36b.
17. *Shulchan Arukh*, Orach Chayim 28:1.
18. Rabbi Eliezer Melamed, *Peninei Halakha, Likkutim* 1 (Israel: Machon Har Beracha,
2006), 195.

of maintaining focused awareness throughout the day is one of the reasons that people stopped the practice of wearing tefillin throughout the entire day. Instead, current Jewish practice requires wearing tefillin only during the morning prayer service.[19] Limiting the wearing of tefillin specifically to the time of prayer ensures that our thoughts will be appropriately focused while wearing tefillin.

This ruling of the *Shulchan Arukh* highlights the challenges of maintaining a consciousness of perpetual holiness. On the one hand, tefillin provide an opportunity to reflect on the ideals that the tefillin symbolize. One the other hand, this mitzva demands a level of awareness that is beyond the capability of most observant Jews. Wearing tefillin during morning prayers reminds us of the opportunity offered and the challenges posed by the mitzva of tefillin.

TEFILLIN AND JEWISH PRIDE

While the sources we have seen thus far focus on the educational and religious opportunities provided by tefillin, the Talmud suggests an additional approach that emphasizes the role that tefillin play in instilling a strong sense of Jewish pride. The Talmud begins by quoting a verse from the Torah: "…all the nations of the world will see that the name of Hashem is called upon you and they will be in awe of you."[20] Expounding this text, R. Eliezer the Great claims that the verse refers to the tefillin worn on the head.[21] In other words, wearing tefillin on our heads results in other nations becoming fearful of God. *Tosafot* explains that it is specifically the tefillin worn on the head that facilitates this fear, as the head tefillin is visible to all, while the tefillin worn on the arm is covered.[22]

Margaliot HaShas offers an alternative suggestion, noting that the homily of R. Eliezer linking the head tefillin to increased fear of God among gentiles uses a specific Hebrew formulation (*tefillin shebarosh*) that can also be translated as "tefillin that are *in* the head."[23] According

---

19. *Shulchan Arukh*, Orach Chayim 37:2.
20. Deut. 28:10.
21. Berakhot 6a.
22. *Tosafot*, ibid., s.v. *elu*.
23. Berachot 80-81, cited in Rabbi Eliyahu Maman, ‏כל שיש לו תפילין בראשו ותפילין בזרעו‎. http://www.yeshiva.org.il/midrash/13861.

to this suggestion, the tefillin generate fear only when the Jewish people, who wear tefillin, internalize the messages of the mitzva "on their heads." In other words, the pride that Jews feel from the values associated with the mitzva cause other nations to realize that God's presence rests upon them. This awareness is what generates the awe that the gentile nations feel towards God and His people.

SUMMARY

In the contemporary experience of wearing tefillin, the mitzva is observed only during the morning prayer service. However, the spiritual lessons that tefillin reflect are intended to inspire us throughout the entire day. Properly meditating on the values that underlie this mitzva allows us to:

- Appreciate the educational role of the tefillin, especially when contrasted with ancient amulets (Dr. Tigay)
- Affirm the theological assumptions of the biblical passages contained in the tefillin (Rabbi Melamed)
- Understand the model of Torah study that tefillin symbolize (Tractate Tefillin, Rabbi Nagen)
- Note the challenges of the perpetual divine awareness demanded by tefillin (*Shulchan Arukh*)
- Reflect on Jewish pride and how internalizing Torah values helps generate an added appreciation of God and His commandments among both Jews and gentiles (Talmud, Margaliot HaShas)

Chapter 9

Prayer
Divine Encounters and Personal Change

Once we have put on tefillin, the next stop on the journey of Jewish law is the experience of daily prayer.

Prayer[1] stands at the center of a traditional Jew's daily routine. According to Jewish law, we are required to pray three times each day: morning, afternoon, and evening.[2] The three daily prayer services all have at their core the *Amida*, the series of nineteen blessings that contain elements of praise, request, and gratitude.

The act of praying three times a day can be quite daunting. Aside from the basic challenge of proper focus, there are philosophical and religious questions that confront anyone engaged in prayer. For example: What are we trying to accomplish when we pray? Are we trying to provide a compelling argument to God so that He will hear our prayers

---

1. While the types of prayers offered in the context of a service differ, the word "prayer" used in this chapter refers to the traditional *Amida* prayer.
2. Traditional authorities differ regarding the scope of a woman's daily prayer obligations. For a discussion of the legal parameters of a woman's obligation to pray, see R. David Brofsky, "Shiur #19-The Obligation to Pray," at: http://etzion.org.il/en/obligation-pray.

and respond favorably? How can we harmonize such a conception of prayer with God's omniscience? How can a finite human being present new information to an infinite and transcendent God?

Beyond the philosophical question of the efficacy of prayer, the act of prayer raises questions about the type of religious posture it seeks to inculcate. By offering praise of God and articulating our endless thanks, are we attempting to highlight our dependency on God's providence? Or is humility our central religious task when we are deeply immersed in the experience of prayer?

Aside from the intellectual appeal of these questions, developing a sophisticated approach to prayer is critical in order to truly appreciate the daily encounter with God through the medium of prayer. Unfortunately, prayer is often experienced as a burden, with congregants rushing to finish the service as quickly as possible. Indeed, the phenomenon of talking during prayer services indicates the extent to which people feel disconnected from the experience of prayer. If we really felt that prayer is a profoundly religious encounter, would talking to our friends while simultaneously conversing with God even be an option? By reflecting on traditional Jewish sources that address these questions, we can build the intellectual and religious foundations necessary for a reinvigorated prayer experience.

PRAYER AS AN ENCOUNTER AND THE CENTRALITY OF *KAVANA* (INTENT)

Before beginning our exploration of the philosophical and theological questions addressed by prayer, it is important to highlight the role that *kavana* (intent) plays in defining the legal contours of the obligation to pray. Rabbi Joseph B. Soloveitchik notes that while Jewish legal authorities debate whether or not we must have proper intent in order to fulfill a mitzva, there is a rabbinic consensus that proper intent is an indispensable requirement of the experience of prayer.[3] Rav Soloveitchik elaborates on this idea, noting that "*kavana* related to prayer is ... not an extraneous addendum, but at the very core of prayer."[4]

---

3. See Rabbi Reuven Ziegler, *Majesty and Humility: The Thought of Rabbi Joseph B. Soloveitchik* (Jerusalem/New York: Urim Publications, 2012), 214.
4. Rabbi Joseph Soloveitchik, *The Lonely Man of Faith* (New York: Doubleday, 1992), 74 footnote 1.

What type of intent should we be striving for when praying? Rabbi Chaim Soloveitchik[5] addresses this question, noting two different types of intent that are part of the exercise of prayer.[6] Basing his position on a careful reading of a few passages in the Rambam's "Laws of Prayer," he states that the first type of intent that is required is an awareness that we are standing before God throughout prayer. This type of intent is so crucial that failure to maintain this awareness negates the prayer experience and prevents us from fulfilling our obligation. The second type of intent relates to the understanding of the words of prayer. This requirement, while certainly ideal, has the potential to neutralize the halakhic significance of prayer only if it is lacking during the opening blessing of the *Amida* (*Avot*).

This first type of intent, emphasizing the need to be mindful of God's presence, has its conceptual roots in the Rambam's statement that during prayer "the mind should be distracted from all other thoughts and one should feel that he is standing in the Divine Presence."[7] Rav Joseph Soloveitchik substantiates this approach, noting that many of the specific laws of prayer reflect the idea that prayer is a direct confrontation with the Divine. Unlike the *Shema*, for example, the *Amida* must be recited in a standing position, facing Jerusalem, and with correct posture. Similarly, proper attire is a prerequisite for prayer. While the *Shema* is an intellectual affirmation of God's sovereignty, prayer is ideally the experience of an encounter with God.[8]

Traditional Judaism thus offers an opportunity for standing in God's presence three times daily. Basic awareness of this idea represents the very foundation of traditional Jewish prayer. Knowing that prayer is meant to be a divine encounter causes us to reflect on the extent to which we view the prayer experience as a genuine dialogue with the Divine.

---

5. Rabbi Chaim Soloveitchik, nineteenth century, Volozhin, Lithuania.
6. *Chiddushei Rabbeinu Chayim HaLevi, Hilkhot Tefilla* 4:1.
7. Laws of Prayer 4:16, translation from Rabbi Joseph B. Soloveitchik, *Worship of the Heart: Essays on Jewish Prayer,* ed. Shalom Carmy (Jersey City: Ktav, 2003), 100.
8. Rabbi Joseph Soloveitchik, *Worship of the Heart: Essays on Jewish Prayer,* ed. Shalom Carmy (Jersey City: Ktav, 2003), 100-101.

PRAYER IS ABOUT CHANGING OURSELVES

While the approach cited above focuses on prayer as a direct encounter with God, it does not address the philosophical question of how an omniscient God can be affected by the prayers of a human being.[9]

One traditional answer to this question is offered by the great medieval sage, Rabbi Yosef Albo,[10] in his work *Sefer Ikarim*. Rabbi Albo deals with this challenge by shifting the focus of prayer from God to man.[11] God is omniscient and cannot possibly change His mind based on the requests of man. Nonetheless, prayers can be answered and the impact of one's prayers can be felt in the physical world. How does this happen? Rabbi Albo explains that the experience of prayer is intended to *change man*, not God. An individual becomes refined through the act of prayer and, ideally, is transformed into a new entity. The change that takes place in us is the medium through which prayers are most likely to become actualized.

Imagine, for example, that there is a divine decree that someone should lose his job. When that person prays and internalizes the lessons of the prayerbook, he becomes a "new person," rendering the original decree irrelevant, since it was intended for a person who no longer exists. God thus hears the prayers of an individual, but He is not convinced by new information that He didn't have before. Rather, God created the world with infinite possibilities that can be actualized based on the changing realities of man. When we pray properly and beseech our Creator, we have the potential to change ourselves, thus allowing our prayers to be realized.

In addition to solving a complex philosophical question, this approach clarifies the role of the siddur as a traditional book of Jewish theology and ethics. The siddur is certainly not a book of magic. On the contrary, authentic prayer requires us to meditate and be truly in tune with the messages of the prayer book. The siddur highlights traditional Jewish themes, such as knowledge, forgiveness, healing, and peace. To

---

9. The philosophy of Jewish prayer is a complex topic. For a survey of traditional Jewish perspectives, see, Shalom Rosenberg, "Prayer and Jewish Thought: Approaches and Problems (A Survey)," in *Prayer in Judaism*, ed. Gabriel H. Cohn and Harold Fisch (Northvale, New Jersey: Jason Aronson Publishers, 1996), 69-107.
10. Rabbi Yosef Albo, fourteenth/fifteenth centuries, Spain.
11. *Sefer Ikkarim* 4:18.

internalize these messages and make them the medium through which we see the world is to adopt the mishnaic advice, "Do His [God's] will as if it were yours so that He may do your will as if it were His."[12] When we align our will with God's will, our prayers are likely to be answered. The prayer book is thus a vehicle for knowing God's will, and the act of prayer allows us to become one with God's vision.

In addition, the siddur helps us prioritize our lives and also reminds us what *not* to pray for. As Rabbi Joseph Soloveitchik explains, "Prayer tells the individual, as well as the community, what his, or its, genuine needs are, what he should, or should not, petition God about."[13] By focusing our attention on themes that are rooted in divine ideals, the traditional Jewish prayer book reminds us of life's ultimate purpose.

PRAYER ACKNOWLEDGES OUR DEPENDENCY

Rabbi Joseph Soloveitchik shifts the conversation away from the philo-sophical challenges posed by prayer and moves the discussion to the question of how prayer can refine our character. According to Rav Soloveitchik, "The efficacy of prayer is not the central term of inquiry in our philosophy of *avoda shebalev* … The basic function of prayer is not its practical consequences, but the metaphysical formation of a fellowship consisting of God and man."[14]

What is the nature of this fellowship that the Rav describes? Rav Soloveitchik's theology of prayer is extremely complex.[15] Nonetheless, we can gain perspective at least regarding one aspect of the religious posture he is describing by highlighting a creative interpretation of a debate between the Rambam and the Ramban about the source of the obligation to pray.

12. Avot 2:4, translated in *The Koren Siddur with Introduction, Translation, and Commentary by Rabbi Jonathan Sacks* (Jerusalem: Koren, 2009), 646.
13. Rabbi Joseph B. Soloveitchik, "Redemption, Prayer and Talmud Torah," *Tradition* 17:2 (1978): 65.
14. Rabbi Joseph Soloveitchik, *Worship of the Heart: Essays on Jewish Prayer,* ed. Shalom Carmy (Jersey City: Ktav, 2003), 35.
15. For an excellent survey of Rabbi Solovetichik's view, see Rabbi Reuven Ziegler, *Majesty and Humility: The Thought of Rabbi Joseph B. Soloveitchik* (Jerusalem: Urim Publications), 213-234.

The Rambam is of the opinion that the obligation to pray is biblical,[16] while the Ramban disagrees and argues that the obligation to pray is rabbinic. However, the Ramban concedes that there does exist a biblical requirement to beseech God *specifically* during times of crisis.[17]

The Rambam also acknowledges an obligation to pray at certain times of crisis arguing that "it is a positive Torah commandment to cry out and to sound trumpets in the event of any difficulty that arises that affects the community."[18]

If both the Rambam and Ramban agree that biblical prayer involves turning to God in moments of crisis, what exactly is the nature of their dispute? Rav Soloveitchik argues that while both the Rambam and Ramban agree that crisis underlies the prayer experience, they differ about the "substance of the experience of *tzara* [crisis] itself."[19] Rabbi Reuven Ziegler explains that according to the Ramban, *et tzara* [times of crisis] refers to periodical external crises, such as "war, famine, or disease." In his view, it is only during these moments of crisis that the Torah requires one to pray. The Rambam, by contrast, believes that "man is perpetually in crisis, for *et tzara* refers to the inner, existential, deep crisis that stems from an awareness of [one's] human limitations, frailties, and finitude."[20] In other words, prayer creates a bond between man and God by acknowledging man's dependency. Crisis is an appropriate occasion for prayer because it makes us aware of human limitations.

It is for this that reason that Rav Soloveitchik views the petitionary elements of prayer as central to the traditional conception of prayer. "The principle topic of Jewish prayer is *techina* [petition] ... . This [focus on petition] is based on our singling out of one particular emotion above all others as the central requisite for prayer, namely dependence and

---

16. Laws of Prayer 1:1.

17. Commentary to Rambam's Book of Commandments, positive commandment 5.

18. Laws of Fast Days 1:1, translated at http://www.chabad.org/library/article_cdo/ aid/951995/jewish/Taaniyot-Chapter-One.htm.

19. Rabbi Joseph Soloveitchik, *Worship of the Heart: Essays on Jewish Prayer*, ed. Shalom Carmy (Jersey City: Ktav, 2003), 30.

20. Rabbi Joseph B. Soloveitchik, cited in Rabbi Reuven Ziegler, *Majesty and Humility: The Thought of Rabbi Joseph B. Soloveitchik* (Jerusalem: Urim Publications), 225.

helplessness."[21] Independent of the potential for prayers to be answered, petitionary prayers highlight mankind's dependency on God. By asking God for help with our own needs, we acknowledge our limited ability to control our destiny. "Man is dissatisfied with himself and he lacks the faith in … the legitimacy of his existence."[22] Prayer therefore reorients mankind and affirms our need for divine assistance.

This approach is particularly critical for modern people in an era of unprecedented technological advancement. Working in an environment that provides enormous opportunity for financial and professional growth, we can easily become desensitized to the temporal nature of existence. Unfortunately, it is often the occurence of tragedy that forces us to reorient priorities and acknowledge the limits of human power. Praying three times daily, and constantly reminding ourselves of our dependency on God's grace, helps us develop a posture of humility throughout prayer itself. Further, when we acknowledge our own limitations during prayer, our entire day takes on the potential for transformation.

PRAYER AND THE TRANSCENDENT SELF

While the Rambam, and Rav Soloveitchik view prayer as arising from some form of existential crisis, some Chassidic thinkers see prayer as primarily a way of neutralizing the ego. Rabbi Betzalel Naor quotes Rabbi Dov Ber of Mezritch:[23] "[When praying,] man must consider himself as naught, and forget himself completely, and throughout his prayer plea for the *Shekhina*."[24] Troubled by the central role of petitionary prayer in traditional liturgy, Rabbi Dov Ber attempts to spiritualize these requests, urging that "when one must ask something of the Creator, one should think that his soul is a limb of the *Shekhina*, like a drop of the ocean. And he should ask for the *Shekhina*, which is lacking that thing."[25] In fact, Rabbi Naor astutely observes that according

---

21. Rabbi Joseph B. Soloveitchik, "Prayer as Dialogue," in *Reflections of the Rav Volume One*, ed. Abraham Besdin (World Zionist Organization, 1979), 84.
22. Rabbi Joseph B. Soloveitchik, *Worship of the Heart: Essays on Jewish Prayer*, ed. Shalom Carmy (Jersey City: Ktav, 2003), 35.
23. Rabbi Dov Ber of Mezritch, eighteenth century, Eastern Europe.
24. Rabbi Betzalel Naor, "Two Types of Prayer," *Tradition* 25:3 (Spring 1991): 29.
25. Ibid.

to these Chassidic thinkers, "earthly wants are of no import, only heavenly goals. And if the ego's craving cannot be put off, it being too permanent a fixture in human life, then it is to be indulged, with the intention that it too, in the final analysis, is a divine desire."[26]

A more tempered version of this Chassidic idea is articulated by Rabbi Dr. Abraham Joshua Heschel.[27] Rabbi Heschel speaks of prayer's ability to "overcome egocentrism and mold a different kind of human self."[28] For Rabbi Heschel, prayer "takes the mind out of the narrowness of self-interest, and enables us to see the world in the mirror of the holy. For when we betake ourselves to the extreme opposite of the ego, we can behold a situation from the aspect of God."[29] As opposed to Rav Soloveitchik, who viewed petition as the centerpiece of prayer, for both Rabbi Dov Ber and Rabbi Heschel, prayer is primarily an act in which the individual affirms that God, and not he, stands at the center of his worldview.

This suggestion has particular relevance for modern Jews, who have a tendency to relate to prayer from the perspective of, "What did I gain from the prayer experience?" or "Did I connect to the prayers that I uttered?" This overemphasis on the self turns religion, in general, and prayer, in particular, into a form of self-worship. The approach articulated by Dr. Heschel reminds us that "the real goal of human life is not to find answers to my questions, but to offer myself as a response to God's."[30]

SUMMARY

Daily prayer stands at the center of a traditional Jew's religious life. Beyond the fulfillment of a halakhic obligation, praying three times daily serves as an effective medium for building a traditional Jewish

---

27. For an excellent discussion of Rabbi Heschel's philosophy of prayer, see, Rabbi Shai Held, *Abraham Joshua Heschel: The Call of Transcendence* (Bloomington/Indianapolis: Indiana University Press, 2013), 198-218.

28. Rabbi Shai Held, *Abraham Joshua Heschel: The Call of Transcendence* (Bloomington/Indianapolis: Indiana University Press, 2013), 201.

29. Rabbi Abraham Joshua Heschel, *Moral Granduer and Spiritual Audacity: Essays*, ed. Susannah Heschel (New York: Farrar, Straus and Giroux, 1996), 343.

30. Rabbi Shai Held, *Abraham Joshua Heschel: The Call of Transcendence* (Bloomington/Indianapolis: Indiana University Press, 2013), 201.

worldview. Specifically, the traditional Jewish prayer book provides a unique opportunity for theological, philosophical, and religious reflection on some of the most central themes of classical rabbinic Judaism. In particular, the act of prayer allows us to:

- Experience a direct divine encounter (Rav Soloveitchik)
- Reflect on prayer's ability to create a more refined character (Rabbi Albo)
- Appreciate how changing ourselves can be an effective medium for having our prayers answered (Rabbi Albo, Mishna Avot)
- Think about the substance of our desires and ask ourselves if our will truly aligns with the will of God (Rav Soloveitchik)
- Appreciate the limited power of mankind and appreciate our ultimate dependence on God (Rav Soloveitchik)
- Neutralize our own ego by acknowledging the often trivial nature of our requests (Rabbi Dov Ber)
- Appreciate prayer's ability to facilitate a God-centered life (Rabbi Heschel)

Chapter 10

Attending a Minyan

Spiritual Teamwork and the Centrality of Jewish Theology

A s we discussed in the previous chapter, the act of prayer can help us to transform ourselves. Praying in the morning, again in the afternoon, and a third time in the evening ensures that the values of the Jewish prayerbook become the medium through which a Jew views his daily existence. But in the Jewish tradition, prayer is an act not only of the individual but of the community. Jewish law holds that prayer should, ideally, take place in a synagogue in the presence of a *minyan* (ten men above the age of bar mitzva).

From the standpoint of the individual, public prayer in a synagogue has a few potential drawbacks. After all, prayer is supposed to be a profoundly meditative and contemplative experience, which some people may prefer to practice privately in the comfort of their own homes. The insistence on public prayer may thus prevent the prayer experience from becoming truly transformative. If clarity of mind is so crucial for the rabbinic conception of prayer, why did the rabbis insist on public prayer in a space where the potential for distraction and loss of focus is significant?

Analyzing traditional sources dealing with this topic will help us understand the larger philosophical vision of rabbinic prayer. It will also help us see how the synagogue serves as an ideal space in which to actualize these virtues.

PUBLIC PRAYER AND THE LOSS OF INDIVIDUALITY

The rabbis were well aware of the potential disadvantages of communal prayer. After citing a statement about the importance of focusing on the meaning of the words we say while praying, the Talmud in Berakhot goes on to discuss the prayer practices of specific rabbinic sages. The practice of R. Akiva is is of particular interest for our discussion:

> When [R. Akiva] would pray together with the congregation, he would shorten [his prayer and be brief] because of the burden [that he would otherwise place] upon the congregation [were they to wait for him to complete a more lengthy prayer]. [Moreover], when he would pray by himself, a person would leave him [standing] in the corner and find him [upon the completion of his prayer] in another corner. [Why was he moving around so much during his prayer?] Because of the bowings and prostrations [in which he engaged while praying].[1]

The Talmud notes how meditatively involved R. Akiva was when praying in private, and acknowledges that he had to compromise on the intensity of his own prayer experience in order to minimize any inconveniencing of the community. Nonetheless, while acknowledging the potential cost of public rather than private prayer, the rabbinic consensus views public prayer as a more ideal form of worship.

This insistence continues into the modern period as well. Rabbi Moshe Feinstein was asked whether it is permitted to study Torah late into the night if that would preclude him from getting up for morning prayers with a minyan.[2] Like the talmudic sages, Rabbi Feinstein asserted that public prayer trumps any personal religious benefit of private prayer. This

---

1. Berakhot 31a.
2. *Iggerot Moshe*, Orach Chayim 2:27.

position of talmudic as well as modern rabbinic authority raises interesting questions about the significance of public prayer and only amplifies the mysterious rabbinic insistence on prayer in the context of community.

CENTRALITY OF A MINYAN: PRAYER AND ITS COSMIC POWER

Despite the potential disadvantages to the individual worshipper, the rabbis attributed to communal prayer a power and efficacy that private prayer cannot possess. The Talmud cites the view of R. Natan: "God does not despise the prayers of the congregation."[3] This position is cited as a matter of law by the Rambam, who writes, "Communal prayer is always heard. Even when there are transgressors among [the congregation], the Holy One, blessed be He, does not reject the prayers of the many. Therefore, a person should include himself in the community and should not pray alone whenever he is able to pray with the community."[4]

Thus, the Talmud and the Rambam attribute cosmic power to public prayer. One might have assumed that the presence of less pious individuals could have an adverse effect on the chances of public prayer being heard by God. The Rambam therefore informs us that public prayer is so powerful that even the presence of people who theoretically deserve to have their prayers rejected cannot alter the positive metaphysical impact of public prayer.

In this rabbinic view, public prayer is almost guaranteed to be heard by God. The philosophical ramifications of this idea are complex and need to be considered in terms of how an omniscient God can reply to the requests of mortal man. Still, it is clear that the rabbis saw public prayer as more efficacious than private prayer. Moreover, the rabbinic insistence on permitting the presence of even those members of the community who are less religiously committed underscores the power of communal prayer to help bring together many different types of Jews into one shared prayer space. Praying in a community reminds us of the transcendent values that bond Jews together despite their differences.

---

3. Berakhot 8a.
4. Laws of Prayer 8:1, translated at http://www.chabad.org/library/article_cdo/aid/920171/jewish/Tefilah-and-Birkat-Kohanim-Chapter-Eight.htm.

THE POWER OF SPIRITUAL TEAMWORK

We may ask why it should be the case that public prayer is more cosmically powerful than private prayer. What is the source of the power of communal prayer?

The Chafetz Chayim[5] addresses this question by referring to the rabbinic notion that mitzvot performed by a group have a much greater impact than mitzvot performed by individuals.[6] The Chafetz Chayim notes that during public prayer, many mitzvot are performed in a collective manner.[7] In addition to prayer itself, the community members fulfill the biblical commandments to wear tefillin, recite the *Shema*, and remember the Exodus from Egypt. A special spiritual energy is created by many Jews performing mitzvot together.

A slightly modified version of this theory is articulated by Rabbi Yehuda Halevi[8] in his philosophical masterpiece, the *Kuzari*.[9] He notes that one of the reasons the rabbis preferred public prayer is that "it is very rare for an individual's prayer to be complete without any mistakes or lapse in concentration." The power of a minyan lies in the fact that some of the "participants might compensate for the mistakes and lapses in concentration of others in the group." The result of this "joint effort is complete prayer said with pure intent."

In other words, he imagines a group coming together to pray as a team might come together. Members of a team complement one another, so they are able to operate at a level that would be impossible for a single individual. In public prayer, each of us has spiritual deficiencies that make it less likely that the prayers will be received favorably. But together, the individuals can spiritually complement each other, thereby enabling a collective prayer that is elevated to heights unachievable for a person praying alone.

This is an important idea for a person to reflect upon before engaging in public prayer. Joining with a minyan means affirming our

---

5. Rabbi Yisrael Meir HaKohen Kagan, twentieth century, Belarus.
6. See Rashi to Leviticus 26:8.
7. Cited in Rabbi Eli Adler, *Tefillat Yesharim: Iyun Emuni BeYesodot HaTefilla* (Kiryat Arba: M'Emek Hevron, 2003), 213.
8. Rabbi Yehuda HaLevi, eleventh/twelfth centuries, Toledo, Spain.
9. *Kuzari* 3:18-19, translated by R. N. Daniel Korobkin, *The Kuzari: In Defense of a Despised Faith* (Jerusalem/New York: Feldheim, 2009), 303-304.

own spiritual limitations and acknowledging the need for assistance in ensuring that our prayers are heard by God. The power of communal prayer rests upon the fact that it is a space in which everyone simultaneously recognizes their own deficiencies and tries to make up for the deficiencies of others.

PUBLIC PRAYER: A MOVE TOWARDS SELF-TRANSCENDENCE

The view that those praying communally are fulfilling a mutual need is confirmed by another passage in Berakhot. Citing the position of Resh Lakish, the Talmud states that "anyone who has a synagogue in his city but does not enter there to pray is called an evil neighbor."[10] One possible explanation is that the reason such a person is considered an 'evil neighbor' is that he neglected to attend the synagogue when he was needed to complete the *minyan*,[11] and as a result, the community could not recite the special prayers reserved exclusively for a prayer quorum of ten. Praying at home can, unfortunately, generate a self-centered religious posture, in which our focus is exclusively on our own spiritual needs. Prayer in public reminds us that we have spiritual responsibilities that extend far beyond ourselves.

This view is reinforced by another passage in Berakhot:

> If two people enter [the synagogue] to pray, and one of them [finished] praying first and he did not wait for his fellow [to finish], but left [the synagogue, leaving the others there alone,] his prayer is tossed aside in front of him [i.e., it is not accepted] … . [Moreover], he causes the Divine Presence to be removed from Israel.[12]

Rabbi Avraham Yitzhak HaKohen Kook explains that if a person is capable of praying, and then leaving without waiting for his friend to complete his own prayers, then that person is probably selfish and thinks only about himself during his prayers.[13] Therefore, he does not deserve to have his prayers answered by God. Moreover, by behaving in such

10. Berakhot 8a.
11. See *Perisha*, Orach Chayim 90:15 for a similar argument.
12. Berakhot 5b.
13. *Ein Aya*, Berakhot 6: 42, s.v. *v'im himteen.*

a manner, he causes the Divine Presence to be removed, since God dwells only in a space where people care for the physical and spiritual well-being of others.

Public prayer thus represents an opportunity to affirm the self-transcendent element of the prayer experience. Praying with a group, and being simultaneously sensitive to the needs of others, allows an individual to remember that, while prayer is about his own needs, it is certainly not exclusively about him. Moreover, when praying with the community, we often have the opportunity to feel that our desires, no matter how critical they seem to us, are insignificant when compared to tragedies that others are experiencing.

This approach compels us to reflect daily on our communal responsibilities, as highlighted by the experience of public prayer. We can easily go about our day and think only about whether or not we are personally behaving in a way that is halakhicly appropriate. Seeing halakhic observance as a type of checklist that we must fulfill can create a posture of self-centeredness, wherein one is only interested in his own religious needs. By insisting that we pray three times daily in a group setting, the rabbis tried to inculcate an ethic of spiritual team-building. Concern for the spiritual welfare of another Jew is not some pietistic practice reserved for rabbis and communal leaders. All Jews are called upon to view their own religious observance as part of a shared communal effort to actualize divine values in the physical world. Praying in a public space daily reminds all of us of the responsibilities we have to the larger Jewish world.

PUBLIC PRAYER AND SANCTIFYING GOD'S NAME

Besides the themes of mutual need and responsibility, the Talmud connects public prayer with the idea of sanctifying God's name. A passage in Berakhot[14] explains the ruling that certain prayers (such as the *Kedusha*) can be recited only in the presence of a minyan, by citing a verse from Leviticus: "I [God] will be sanctified among the children of Israel."[15] According to the Talmud, this verse teaches that "all matters

14. Berakhot 21b.
15. Lev. 22:32.

of sanctity" cannot be recited without the requisite minyan. Since the *Kedusha* prayer deals with the theme of the sanctity of God, it may be recited only in the presence of a group.

The relationship between public prayer and sanctity is reflected in the case of R. Eliezer, who freed his slave in order to complete a *minyan* of ten men.[16] Questioning R. Eliezer's behavior, the Talmud wonders how he could free his slave; after all, the Torah states regarding a Cananite slave, "You [Jewish people] shall work them forever."[17] The Talmud explains that R. Eliezer was allowed to free his slave because "a communal mitzva," such as the public declaration of *Kedusha* by a *minyan*, is different; in this case, there is an allowance to free a slave.[18] The Rosh explains that the positive mitzva of publicly sanctifying God's name by reciting *Kedusha*, which is incumbent upon a group, overrides a commandment that applies only to an individual, such as not freeing a slave.[19] This explanation highlights the extent to which public prayer serves as an important medium for people to come together and publicly affirm fundamental tenets of Jewish theology, thus sanctifying God's name. Creating a robust public prayer space is thus an important means for Jews to publicly declare their commitment to central aspects of traditional Jewish dogma.

Unfortunately, Jewish law can often feel detached from its theological roots. Viewing Jewish law exclusively from the perspective of facilitating Jewish continuity can create a situation in which observance of the law is disconnected from the ideals that it attempts to represent. The presence of "Kiddush clubs" in contemporary synagogues demonstrates this tension. Someone who leaves the synagogue service during the weekly reading of the *haftara* in order to have a drink with friends essentially assumes that there is no transcendent message to be learned from listening attentively to the words of the *haftara*. In truth, however, public prayer is much more than an opportunity to socialize.

---

16. Cannanite slaves are converted to Judaism. However, their legal status is unique and therefore cannot be counted in a minyan. Once the slave is freed however, he is able to count in a minyan. See Talmud Bavli Tractate Berachos 47b, *The Shottenstein Daf Yomi Edition Volume 1* (Brooklyn: Artscroll Mesorah Publications, 2000), footnote 36.

17. Lev. 25:46.

18. Berakhot 47b.

19. Rosh, Berakhot 7:20.

It is a critical medium for committing to the larger Jewish ideas that the halakha attempts to actualize. Once we understand this, we can begin to appreciate what various aspects of the public prayer service, such as the *haftara*, seek to accomplish.

PUBLIC PRAYER: TESTING OUR THEOLOGICAL INTUITIONS

The sources cited thus far highlight the importance of public prayer as part of rabbinic Judaism's general worldview. Given its centrality, we would expect codifiers of Jewish law to articulate the requirement to pray with a minyan as a clear and unequivocal obligation. It is therefore particularly surprising that in the *Shulchan Arukh*, there is a rather vague formulation about the need to pray with a community. According to the *Shulchan Arukh*, a person should "try his best to pray with the community." If he is unable to attend synagogue, however, he should still try to pray at the same time that the community prays.[20] Some scholars maintain that, in fact, there is no formal obligation to pray with a minyan.[21] While everyone agrees that it is certainly ideal, these authorities conclude that public prayer, while religiously optimal, is not obligatory.

Rabbi Moshe Feinstein argues, however, that public prayer is indeed an obligation, even according to the *Shulchan Arukh*, in which we find the language of "trying one's best" to pray with the community. A particularly striking argument of Rabbi Feinstein is that, according to both the Talmud and the Rambam, communal prayer is always heard by God. Since the act of prayer fundamentally assumes that we want to have our prayers answered, how can it not be obligatory to enter a prayer space that nearly guarantees a successful prayer experience?[22]

This approach in particular compels us to reflect on our own beliefs regarding the impact our prayers have on our lives. Have we truly internalized the extent to which God can intervene in our lives through the medium of prayer? If so, how could we not make every effort to pray

---

20. *Shulchan Arukh*, Orach Chayim 90:9.
21. See Rabbi Ari Pumarnchik, *Emek Berakha,* Birchot Keriat Shema: 1.
22. *Iggerot Moshe*, Orach Chayim 2:27.

with a minyan, through which, according to Jewish tradition, our prayers are most likely to be answered?

THE CENTRALITY OF THE SYNAGOGUE

In addition to emphasizing the centrality of public prayer, the talmudic sages saw great value in communal prayer specifically in a synagogue. Quoting the view of Abba Binyamin in the Talmud, "[A] person's prayer is heard only [if he recites it] in a synagogue."[23] Similarly the Talmud cites the view of Ravin bar R. Adda in the name of R. Yitchak, that God's presence is found in the synagogue, as the verse states that "God stands in the divine assembly."[24] This view is codified by the Rambam, who states that "one should always spend the early morning and evening [hours] in the synagogue, for prayer will not be heard at all times except [when recited] in the synagogue."[25] In fact, Rabbi Yonah notes that, even if we need to pray privately, we should try to pray in a synagogue, even if there is no *minyan*.[26]

What is the significance of praying specifically in a synagogue? In the *Lechem Mishneh*,[27] it is argued that prayer in a synagogue is always heard by God, and it is therefore more metaphysically meaningful, even when performed by an individual alone.[28] The Chafetz Chayim, by contrast, notes the importance of a synagogue in creating a centralized sacred space.[29] When we come to the synagogue to pray, we encounter, for example, a place that is often the forum for Torah classes before and after the prayer services. The power of the synagogue is less about its ability to transform the prayers themselves, and more a function of its power to connect us to a sacred space that will facilitate involvement in holy activities.

---

23. Berakhot 6a.
24. Ibid., quoting Psalms 82:1.
25. Laws of Prayer 8:1, translation from http://www.chabad.org/dailystudy/rambam.asp?tDate=5/26/1840&rambamChapters=3.
26. Berakhot 4a.
27. Rabbi Avraham b. R. Moshe de-Boton, sixteenth century, Salonika.
28. Laws of Prayer 8:1.
29. Cited in Rabbi Eli Adler, *Tefillat Yesharim: Iyun Emuni BeYesodot HaTefilla* (Kiryat Arba: M'Emek Hevron, 2003), 210.

This rabbinic insistence, therefore, reminds us about the impact of a religiously positive environment in fostering a passionate Jewish identity. Many young people say that the most important factor in building a robust commitment to halakhic observance on university campuses is daily minyan attendance. Connecting to a community that is committed to the values that the prayer book advocates is so important. It provides a critical social framework for actualizing the ideals of traditional Jewish life. By insisting that Jews pray with a committed community, the rabbis helped engender this deep engagement in Jewish living.

For many Jewish communities today, the synagogue serves as the center for much of Jewish life. Beyond daily prayer services, Jewish cultural and religious events regularly take place in synagogue social halls and chapels. Additionally, the synagogue plays a crucial role in fortifying traditional Jewish identity. Jews gather together in a synagogue space to study, pray, and socialize in a religious context.

SUMMARY

Prayer with a minyan provides a gateway to upgrading the quality of our prayer experience. As demonstrated in this chapter, prayer in a communal setting has significant religious benefits beyond the social and communal dimensions. The rabbinic admonition to pray daily with a minyan thus provides another example of the rabbis' attempt to facilitate a broader religious conversation through the practical medium of daily Jewish living. In particular, public prayer allows us to:

- Appreciate the cosmic efficacy of communal prayer (Talmud, Rambam)
- Experience prayers related to the sanctity of God that are recited only in the presence of a *minyan* (Talmud)
- Recognize the impact of mitzvot performed by a group versus those performed by individuals (Chafetz Chayim)
- Reflect on our own spiritual shortcomings and how we need others to complement us in our experience of prayer (Kuzari)
- Highlight prayer as an experience of self-transcendence, as thinking of others is an essential part of what it means to pray (Talmud, Rabbi Kook)

- Collectively sanctify God's name by affirming our shared theology in a group setting (Talmud, Rosh)
- Affirm our own confidence in the efficacy of prayer (Rabbi Moshe Feinstein)
- Acknowledge the central power of the synagogue to create a shared sacred space for the community (Chafetz Chayim)

Chapter 11

Fixed and Spontaneous Prayers

Self-Awareness Through Self-Transcendence

In previous chapters, we discussed the underlying philosophical vision of traditional Jewish prayer, as well as the religious significance of the rabbinic advocacy of public prayer. But even after we understand the profound spiritual opportunities provided by daily prayer, it is still possible to struggle with the rabbinic insistence on praying specifically from a fixed prayer book.

After all, prayer is an extremely complex exercise. On the one hand, the act of praying allows us to tap into our deepest desires and dialogue with God about our wants and needs. On the other hand, the requirement to pray from a siddur seems to limit the way we communicate with God to a predetermined and fixed text. In the words of Rabbi David Hartman:

> When prayer is regulated and standardized using fixed linguistic formulas and prescribed times and format, the psychological/religious qualities of inwardness and spontaneity, which are generally

considered necessary conditions for experiencing relational passion towards God, become problematic.[1]

On the flip side, however, prayer without any default text runs the risk of becoming an exercise in self-worship. Such a prayer model would allow us to beseech God whenever we feel the need, without providing any parallel context for the values and virtues for which he should be yearning.

Jewish law acknowledges this tension, and the laws of prayer reflect an attempt by the sages to allow for personalized and spontaneous prayer within the framework of a fixed and formalized text. Reflecting on the sources that struggle with these ideals will help us gain greater appreciation for the dialectic experience of Jewish prayer.

BIBLICAL PRAYER: PRAYER DURING TIMES OF CRISIS

A cursory reading of the Bible reveals that biblical figures do not pray from a fixed script, nor do they beseech God at specific times of day. Instead, they pray whenever they have a need to communicate with the Divine.

This model is reflected in the position of the Ramban that we previously noted. The Ramban maintains that prayer in general is a rabbinic requirement, but he concedes that there is a biblical requirement to beseech God *specifically* during times of crisis. Thus, he states:

> We should learn Torah and pray to [God] in times of crisis, and our eyes and hearts should be towards Him alone like the eyes of slaves to their masters. This is similar to the command from the Torah, "And when you go to war in your land against the adversary that oppresses you, then you shall sound an alarm with the trumpets; and you shall be remembered before the Lord your God, and you shall be saved from your enemies" (Numbers 10:9). It is a mitzva to respond to every crisis that the community will face by crying out to Him in prayer.[2]

---

1. Rabbi Dr. David Hartman, "Prayer and Religious Consciousness: An Analysis of Jewish Prayer in the Works of Joseph B. Soloveitchik, Yeshayahu Leibowitz and Abraham Joshua Heschel," *Modern Judaism* 23:2 (2003): 106.

2. Comments on the Rambam's Book of Commandments, #5, translated at http://etzion.org.il/en/obligation-pray.

The Ramban's approach emphasizes the awareness of humanity's dependence on divine mercy. Biblical prayer is spontaneous and reinforces man's ability to connect with God by opening up his heart to God during the most difficult times. A formal text with fixed times is fundamentally alien to this model. Prayer must be spontaneous in order to truly reflect the biblical ethic emphasizing God's intervention in human affairs. By turning to God in its darkest moments, the community of Israel demonstrates its faith in God's redemptive powers.

RABBAN GAMLIEL: THE POWER OF FIXED PRAYER

The Mishna expands the conversation beyond the limited question of prayer in times of crisis, citing a dispute about prayer from a fixed text.

The Mishna begins by citing the view of Rabban Gamliel, who states that "every single day, a person must pray [the] eighteen blessings."[3] As Rabbi Yakov Nagen notes, Rabban Gamliel lived after the destruction of the Temple, and he needed to help fill the religious void created as a result of the Temple's destruction. Fixed prayer with a formalized text helped unify a fractured community and provided a stable medium for the Jewish people to dialogue regularly with God.[4]

Rabbi Nagen traces Rabban Gamliel's insistence on a fixed text for prayer to R. Yehoshua ben Levi's statement that prayer was instituted to correspond to the daily *tamid* (regular) offerings,[5] which were offered twice daily in the Temple. R. Yehoshua ben Levi's position implies that an individual cannot stand before God only when he feels inspired. Consistency is as necessary as inspiration to a life of commitment. Rabban Gamliel's insistence on a fixed text expresses a religious orientation that prioritizes the daily, sometimes tedious, religious act over the infrequent burst of religious enthusiasm.

Rabban Gamliel's ruling has religious and spiritual significance beyond the formal act of prayer itself. After all, in addition to the experience of praying from a fixed text, the daily ins and outs of Jewish

---

3. Berakhot 28b.
4. Rabbi Yakov Nagen, *Tefilatam Shel Tannaim: Bein Keva L'zerima,* http://www.daat. ac.il/chazal/maamar.asp?id=139.
5. Berakhot 26b.

observance can often seem tedious and repetitive. Rabban Gamliel teaches us that it is only through engagement in the ordinary that we can gain access to the extraordinary.

An appropriate analogy can be drawn from the idea of exercise. If we work out only when we feel inspired, what are the odds that we will actually build a heathy body? On the other hand, if we exercise daily, the exercise itself will become more enjoyable and effective. Although we may not be in the mood to exercise every day, it is only through the daily routine that we have the potential to experience the transformative power of a healthy lifestyle. Similarly, Rabban Gamliel reminds us that spiritual intimacy can be achieved only through hard work. Religious highs are powerful, but they cannot serve as a replacement for the daily religious grind.

R. ELIEZER: A RETURN TO SPONTANEITY

At the opposite end of the tanaaitic spectrum on this issue is the position of R. Eliezer.[6] Responding to Rabban Gamliel's belief in a fixed text for prayer, R. Eliezer argues that "one who makes his prayers fixed, his prayers are not genuine supplications." R. Eliezer emphasizes the risks inherent in Rabban Gamliel's position. How can the same text, recited three times daily, truly capture the inner feelings of a person praying before God?

The talmudic discussion of R. Eliezer's position wonders what, exactly, is so problematic about a prayer model that is fixed.[7] The first view is cited in the name of R. Oshaya, who argues that a fixed text is problematic because it can lead to a prayer experience that is perceived as a burden. Rashi explains that R. Eliezer is concerned that when we use a formal prayer book, we might consider the act of prayer to be a chore.[8] A second view cited by the Talmud argues that fixed prayer is problematic because it implies that prayer is not a supplication. When we come before God and plea for help and mercy, we affirm the prayer experience as a heartfelt dialogue between man and God.

---

6. Mishna Berakhot 4:4.
7. Berakhot 29b.
8. Rashi, Berakhot 29b, s.v. *kemasui*.

If our prayers are fixed, however, the prayers themselves may seem artificial and forced, void of the supplicatory element that defines classical prayer. R. Eliezer therefore reminds us that prayer lacking this component is simply not prayer at all. Prayer is a fundamentally unique ritual, in that it assumes our ability to express our most intimate emotions before God. The moment prayer becomes habitual, it loses this critical element.

R. YEHOSHUA: A COMPROMISE VIEW

While R. Eliezer and Rabban Gamliel represent the two extreme positions in the debate surrounding the question of fixed versus spontaneous prayer, R. Yehoshua advocates a compromise position.[9] According to R. Yehoshua, we should recite an abridged version of the eighteen required blessings daily. Attempting to define what exactly an "abridged" *Amida* prayer would look like, the Talmud provides two explanations. According to Rav, R. Yehoshua's position advocates an abridgement of the middle thirteen blessings by reciting only the opening words and concluding blessing of each unit. Shmuel suggests an alternative understanding of R. Yehoshua, according to which abridged prayer involves condensing all of the middle thirteen blessings into one long blessing that incorporates all the major themes cited in the thirteen blessings.[10]

Rabbi Yakov Nagen argues that, like Rabban Gamliel, R. Yehoshua requires a fixed time of prayer, but unlike Rabban Gamliel, he does not demand a fixed text. Rather, he insists that we maintain *fixed themes* that define our prayer experience. Abridged prayer requires that the practitioner reference the eighteen themes of the *Amida* during his daily prayer. However, while R. Yehoshua advocates a more fluid and individual model than that of Rabban Gamliel, he does not go as far as R. Eliezer, who rejects any attempt to formalize the act of prayer. R. Yehoshua's approach ensures that prayer does not become an exercise in self-worship, since it mandates the incorporation of the central themes of traditional Jewish prayer. By legislating only themes and not

9. Mishna Berakhot 4:3.
10. Berakhot 29a.

specific texts, R. Yehoshua maintains the personal connection we feel to the prayer experience.

R. YOSEF KARO: SPONTANEITY IN THE
CONTEXT OF THE ORDINARY

The talmudic text cited above presents two perspectives on the challenges of fixed prayer. Interestingly, the *Shulchan Arukh* rules stringently in accordance with both opinions, stating that prayer cannot be a burdensome experience *and* it must be supplicatory in nature.[11] The *Magen Avraham* explains that this ruling implies that even if we pray in a supplicatory manner, it is still improper to pray if we perceive prayer as a burden or chore.[12] The *Machatzit HaShekel*[13] claims that the converse is true as well. If we are excited to pray and do not perceive it to be a burden, yet fail to pray in a manner that is heartfelt, the prayers do not represent religious ideals.[14] In fact, the *Mishna Berura* notes that, at least ideally, we must be extremely cautious about that our prayer is not burdensome, but rather supplicatory. Indeed, he notes that according to many halakhic authorities, we would have to repeat our prayers if we lack these components.[15]

In order to preserve the more spontaneous and heartfelt aspects of prayer while utilizing a fixed text, Rabbi Yosef Karo rules that one is permitted to add personal supplications that are thematically connected to the eighteen required benedictions that must be recited daily. For example, a prayer for a specific sick person may be inserted[16] into the standard blessing for healing. Similarly, we may add personal prayers for physical sustenance during the prayer for prosperity. Moreover, during the blessing beginning "Hear our voice," we are permitted to add any personal supplications, since that blessing is intended to include space for any personal requests.[17]

---

11. *Shulchan Arukh*, Orach Chayim 98:3.
12. Ibid. 98:3-4.
13. Rabbi Shmuel b. R. Natan Nata HaLevi Keilin, eighteenth century, Germany.
14. *Machatzit HaShekel*, Orach Chayim 98:4.
15. *Biur Halakha* Orach Chayim 98, s.v *yitpallel*.
16. The Rema (Orach Chayim 119:1) notes that one adds these requests after beginning the formal prayer.
17. *Shulchan Arukh*, Orach Chayim 119:1.

In this model, we preserve the stability of prayer as a daily encounter with God through the medium of a fixed text that compels us to have a three-time-daily confrontation with the Divine. In addition, our prayer remains a self-transcendent experience, since the presence of the eighteen blessings reminds us what we *should* be striving for. At the same time, Jewish law enables us to insert our own personal feelings and reflections into our prayers so that they maintain their vibrancy and personal relevance. This dialectic allows us to truly find ourselves by locating our personal needs in the context of the needs of the community.

ELOKAI NETZOR: A PRAYER WITHOUT LIMITS

While the approach of Rabbi Karo provides opportunities for us to inject a more personal voice into our prayer experience, the Talmud in Tractate Berakhot suggests the possibility of doing so, namely by attaching personal prayers to the end of the daily *Amida*. It gives a long list of such prayers offered by great rabbis, including that of Mar, the son of Ravina. Upon completing the *Amida*, he would state:

> My God, guard my tongue from evil and my lips from speaking deceit. And to those who curse me, let my soul be silent and let my soul be like dust to everyone. Open my heart to Your Torah and let my soul pursue Your commandments, and save me from evil mishap.... May the expressions of my mouth and the thoughts of my heart find favor before You, Hashem, my Rock and my Redeemer.[18]

While this text was a personal prayer recited by Mar, the son of Ravina, over time a derivative of this prayer became the standard supplication used by all Jews at the end of the *Amida*. Professor Gerald Blidstein comments: "Talmudic preservation of the meditations of great individuals can only be explained as an attempt to bequeath their creativity to succeeding generations."[19] Continuing to recite this text daily humbles us and facilitates an awareness that the traditional paragraphs may express our feelings better than we could ourselves.

---

18. Berakhot 17a.
19. Gerald Blidstein, "Kaddish and Other Accidents," *Tradition* (Spring 1974), 81.

However, while we are required to recite this text daily, the presence of the prayer of Mar, the son of Ravina, in our prayer book reminds us that at the end of the *Amida*, we are granted license to construct our own personal supplications without the formal language of a blessing to express our individual religious needs. Rabbi Yonah states this explicitly, noting that after the *Amida*, we may recite prayers that relate to personal as well as communal needs, as we see fit.[20] This legal allowance for personal reflection at the end of the *Amida* provides a daily mechanism for us to reflect on any aspects of our identity that are not covered by the formal prayer requirements.

SUMMARY

The daily prayer experience is a dialectic exercise enabling personal expression, as well as providing a structured framework to contextualize our wants and desires. Praying daily using the traditional prayer book, while simultaneously adding personal supplications into the fixed liturgy, allows us to:

- Connect to God during moments of crisis, highlighting man's dependence on the Divine (Ramban)
- Emphasize prayer as an exercise in religious consistency (Rabban Gamliel)
- Focus on prayer as a spontaneous encounter with God (R. Eliezer)
- Locate personal meaning within a fixed system (R. Yehoshua)
- Ensure that our prayer experience is supplicatory and not burdensome (Rabbi Yosef Karo)
- Existentially reflect on our current religious state and identify aspects of our lives that are not addressed by the formal liturgy (Mar, son of Ravina)

---

20. Cited in *Beit Yosef* 119:1.

Chapter 12

Prayer in the Vernacular and in Hebrew

Personal Reflections and Communal Identity

Even if we fully comprehend the religious philosophy of prayer and the significance of praying from a fixed text, the language of prayer can be extremely intimidating. While the traditional prayer book is written in Hebrew, the majority of Jews worldwide are not fully conversant in this holy language. Traditional Jewish sources refer to the prayer experience as "worship of the heart,"[1] but is it really possible for Jewish law to expect us to have a heartfelt experience of prayer if we cannot understand the words we are saying?

On the other hand, praying in Hebrew has enormous cultural and religious benefit. By preserving Hebrew as the international language of prayer, we ensure that Jews worldwide can walk into any synagogue and join together in a collective worship of God.

---

1. Rambam, Laws of Prayer 1:1.

Jewish law recognizes the complexity of the questions surrounding prayer in the vernacular. By analyzing traditional sources that struggle with these often-clashing values, we will be able to more fully appreciate the challenges involved in choosing a language for prayer.

TALMUDIC ACCOUNT: THE STORY OF THE HEART

The Mishna lists a variety of prayers and ritual texts that can be recited in "any language."[2] Included in this list is the daily *Amida*. The Gemara attempts to locate the biblical sources that substantiate the Mishna's claim that each of these texts may be recited in any language. For example, when discussing the recitation of *Shema*, the Gemara asks, "From where do we know that *Shema* can be recited in any language?" The Gemara answers by citing the verse in Deuteronomy, "Hear, O Israel," which is understood in the Gemara to imply that *Shema* may be recited in "any language that you understand." This same pattern of looking for a source to explain the rulings of the Mishna is used to understand the entire mishnaic list – until the question of prayer in the vernacular.

Here, the Gemara does not seek scriptural support, but rather offers an intuitive justification to explain the mishnaic allowance. After all, according to the Gemara, prayer is a request for divine mercy, and it therefore must be permissible for us to pray in our mother tongue. Limiting prayer exclusively to Hebrew would compromise the quality of the prayer experience.

The Gemara goes on to question this permissive ruling, based on a statement by R. Yehuda:

> Is it indeed so that prayer may be recited in any language? For R. Yehuda has said: A person should never request his needs [from God] in Aramaic, because R. Yochanan said: If one requests his needs in Aramaic, the ministering angels do not pay attention to him, since the angels do not know Aramaic. [The Gemara replies: There is] no difficulty, [since] this [ban on praying in Aramaic applies to] an individual, whereas this

2. Sota 32a.

[permissive mishnaic ruling permitting prayer in any language applies] to a congregation.[3]

The Meiri[4] interprets the reference here to the ministering angels metaphorically, explaining the logic behind the resistance to prayer in the vernacular. According to the Meiri, the talmudic ruling assumes that people are more familiar and comfortable with prayer in Hebrew. Praying in Hebrew generates increased devotion, and it therefore is the preferred form of prayer and is most likely to be received favorably by God. The need for added devotion is particularly relevant when praying alone, and therefore praying in the vernacular is forbidden in that situation. Praying in public, by contrast, allows one access to the community and facilitates a more devotional prayer experience. Therefore, in a public quorum, prayer in the vernacular is permissible.[5]

According to the Meiri, the question of prayer in a foreign language is directly related to the question of how to ensure that prayer is, in fact, "worship of the heart." While one can certainly challenge the Meiri's reading of the Talmud, his view reinforces the talmudic position that prayer is, at its core, an appeal to divine mercy. The challenge is to find the most halakhically permissible yet devotionally plausible way to accomplish this goal.

THE RIF: PRAYER AND ANGELIC INTERCESSION

While the Meiri's reading of the Talmud limits the discussion to the subject of devotional prayer, the Rif takes a more literal reading of the Gemara and expands the dialogue to discuss the role of angels in the petitionary prayer experience. According to the Rif, Jewish law prohibits vernacular prayer in private, while permitting it in public, because private prayer requires some type of angelic intercession in order to maximize the chances for the prayers to be answered. Public prayer, by contrast, is metaphysically more effective, and therefore does not

---

3. Sota 33a.
4. Rabbi Menachem b. Shlomo Meiri, thirteenth/fourteenth centuries, France.
5. Shabbat 12b.

need any angelic help. As a result, public prayer in the vernacular is permissible.[6]

This approach highlights the experiential challenges of ensuring that prayer is devotionally meaningful while maximizing the chances for our prayers to be answered. Regardless of how we understand the metaphysical role of angels as intermediaries, it is often challenging to experience prayer as a devotional exercise. By introducing the angelic role into the conversation, the Rif challenges us to ask ourselves if our prayers are recited with sufficient devotion to allow God to receive them favorably. By prohibiting prayer in the vernacular in private, the Talmud compels us to reflect on our encounter with daily prayer and to struggle to find the most effective medium to ensure that our prayers are answered.

ROSH: THE IMPORTANCE OF PRECISION IN LANGUAGE

The Rosh adds an additional layer, understanding this talmudic passage as referring exclusively to the challenges of praying in Aramaic.[7] According to the Rosh, prayer in the vernacular is permissible both in public and private. Praying in Aramaic, however, is permissible only in public. The Rosh views Aramaic as a corrupted form of Hebrew, and this explains why angels choose to ignore prayers uttered in that language.

This approach highlights the significance of linguistic precision when beseeching God in prayer. Whether or not we accept the position of the Rosh, his view provides a means of appreciating the challenges of verbalizing our prayers before God and the importance of choosing the most refined language possible.

SEFER HASIDIM: A PRIORITIZATION OF INTENT

The sources cited thus far offer guidance regarding the question of when we are allowed to pray in the vernacular. What remains unclear is whether there is a preference for praying in Hebrew even in those instances when prayer in the vernacular is permissible. Rabbi Yehuda

---

6. Rif, Berakhot 7a.
7. Rosh, Berakhot 2:2.

HaChasid[8] addresses this question, discussing a case of a God-fearing individual who does not understand Hebrew and wishes to pray. According to Rabbi Yehuda HaChasid, we instruct this person to pray in his native tongue, since prayer is fundamentally an exercise of the heart and mind, and "if the heart does not understand [the words of prayer], what possible effect [can the prayers have]?"[9]

This perspective places a heavy emphasis on the devotional aspect of the prayer experience and assumes that the laws of prayer must facilitate this religious ideal. This view is particularly critical since it reminds us that prayer is intended to be an existentially reflective encounter. Understanding the meaning of the prayers is critical in order to achieve this lofty goal.

THE *MISHNA BERURA*: THE METAPHYSICS OF THE HEBREW LANGUAGE

While the position of the *Sefer Chasidim* seems to prefer prayer in the vernacular for an individual who is not conversant in Hebrew, the *Mishna Berura* limits this ruling to a pious individual who will almost definitely have proper intent in the vernacular. An ordinary person who struggles with Hebrew but cannot guarantee an elevated level of intent in his native language should, preferably, pray in Hebrew.

The *Mishna Berura* explains the preference for Hebrew prayer by noting the metaphysical uniqueness of the Hebrew language. He notes that Hebrew is the language that God used to dialogue with the prophets and, according to the rabbis, is the language through which God created the world. Moreover, the liturgy of the traditional Jewish prayer book was written by sages – some of whom were prophets – with a profound mystical worldview, who imparted mystical secrets into the text itself. Prayer in Hebrew is effective because the words themselves have momentous cosmic impact. Prayer in the vernacular, by contrast, is not guaranteed to be equally efficacious.[10]

---

8. Rabbi Yehuda b. R. Shmuel HaChasid, twelfth/thirteenth centuries, Germany.
9. *Sefer Chasidim* 588.
10. *Biur Halakha* Orach Chayim 101:4, s.v. *yakhol.*

THE *MISHNA BERURA*/ RABBI MOSHE SOFER:
HEBREW AND THE CHALLENGES OF TRANSLATION

Besides expressing a clear preference for prayer in Hebrew over prayer in the vernacular, the *Mishna Berura* adds another perspective, emphasizing the challenges of ensuring that translated prayers capture the profundity and depth of the Hebrew original. He notes that there are some words in the liturgy whose meaning is unknown and wonders how we would go about translating these problematic phrases. Moreover, he points out that some Hebrew phrases have multiple meanings, and translation involves choosing one meaning over another.[11] Thus Hebrew is always to be preferred because it guarantees that the multi-layered meaning inherent in the text of the prayer book is most effectively captured.

In a long and detailed responsum, Rabbi Moshe Sofer (Hatam Sofer)[12] rules that public prayer in the vernacular is permissible only on an *ad hoc* basis.[13] Aside from the challenging issues of translation, he notes that the Men of the Great Assembly chose Hebrew as the language of the prayerbook despite the fact that many Jews of their period were ignorant of the Hebrew language. Furthermore, rabbinic prayer was at least partially intended to help fill the religious void created by the destruction of the Temple. The sages composed the Jewish prayerbook in Hebrew in order to capture the motifs and themes that helped, and continues to help, the Jewish people to cope with the tragic loss of the centralized house of worship. The Hatam Sofer also argues that we should pray in Hebrew because Hebrew is God's language, just as we would want to converse with a king in the language of the kingdom. In the Hatam Sofer's opinion, the best way to respond to Hebrew illiteracy is to educate people in the holy tongue, not to move away from a Hebrew-centered prayer experience.

RABBI ELIEZER FLECKELES: HEBREW
AS AN INTERNATIONAL UNIFIER

Rabbi Eliezer Flekeles[14] also expresses a strong preference for prayer in Hebrew, especially in a synagogue setting. Rabbi Fleckeles explains

---

11. *Mishna Berura* Orach Chayim 62:3, s.v. *bekhol lashon*.
12. Rabbi Moshe Sofer, eighteenth/nineteenth centuries, Austria-Hungary.
13. Responsa *Hatam Sofer* 6:84.
14. Rabbi Eliezer b. David Fleckles, eighteenth/nineteenth centuries, Prague.

that Hebrew serves as an international unifier, allowing Jews visiting any city in the world to enter a synagogue and feel comfortable praying with people who speak an entirely different language. He argues that if praying in the vernacular were permitted, then visitors to a foreign country would not understand the language of prayer and would not know when to reply during responsive sections of the prayer service. Such a reality would not only have negative consequences on synagogue life, but it would also create a rupture in Jewish communities, as people would be able to pray only with those with whom they are able to converse. By preserving Hebrew prayer, we preserve the unity of the Jewish people, at least when it comes to synagogue services.[15]

This approach has particular appeal in a world in which corporate travel is constantly increasing. A management consultant, for example, may be asked to travel to several countries over the course of a few months in order to advise different companies on business strategy. Imagine how his prayer experience would be affected if a different language of prayer were used in every country he visited! Maintaining a uniform model of prayer in Hebrew allows this individual to be religiously connected to Jews around the world, as they share the same language of communal prayer.

RABBI YECHIEL YAAKOV WEINBERG: HEBREW AND
THE PRESERVATION OF COMMUNAL IDENTITY

Rabbi Yechiel Yaakov Weinberg gives an additional perspective on the importance of Hebrew prayer.[16] He stresses the educational role of prayer in Hebrew, in the context of the synagogue, which serves as the sanctuary of traditional Jewish identity in the modern period. After citing Rabbi Moshe Sofer's opposition to prayer in the vernacular based on the fear that this type of prayer could cause the Hebrew language to be forgotten, Rabbi Weinberg continues to list other disadvantages of prayer in the vernacular. In particular, he writes:

> As a result of our great sins, the synagogue remains the last remnant of pure and complete traditional Judaism. As a result, we

---

15. Responsa *Teshuva MeiAhava*, cited in Responsa *Mishneh Halakhot* 3:83.
16. Rabbi Yechiel Yaakov Weinberg, twentieth century, Russia/Germany.

must ensure that Hebrew remains [the language of the syna-
gogue].... Prohibiting prayer in the vernacular in the synagogue
emphasizes the need [for community members] to learn Hebrew.[17]

Rabbi Weinberg's opposition to prayer in a foreign language highlights
the educational function of the synagogue in promoting increased Jewish observance. Particularly with rising assimilation, the synagogue has
become a safe haven for Jews seeking to experience traditional Judaism.
Prayer in Hebrew not only promotes Jewish cultural values by exposing
worshippers to our holy language, but it also encourages these Jews to
increase their Judaic knowledge by learning Hebrew, and thus to become
more familiar with Jewish tradition in general and the siddur in particular.

RABBI NACHMAN OF BRESLOV:
CONVERSATION VERSUS PRAYER

Despite the many advantages of Hebrew prayer, prohibiting prayer in
the vernacular can generate frustration by limiting the ability of prayer
to become personally transformative. In fact, in the Talmud Yerushalmi,
it is argued that prayer can be recited in any language "so that a person
will know how to ask for his needs."[18]

Beyond its role to appeal to divine mercy, prayer helps us organize
our thoughts and get in touch with our needs and desires. How can this be
accomplished if prayer is limited exclusively to Hebrew? Rabbi Nachman
of Breslov answers this question with a solution outside the framework
of formal prayer. Instead of praying in the vernacular during daily services, Rebbe Nachman advocates spontaneous "conversations" with God,
without the halakhic limitations associated with traditional prayer. Rebbe
Nachman demands that every Jew observe traditional Jewish law and pray
three times daily. However, he suggests *also* engaging in regular dialogue
with God, which should be conducted in everyone's native language:

In the holy tongue [Hebrew], it will be difficult for him to
express whatever he wants to say, and also the heart will not flow

---

17. Responsa *Seridei Eish* 1:9, 20.
18. Sota (Vilna) 7:1.

after the words because he is not used to the language ... . [In the vernacular, by contrast,] he can express whatever he wants to say and ... whatever is in his heart ... . [He can speak] ... before Him, blessed be He, whether it be regret and penitence about the past, or entreaties to merit actual nearness to Him from this day on.[19]

This approach allows us to preserve Hebrew as the language of formal prayer while providing an additional venue for those who are limited in the Hebrew language to express their wants and desires before God.

SUMMARY

While the experience of daily prayer can certainly be challenging, analyzing the messages that underlie the discussion of prayer in the vernacular provides insight into the spiritual opportunities of daily prayer. Praying daily in Hebrew – or in the vernacular when halakhically permissible – allows us to reflect upon:

- Prayer as an appeal to divine mercy (Talmud)
- Maximizing the chances for our prayers to be heard (Rif)
- Prayer and the role of angelic intermediaries (Rif)
- Importance of precise language in daily prayer (Rosh)
- The primacy of proper intent when praying (*Sefer Hasidim*)
- The unique metaphysical status of the Hebrew language (*Mishna Berura*)
- Prayer and the challenges of proper translation (*Mishna Berura*, Rabbi Moshe Sofer)
- Prayer and its role in unifying Jews worldwide (Rabbi Eliezer Fleckeles)
- The role of Hebrew in preserving communal identity (Rabbi Yechiel Yaakov Weinberg)
- Prayer as a means of facilitating fluid conversation with the Divine (Rabbi Nahman of Breslov)

---

19. Cited in R. Elyakim Krumbein, *Mussar For Moderns* (Jersey City: Ktav, 2004), 114.

Chapter 13

The Shema

History, Identity, And the Centrality Of Intent

As we discussed in the previous chapters, the experience of prayer is multifaceted. Each time we enter the synagogue and begin to pray from a traditional siddur, we have an opportunity to be truly transformed by the spiritual messages linked to prayer. Beyond the daily *Amida*, the siddur includes many prayers that express powerful concepts.

One of the most famous parts of the prayer service is the recitation of the *Shema*. In addition to being the prayer traditionally recited by Jews during moments of martyrdom, the *Shema* has also served as an important symbol of hope and commitment for Jews looking towards a better future. Indeed, Rabbi Norman Lamm highlights the centrality of the *Shema* to Jewish identity by noting that it served as a signal during the "failed revolt of Jewish inmates in Auschwitz." During this revolt, a "medallion engraved with the first verse of the *Shema* was passed" from Jew to Jew to indicate that the uprising was to begin. The leaders of the rebellion knew that all Jews would be familiar with the *Shema* and that its image would activate a sense of hope and optimism before the beginning of the revolt.[1]

Beyond its social and communal relevance, the *Shema* is invested with great halakhic significance. According to Jewish law, we are required to recite the *Shema* twice daily, once in the morning and again in the evening. Moreover, the *Shema*'s uniqueness is attested to by the fact that having proper *kavana* (intent) is a critical component of the mitzva itself. Failure to recite certain parts of the *Shema* with the requisite mindset nullifies the fulfillment of the mitzva.[2]

The unique features associated with the *Shema* raise interesting questions about the philosophical and religious significance of the mitzva. Why are Jews required to recite the *Shema* twice daily? Shouldn't a once-daily recitation suffice? Furthermore, why is proper intent such a critical component of the commandment? Lastly, why has the *Shema* become so intertwined with the national story of the Jewish people? Is there something inherent in its message that renders it the appropriate prayer for Jews during moments of both tragedy and opportunity? Reflecting on these questions will help us to better understand the centrality of the *Shema* in our daily lives, as well as its larger role in shaping traditional Jewish identity.

SHEMA AND TORAH STUDY

Before beginning our investigation into the *Shema* as an independent mitzva, it is important to note a rabbinic view that underscores a significant conceptual link between the recitation of the *Shema* and Torah study. The source for the obligation to recite *Shema* daily is the statement in Deuteronomy 6:6-7, which is recited as part of the *Shema* itself:

> These matters that I command you today shall be upon your heart; you shall teach them thoroughly to your children and you shall speak of them while you sit in your home, while you walk on the way, when you retire, and when you arise.

---

1. Rabbi Norman Lamm, *The Shema: Spirituality and Law in Judaism* (Philadelphia/Jerusalem: Jewish Publication Society, 2000), 4.
2. *Shulchan Aruch*, Orach Chayim 60:5.

What is the subject of these verses? What are "these matters" that must be transmitted to others and remembered at all times?

Interestingly, the Talmud quotes the view of Abaye, who argues that these verses do not refer to any formal obligation to recite the *Shema* twice daily. Rather, the subject of these verses is the requirement to be perpetually involved in the study of Torah. Abaye argues that the requirement to recite *Shema* daily lacks a biblical source and is, in fact, only rabbinic in nature.[3] Dr. Yitzchak Gilat notes that according to Abaye's position, the obligation to recite *Shema* daily was instituted with the specific goal of providing structured Torah learning for the average Jew both in the morning and evening.[4] Indeed, the Raavan,[5] explicitly asserts that the *Shema* was legislated in order to fulfill the mitzva of Torah study.[6]

On the surface, this approach seems to prescribe the *Shema* as a technical means of fulfilling a halakhic obligation: by reciting this biblical passage, one has studied Torah. However, Rabbi Mayer Lichtenstein[7] argues for a more fundamental connection between *Shema* and Torah study.[8] Quoting his grandfather, Rabbi Joseph Soloveitchik, Rabbi Lichtenstein notes that traditional Judaism views Torah study as more than an intellectual exercise. Torah study is a transformative religious experience, in which the student commits to observe the obligatory statutes that emerge from his study. In fact, the Talmud Yerushalmi states that it would be better not to be born than to study Torah with no intention of committing to the *halakhot* that one studies.[9] Legislating the *Shema* specifically as the vehicle for Torah learning connects the intellectual aspect of study with the larger imperative to accept divine sovereignty upon oneself. The *Shema* is not just a passage to be recited in fulfillment of the requirement to study Torah. Rather, it is an affirmation of

3. Berakhot 21a.
4. Yitzchak Gilat, *Perakim BeHishtalshelut HaHalakha* (Ramat Gan: Bar Ilan University, 1992), 284.
5. Rabbi Eliezer b. Natan, eleventh/twelfth centuries, Germany.
6. Raavan, Berakhot 155, s.v. *amar Rav Yehuda*.
7. Rabbi Mayer Lichtenstein, twenty-first century, Israel.
8. Rabbi Mayer Lichtenstein, "Hadevarim Haeleh: The Connection Between Keriat Shema and Torah Sudy," *Mishlav* 31 (1997): 40.
9. Shabbat 1:2 (Vilna edition).

our commitment to Torah study as a basis for observing Jewish law and connecting to God.

The view that the *Shema* is a rabbinic obligation is a minority voice in classical literature. Nonetheless, it highlights an important undercurrent regarding the nature of *Shema's* recitation. The ultimate goal for a Jew is to connect to God and be transformed by His statutes. There is a risk, however, that the intellectual excitement of Torah study will erroneously lead an individual to connect cognitively to Torah study without simultaneously submitting to the dictates of the law. The *Shema* reminds us that all of our actions – even those that seem intuitively religious – should further the larger ideal of accepting God's sovereignty.

SHEMA AND JEWISH THEOLOGY

The majority voice in the Jewish tradition views reciting *Shema* as an independent Torah obligation. While halakhic authorities debated which paragraph of the *Shema* is obligatory according to the Torah, traditional codifiers assume that one must recite three paragraphs twice daily. Thematically, the first paragraph (Deuteronomy 6:4-9) deals with topics such as accepting God's sovereignty, His oneness, and the requirement to love God. The second passage (Deuteronomy 11:13-21) adds the themes of commitment to a life of mitzvot and reward and punishment. The last paragraph (Numbers 15:37-41) mentions the Exodus from Egypt, reminding us of God's providence.

The specific order of the three paragraphs is addressed in the Mishna.[10] The order certainly cannot be based on chronology, since the passage from Numbers is read last, after two chapters from the book of Deuteronomy. *Tosafot* notes that this question implies that the second paragraph of the *Shema* should have been recited first, since it is written in the plural form, addressing the entire nation of Israel, while the first paragraph is written in the singular.[11] The Mishna notes that the paragraphs are arranged in this order so that "one should first accept upon himself the yoke of God's sovereignty,[12] and [only] then accept upon himself the yoke of the

---

10. Berakhot 13a.
11. Tosafot, Berakhot 14b, s.v. *lama*.
12. By reciting the verse, "Hear O Israel, Hashem is our God, Hashem is One."

commandments."[13] One way to understand this mishnaic formulation is that anyone who does not accept God's sovereignty most likely will not observe the commandments.[14] However, another way to understand this mishnaic statement is as an assertion of the centrality of theology in fostering a more elevated form of observance. A Jew may indeed follow the statutes of the law even without accepting Judaism's basic tenets. However, such an observance would be fundamentally flawed. Traditional Jewish beliefs provide the broader theological framework for Jewish observance. Without a firm belief in God and His sovereignty, observance of the precepts is religiously lacking.

An illustrative example will be helpful in highlighting the centrality of traditional Jewish dogma.[15] Imagine two people who are both very kind to animals. One person's kindness is a reflection of his larger belief in the immorality of cruelty to any living thing. The other individual treats animals with dignity because he thinks they are gods. While the bottom line behavior for both is identical, the qualitative experience of kindness towards animals would be different, depending on one's beliefs.

The *Shema* has historical and national significance as well. Dr. Jeffrey Tigay notes:

> [The word *echad* in the *Shema* provided] a suitable response to the many theological challenges that Jewish monotheism confronted throughout history... in the face of polytheism, it meant that the Divine is one, not many; in the face of Zoroastrian and Gnostic dualism, it meant one, not two; in the face of Christian trinitarianism, it meant one, not three; and in the face of atheism, one and not none.[16]

Thus, the *Shema* serves as the perfect meeting point between theology and history, reminding Jews daily of our theological roots and of the opposition the Jewish nation has overcome throughout the ages.

---

13. By reciting the verse, "And it will be that if you hearken to My commandments," etc.
14. See Meiri, Berakhot 14b, s.v. *hamishna* for a similar explanation.
15. This example is adapted from an analogy of Rabbi Yitzchak Blau in his excellent article, "Flexibility with a Firm Foundation: On Maintaining Jewish Dogma," *The Torah U-Madda Journal* 12 (2004): 179-191.
16. Jefferey Tigay, *The JPS Torah Commentary: Deuteronomy* (Philadelphia/New York: The Jewish Publication Society, 1996), 440.

SHEMA AND THE POWER OF BELONGING

Beyond the required three paragraphs of the *Shema*, the Talmud notes one additional line that we are obligated to recite during the *Shema's* recitation: "Blessed is the Name of the glory of the kingdom forever." Articulating the rationale behind reciting this line, the Talmud cites a powerful midrashic dialogue between [Yaakov] and his children at the end of [Yaakov's] life:

> [Yaakov] wished to reveal to his sons the end of days, but the Holy Spirit withdrew from him. He said, "Perhaps, Heaven forbid, there is a defect in my bed, like Avraham, from whom Yishmael was [born], and from my father Yitzhak, from whom Esau was [born]." His sons said to him, "Hear O Israel, the Lord is God, the Lord is One! Just as there is only One in your heart, so there is only One in our hearts." Then did our father Yaakov recite, "Blessed is the Name of the glory of His kingdom forever."[17]

What is the relationship between this midrash and our daily recitation of the *Shema*? Rabbi Joseph Soloveitchik claims that the talmudic account underscores the inherent interconnectedness of the *Shema* and its theology with the earliest origins of Jewish history. He writes, "The solemn declaration is perhaps the first truth which our great patriarchs discovered. It became their motto and dominant motif in life."[18]

However, in addition to its relevance as a feature of traditional Jewish theology, the *Shema's* meaning extends far beyond the philosophical plane. Jews who recite the *Shema* daily connect themselves with the millions of Jews who have been reciting the *Shema* since the time of our forefathers. In particular, they affirms the *Shema* as a "living doctrine … which keeps us together as one, spanning almost the whole course of ages, uniting us with our patriarchs, drawing them into our temporal ontic circle, thus lending to our own existence the tenor of

17. Pesachim 56a, translated in *Worship of the Heart: Essays on Jewish Prayer* by Rabbi Joseph B. Soloveitchik, ed. Shalom Carmy (Jersey City: Ktav, 2003), 110.
18. Rabbi Joseph B. Soloveitchik, *Worship of the Heart: Essays on Jewish Prayer*, ed. Shalom Carmy (Jersey City: Ktav, 2003), 111.

timelessness."[19] In the midrashic account, Yaakov was worried about his children's commitment to the tradition that he loved. His declaration of the phrase, "Blessed is the Name of the glory of His kingdom forever," testified to his own confidence that his progeny would remain loyal to the covenant of the forefathers. Every time contemporary Jews recite the *Shema* and say "Blessed is the Name of the glory of His kingdom forever," they similarly affirm the hope that they will pass on the tradition to their children in a way that maximizes the chances that their offspring will continue to keep the tradition of Avraham alive. In this way, we are able to engage in a conversation that spans the generations and allows us to converse with the partriarchs, who "though they died a biological death, have been reincarnated time and again in our historical experience."[20]

The *Shema* thus facilitates a profound sense of belonging and responsibility. Each Jew is a part of an ongoing story that began with Avraham and continues to this very day. This sense of connectedness to the extraordinary narrative of the Jewish people simultaneously provides comfort and imposes obligation. The modern Jew reciting *Shema* can think back to Avraham, Yitzchak, Yaakov, Moshe, the Rambam, and the Ramban, as well as all of the other great Jewish thinkers who continue to crystallize and articulate traditional Judaism's unique theological message. However, we must also affirm that this theology is not intended solely as an intellectual abstraction. Our collective history serves as a reminder for us to keep the story alive in a way that perpetuates the legacy of our ancestors.

SHEMA AND THE CENTRALITY OF KAVANA

Given the profound theological and historical messages of the *Shema*, it is not surprising that Jewish law requires added concentration when performing this mitzva. In fact, the *Shulchan Arukh* rules that if we recite the first two lines of the *Shema* ("Hear O Israel" and "Blessed is the Name") without proper intent, we do not fulfill our obligation.[21]

---

19. Ibid.
20. Ibid., 112.
21. *Shulchan Arukh*, Orach Chayim 60:5, and comments of the *Mishna Berura*, Orach Chayim 63:12.

Rav Soloveitchik articulates why the requirement of intent is more stringent for the *Shema* (and the *Amida*) than for other mitzvot. *Kavana* (intent) with regard to most mitzvot requires "only normative heedfulness... and intention of action in accord with the divine will, which decreed the norm."[22] This obligation of *kavana* is external to the specific mitzva being performed. Intent during the recitation of *Shema* (and *Amida*), however, "forms the core of accomplishment, the central idea and the intrinsic content of the mitzva." Reciting *Shema* is ultimately about accepting divine sovereignty and acknowledging the "universal and eternal authority of God."[23] Saying the words of the *Shema* without the proper intent renders the internalization of the *Shema's* messages impossible and therefore cannot constitute a fulfillment of the mitzva. The mouth is the formal medium for the fulfillment of the mitzva, but ultimately the messages of the *Shema* must penetrate the heart.

Since *kavana* is particularly critical in the first two lines of the *Shema*, it is crucial to define the concepts that we should be focusing on while performing the mitzva. Having addressed the meaning behind the phrase, "Blessed is the Name of the glory of His kingdom forever," we still need to delineate the theological significance of the first line of *Shema* ("Hear O Israel"), which focuses on God's oneness.

Medieval interpreters differ regarding the significance of this declaration of God's oneness. For Rashbam,[24] the phrase "our God" in the first line focuses our attention on the fact that we worship God alone, and not any other foreign deities – Hashem is our God, and no other. The phrase "God is One" (*Hashem Echad*) then extends this theme from God's vantage point: just as we worship only the One True God, God is able to act alone without the assistance of any other power.[25] Rashi understands the *Shema* in more eschatological terms: right now Hashem is "our God," and not the God of the other nations, but at the end of

---

22. Rabbi Joseph B. Soloveitchik, *Worship of the Heart: Essays on Jewish Prayer*, ed. Shalom Carmy (Jersey City: Ktav, 2003), 89.
23. Ibid., 88.
24. Rabbi Shmuel b. Meir, twelfth century, France.
25. Rashbam, Deuteronomy 6:4.

days, God's providence and sovereignty will be accepted by all and He will be "One."[26] Lastly, the Rambam emphasizes God's oneness from a philosophical perspective. God is unique in His oneness and is fundamentally different from anything physical.[27] God is not one unit that is comprised of multiple parts. God's oneness is a transcendent philosophical category that cannot be experienced by mankind.

The *Shema* is thus a vehicle for us to affirm these philosophical axioms. If we combine all three interpretations, the first line of the *Shema* becomes a powerful medium for contemplating God's oneness from a national, eschatological, and philosophical perspective. Being a Jew means being part of a theological worldview that is profoundly unique, and God's omnipotence affirms our monotheistic worldview. In this way, *Shema* serves as a nationalistic calling card. However, we also yearn for a time when our basic theological assumptions of God will be shared by all. Reciting the *Shema* reminds us that history is constantly moving ahead and our mission is to ensure that it continues to move in a direction that helps facilitate this understanding of God. Lastly, the *Shema* affirms Judaism as a theological system rooted in a philosophical vision of the world. God's oneness is not a concept to be explored exclusively by Jewish mystics. Rather, by reciting the *Shema* daily, we declare that God's oneness is something that all Jews can philosophically affirm.

SUMMARY

Given the *Shema*'s rich history and philosophy, it is not surprising that it has become a central component of traditional Jewish identity. Our study of the ideals that underlie the laws of the *Shema* provides another illustrative example of the powerful ideas that are at the root of our daily observance of Jewish law. In particular, our daily recitation of the *Shema* allows us to:

- Appreciate the way *Shema* affirms Torah study as a religious experience and not just an intellectual exercise (Rav Soloveitchik)

---

26. Rashi, Deuteronomy 6:4.
27. Rambam, Laws of the Foundations of the Torah 1:7.

- Reflect daily on central theological concepts, such as God's oneness, divine providence, reward and punishment, and the Exodus from Egypt (verses in Deuteronomy 6:4-9, 11:13-21, and Numbers 15:37-41)
- Reflect on the centrality of Jewish theology and how it provides the proper context for authentic Jewish observance (Mishna Berakhot)
- Understand the *Shema*'s unique role in defending traditional Jewish theology from external threats (Dr. Tigay)
- Feel a profound connection to the millions of Jews who lived before us and affirmed their faith by reciting the *Shema* (Rav Soloveitchik)
- Affirm a commitment to trying our best to pass on the tradition of our forefathers to our children (*Pesachim* 56a)
- Have the requisite intent and fully accept God's sovereignty and oneness (*Shulchan Arukh*)
- Appreciate Judaism's unique theology and its national, philosophical, and eschatological significance (Rashi, Rambam, Rashbam)

Chapter 14

The Obligation of Torah Study

Religious Inspiration and Communal Obligation

T he primary premise of this book is that mitzvot represent profound opportunities for divine encounters and serve as the medium through which we interact with God. Jewish law prescribes that, immediately following morning prayers, we should take time before beginning the work day to immerse ourselves in Torah study.[1] Why does the halakha demand that we begin our day with a foray into the world of traditional Jewish study?

Traditional rabbinic sources assume that Torah study is not merely an intellectual exercise. Rather, it has the potential to be a transformative divine encounter. Rabbi Joseph Soloveitchik describes Torah study as a "total, all-encompassing, and all-embracing involvement of the mind and heart, will and feeling – the very center of the human

---

1. *Shulchan Aruch*, Orach Chayim 155:1.

personality."[2] Nonetheless, there is an awareness in rabbinic texts of the varied nature of the obligation to study Torah. Far from viewing the obligation of Torah study as a uniform requirement, talmudic sources identify Torah study as a contextual obligation based on the intellectual and spiritual capacity of the individual.

Reflecting on sources that define the contours of the obligation to study Torah daily will help generate an appreciation for the rabbinic requirement that Torah study be an integral part of our daily routine. Additionally, by providing a narrative framework for Torah study, we will ensure that it is experienced as a divine encounter, and not simply as an academic discipline.

THE VIEW OF R. YISHMAEL: THE PRIMACY OF TORAH STUDY

The Talmud in Tractate Berakhot cites a *beraita* that quotes an interesting position of R. Yishmael:

> [The verse states:] "And you will gather in your grain." For what reason did Scripture have to say this? For since it is stated: "This book of the Torah shall not depart from your mouth," it would be possible [to think that] the words [of Scripture here are meant] as they are written, [i.e. that one must study Torah every waking moment, precluding one from earning a livelihood]. The Torah therefore states, "And you will gather in your grain," [which bids us to lead a life of] Torah study conducted in the way of the world [i.e. Torah study should be combined with the earning of a livelihood]. These are the words of R. Yishmael.[3]

According to the view of R. Yishmael, the obligation to study Torah must be reconciled with the directive to earn a living. Both are eternal Torah values, and each one therefore deserves its own attention. Rashi argues that R. Yishmael's insistence on balancing Torah study with work is based on the assumption that relying on others for livelihood

---

2. Rabbi Joseph B. Soloveitchik, cited in R. Aaron Rakeffet-Rotthkoff, *The Rav: The World of Rabbi Joseph Soloveitchik, Volume Two* (New Jersey: Ktav, 1999),202.
3. Berakhot 35b.

will adversely affect our Torah study.[4] A career that offers fiscal stability for our families allows us to focus attention properly during studies, without the anxiety of financial instability.

R. Yishmael is cited in Tractate Menachot as quoting the same verse from Joshua – "The book of the Torah shall not depart from your mouth; rather you shall contemplate it day and night"[5] – but with a very different message. Here, he quotes this verse in response to a question from his nephew regarding the permissibility of studying "Greek wisdom" after completing the entire Torah. Expounding on this citation, R. Yishmael tells his nephew to "seek a moment that is neither of the day nor of the night and study in it Greek wisdom." Here it seems that the verse in Joshua demands constant study of Torah, and therefore even one who has completed the Torah in its entirety may not engage in the study of other disciplines.[6]

Many scholars have attempted to harmonize R. Yishmael's insistence on combining Torah study with a profession with his firm opposition to studying Greek wisdom. One explanation is that R. Yishmael is generally resistant to diverting attention from Torah study unless the diversion, itself, will ultimately facilitate increased Torah study. Learning a profession falls into this category, since the stability that it provides facilitates the proper peace of mind that allows for more concentrated study. This explains R. Yishmael's belief in combining Torah study with a profession. Greek wisdom, by contrast, does not facilitate increased Torah study and is therefore frowned upon.

THE VIEW OF RASHBI: TORAH AND
THE METAPHYSICS OF LIFE

In contrast to R. Yishmael, R. Shimon bar Yochai (Rashbi) maintains that we may not divert attention from Torah study even to learn a profession. He argues, "If a man plows at the time of plowing and sows at the time of sowing... what will become of the study of Torah?" In other words, involvement in the material world creates a risk that a person will become excessively focused on materialism and, as a result, neglect the spiritual pursuit of Torah learning. Responding to the question of

---

4. Rashi, Berakhot 35b, s.v *minhag*.
5. Josh. 1:8.
6. Menahot 99b.

who will provide for the Jewish people's physical needs if everyone is fully immersed in Torah study, Rashbi replies that "when the people of Israel do the work of the Omnipresent, their work is done for them by others."[7] Rashbi understands that the need to engage in physical labor is a sign of divine disapproval with human behavior. In the ideal world of divine metaphysics, Jewish people engage exclusively in Torah study and their physical needs are provided for by God.

While this view seems fairly extreme, it is significantly tempered by a parallel statement of Rashbi cited in Menachot. There, he says that we can fulfill our obligation to study Torah daily by minimally reciting the *Shema* in the morning and evening.[8] On the surface, this citation seems difficult to reconcile with Rashbi's uncompromising stance cited in Berakhot. How can Rashbi prohibit even engaging in a profession because of the expansive requirement to study Torah and simultaneously maintain such a minimum standard for the requirement of Torah learning?

One possibility is that, while ideally R. Shimon does insist on full-time Torah study, he acknowledges that this approach is not possible for every Jew. Individuals who are not capable of living up to the rabbinic ideal and must preoccupy themselves with worldly endeavors are nonetheless required to study Torah. The minimal requirement for this subset of the Jewish community is the recitation of the *Shema* in the morning and evening.

SHULCHAN ARUKH HARAV: MAXIMIZED TORAH STUDY

Referencing the debate between R. Yishmael and Rashbi, the Talmud cites the view of Abaye, who states that "many did as R. Yishmael," combining Torah study with a livelihood, and achieved success both fiscally as well as in Torah scholarship. Conversely, Abaye reports that others followed the view of Rashbi and experienced limited success. The clear implication of this passage is that while the view of Rashbi may be relevant for a few exceptionally pious individuals, the default traditional assumption is that Jews should commit themselves to Torah study while investing sufficient effort to provide financially for themselves and their families.

---

7. Berakhot 35b.
8. Menahot 99b.

This position is articulated by Rabbi Shneur Zalman of Liadi in his classical work *Shulchan Arukh HaRav*. While ruling that Jewish law does not demand full-time Torah study and requires one to find a profession, Rabbi Shneur Zalman states that this permissive ruling allows us to divert time away from Torah learning only for the specific purpose of earning a living. However, the moment we take a break from earning a living, the obligation to study Torah is reactivated.[9]

This position raises interesting questions about the rabbinic attitude towards activities that are not connected to any profession but are still experientially valuable. For example, what room is there within the rabbinic tradition for relaxation, exercise, and socializing? Is the rabbinic ideal intended to create Torah scholars engaging exclusively in Torah study and the pursuit of a livelihood? Rabbi Moshe Feinstein indirectly addresses this question in a responsum dealing with a student who wanted to leave yeshiva early in order to pursue academic studies. Discussing the larger ideal that Jews should strive for in regulating their schedules, Rabbi Feinstein writes that we truly experience soulful satisfaction only when we engage in activities that are by definition spiritual and value-centered. "Correct and proper activities," as well as Torah study, fall into this category and should be encouraged.[10]

This loosely defined category of "correct and proper activities" seems difficult to formalize. Presumably, Rabbi Feinstein maintains that we require special dispensation to engage in earning a livelihood because economic sustenance is, by definition, a material venture. While the act of fiscally providing for one's family is certainly a mitzva, the risks involved in engaging in material ventures are so significant that we require a special source-based dispensation. However, other activities that are value-centered rather than driven by material considerations are permissible even without the support of the biblical text.

Although this model focuses heavily on the centrality of Torah study and assumes that one's default activity should be Torah learning, Rabbi Feinstein's explanation allows us to view Torah study as

---

9. *Shulḥan Arukh HaRav*, Laws of Torah Study 3:6-7.
10. *Iggerot Moshe*, Yoreh Deah 4:36.

representative of a class of activities that are not materially motivated and have significant spiritual potential.

ARUKH HASHULCHAN: TORAH STUDY
AND INDIVIDUAL EXPRESSION

While the *Shulchan Arukh HaRav* presents a demanding model that focuses heavily on Torah learning as our daily default activity, the *Arukh HaShulchan*[11] acknowledges that the demand of Torah study should fluctuate based on the intellectual and spiritual posture of the individual in question. According to the *Arukh HaShulchan*, the talmudic requirement for an individual to make his Torah learning primary while ensuring that everything else is secondary applies only to a great scholar, who has higher learning standards. An ordinary Jew is required to ensure only that Torah study is part of his overall schedule.[12]

The *Or Same'ach*[13] offers the philosophical underpinnings for the idea that the obligation to study Torah is contextual, based on the uniqueness of each individual. According to the *Or Same'ach*, the Torah can legislate mitzvot only according to a minimum standard that is uniform for the entire Jewish people.[14] Rabbi Yitzchak Blau notes that "this universalizing quality of mitzvot conveys the idea that Judaism is not reserved for a small elite and applies equally to all."[15] For example, the Torah can mandate that each person shake the lulav at least on the first day of Sukkot and recite Kiddush on Shabbat. However, there is another genre of mitzvot that are circumstantial, based on the spiritual make-up of the individual. The classic example of the second category is the Torah's lack of formal demands in the realm of ethics. Since the extent that one should experience feelings of pride, for example, changes based on person and context, the Torah provides only general – not definitive – guidelines.

The *Or Sameach* asserts that Torah study falls into this second category. After all, it is not reasonable for the Torah to formulate clearly

---

11. Rabbi Yehiel Michel b. Rabbi Aharon HaLevi Epstein, nineteenth century, Russia.
12. *Arukh HaShulchan*, Orach Chayim 156: 1-2.
13. Rabbi Meir Simha HaKohen, nineteenth/twentieth centuries, Dvinsk (Latvia).
14. *Or Sameach*, Laws of Torah Study 1:2.
15. Rabbi Yitzchak Blau, *Fresh Fruits and Vintage Wine: The Ethics and Wisdom of the Aggada* (Brooklyn: Ktav, 2009), 59.

defined regulations as to the specific amount of Torah learning required each day, since each individual possesses unique intellectual and spiritual capabilities. Therefore, the rabbis set a minimum standard, requiring only the daily recitation of *Shema* in the morning and evening and leaving any further study to personal choice.

In addition to creating a more flexible halakhic standard, this ruling highlights the personal element in Torah study. Each individual is endowed by God with a unique identity, and the nature and scope of our daily Torah learning should reflect our personal situation. This allows an us to assume personal responsibility for the success or failure of our Torah study. Students often wonder how best to integrate Torah study with their university studies. Instead of imposing a uniform external standard, the approach suggested by the *Or Sameach* encourages them to personally reflect and honestly assess what would be the most effective strategy for successful Torah study, given their personal schedules and character traits. This model ultimately inspires sophisticated Torah study while acknowledging the individual nature of each of us and our special relationship to the world of Torah learning.

TORAH STUDY AND SHARED RESPONSIBILITY

While the sources cited above focus on the parameters of an individual's obligation to study Torah, additional sources focus on the responsibility for sharing Torah knowledge with others. The primary source for this idea is a statement by Shammai, cited in Tractate Avot, that we must make our Torah study "fixed" or "permanent."[16] The Mishna is interpreted in the *Mishna Berura* as mandating daily study as a permanent feature of our schedule.[17] For example, if we study Torah daily, after the morning prayer service, we should make sure that we don't neglect this fixed Torah learning under any circumstances. In the event that we have to skip this study for reasons beyond our control, we should double our efforts the next day in order to "make up" the Torah study we missed.

According to this approach, the mishnaic requirement highlights the centrality of Torah learning by incorporating study as a fixed part

---

16. Avot 1:15.
17. *Mishna Berura* Orach Chayim 155:4, s.v. shelo.

of our daily routine. Activities that we perform daily are those we feel most passionate about. Making Torah study permanent keeps it high on our list of daily priorities.

While the *Mishna Berura* focuses on an individual's requirement to study Torah daily, *Avot DeRebbe Natan* claims that the mishnaic phrase "fixed" generates an obligation for each Jew to promote Torah learning as a "fixed" part of the entire Jewish people's communal discourse. According to *Avot deRebbe Natan*, if we study Torah, we have a duty to share whatever we learn with others. Citing Biblical support for this notion, *Avot DeRebbe Natan* brings Ezra the Scribe as the model of someone who studied Torah while simultaneously taking responsibility for the spiritual welfare of his fellow Jews.[18] Rabbi Aharon Lichtenstein[19] explains:

> The Jews returning from the Babylonian exile [at the time of Ezra] had a very tenuous relationship to Torah…. [As a result,] Ezra was faced with a tremendous challenge: to ensure that Torah would become permanent within *that* community. Ezra did not just explain and extend Torah Rabbinic enactments, but saw to it that the people understood that adherence to Torah was not negotiable; it is part of what being *Klal Yisrael* means.[20]

This perspective extends the nature of the obligation to study Torah beyond the personal and into the communal sphere. Students of Torah are thus not people who cares only about their own spiritual needs. Rather, by learning and sharing Torah with others, they affirm their commitment to the spiritual well-being of the entire Jewish people.

SUMMARY

As we have demonstrated in this chapter, Torah study is much more than an intellectual exercise. Jewish law asks us to take time out of

---

18. *Avot DeRabbi Natan, nuscha* 1:13, s.v. *aseh.*
19. Rabbi Aharon Lichtenstein, twentieth/twenty-first centuries, United States/Israel.
20. Rabbi Aharon Lichtenstein, "Make Your Torah Permanent: The Centrality of Torah Study," adapted by Rabbi Reuven Ziegler, http://etzion.org.il/en/make-your-torah-permanent-centrality-torah-study.

our schedules, every morning after leaving the synagogue, to invest in Torah learning. By meditating on the nature of Torah study, as well as the values that underlie the texts that we choose to learn, we are guided toward implementing divine ideals in the real world. In addition, as we enter our work space, our initial morning encounter with Torah study reminds us of our broader communal responsibility to share Torah with our fellow-Jews.

Studying Torah daily while contemplating its underlying philosophy allows one to:

- Reflect on the primacy of Torah study in rabbinic tradition (R. Yishmael, Rashbi)
- Think about how Torah study can have a metaphysical impact (Rashbi)
- Highlight the challenge of balancing our time between the physical and spiritual (R. Yishmael, Rabbi Moshe Feinstein)
- Focus on Torah study and the uniqueness of each individual (*Or Sameach*)
- Ensure that Torah study is a permanent fixture in our daily schedules (*Mishna Berura*)
- Remember that Torah study should generate a sense of communal responsibility (*Avot DeRebbe Natan*)

Chapter 15

Choosing a Text

Finding Personal Meaning
Within A Structured System

I n the previous chapter, we examined the religious messages underlying the halakhic mandate that morning prayers be followed immediately with Torah study. We now ask what type of Torah learning we are
obligated to engage in? Is the text that we use to fulfill this obligation
simply a matter of personal preference, or does halakha prescribe a specific daily curriculum?

Answering these questions is critical in order to fully appreciate
the larger religious agenda of the rabbinic requirement of daily Torah
study. Analyzing sources that grapple with these issues will allow us to
better appreciate the requirements of Torah learning and the opportunities that Torah study provide for a Jew to assert individuality within
a formal structured system.

TRACTATE AVODA ZARA: PERSONAL PREFERENCE

One of the central texts addressing the obligation of daily Torah learning
is a passage in Tractate Avoda Zara. The Talmud records a statement of

R. Yehuda haNasi that highlights the importance of feeling personally connected to the material being studied. According to R. Yehuda, "A person can learn Torah [successfully] only from the area [i.e. within the topic] that his heart desires." In order to substantiate Rabbi's claim, the Talmud relates an incident that demonstrates the significance of personal connection in choosing a subject of study:

> Levi and R. Shimon the son of Rabbi sat before Rabbi [their master] and were studying Scripture. They concluded a book [and debated which book to study next]. Levi said, "Let Proverbs be brought to us." R. Shimon the son of Rabbi said, "Let Psalms be brought to us." R. Shimon prevailed over Levi, and the book of Psalms was brought. When they reached the verse, "But his desire is in the Torah of Hashem," Rabbi explained and said, "A person can learn Torah only from the area that his heart desires." Levi [then] said, "My master, you have [hereby] given me permission to rise [and retire, since I currently wish to study Proverbs]!"[1]

While this story demonstrates the importance of each student's personal connection to the material being studied, it neglects to explain why this personal connection is so central to the experience of Torah study. Rashi explains that R. Yehuda's dictum requires a teacher to teach a specific talmudic tracate that a student requests; for if a teacher insists on teaching a tractate other than the one requested by the student, the student's learning will be compromised, since his attention will be focused on the material that he would rather be studying.[2]

According to Rashi's understanding, R. Yehuda's concern was primarily pragmatic. Every teacher wants his students to maximize their learning potential. R. Yehuda understood that, by affirming the personal learning preference of every student, we provide each student with the proper framework to foster success.

This view challenges us to think about our own Torah study – how productive it is and whether it accomplishes the goals we wish to

---

1. Avoda Zara 19a.
2. Rashi, Avoda Zara 19a, s.v. *mimakom shelibo*.

achieve. Choosing for ourselves the text that we study every day maximizes our chances for success, since we will feel personally connected and invested in the material that we study. For example, imagine that someone chooses to study Mishna daily, with the goal of completing the entire Mishna during a three-year cycle. The halakha did not obligate that person to choose this specific project. Providing a broad obligatory framework for Torah learning, while also encouraging students to feel personally connected to the texts they choose, facilitates a high probability that the student will accomplish their desired learning goals.

TALMUD KIDDUSHIN: FORMAL STRUCTURE REVISITED

While the talmudic account in Tractate Avoda Zara stresses the importance of all students choosing the material that they wish to study, a passage in Tractate Kiddushin advocates a more formal and rigid approach. Citing the view of R. Safra in the name of R. Yehoshua ben Chananya, the Gemara holds that we should always divide our learning time into thirds, spending a third studying Scripture, a third studying Mishna, and a third studying Gemara.[3]

According to Rashi, R. Yehoshua ben Chananya's view demands that *weekly* learning be split into thirds: two days should be devoted to Scripture, two days to Mishna, and two to the study of Gemara.[4] In *Tosafot*, by contrast, it is argued that *daily* learning should be divided into the talmudically-mandated three-part division.[5] Whether we accept the position of Rashi or *Tosafot*, this approach leaves much less room for personal initiative than the approach in Avoda Zara. While it does allow some room for choosing one book of Scripture over another, for example, it places Torah study into a neatly divided format that clearly limits freedom in determining which topics to study.

In addition, this text in Kiddushin reminds us that the Torah encompasses a wide range of ideas and ideals to be studied. Excessive focus on the study of one aspect of the Torah could cause an imbalance in terms of the spiritual messages that we encounter during Torah learning. And finally, there are pragmatic elements of Torah study that we must be

---

3. Kiddushin 30a.
4. Rashi, Kiddushin 30a, s.v *leyomei.*
5. *Tosafot,* Kiddushin 30a, s.v. *lo tzrikha.*

exposed to in order to live lives dedicated to the dictates of Jewish law. For example, how can we know how to properly observe Shabbat if we don't spend any time dedicated to the texts that address Shabbat observance?

RITVA: PERSONAL MEANING IN THE CONTEXT OF A FORMAL SYSTEM

Attempting to reconcile the tension between personal preference and imposed requirements, the Ritva reads the seemingly formal passage in Kiddushin through a more personal lens. According to the Ritva, the obligation to divide study time among Scripture, Mishna, and Gemara requires devoting *some* time to each of the three areas. However, the exact nature of the division and how much time spent on each is a function of personal preference.[6] For example, according to the Ritva, if we feel personally connected to the study of Mishna, we would be permitted to spend significantly more time working through the mishnaic corpus, even at the expense of time spent on talmudic study.

The Ritva's approach preserves the balanced curriculum advocated by the the passage in Kiddushin, thus ensuring exposure to a wide range of biblical and rabbinic teachings. Nonetheless, by allowing for a slightly looser division of the required texts, the Ritva ensures that Torah study should be generally guided by a sense of personal preference, with an eye towards texts that will be more personally and religiously transformative.

RABBEINU TAM: THE CENTRALITY OF GEMARA AND THE UNITY OF JEWISH LEARNING

Rabbeinu Tam[7] offers an alternative understanding, emphasizing the prominence of the study of Talmud in the academies of Jews in twelfth-century Franco-Germany. Despite the clear talmudic directive requiring the division of time into thirds, rotating among Scripture, Mishna, and Gemara, Rabbeinu Tam notes that the common practice in his time was to study Gemara exclusively. In order to justify this practice, Rabbeinu Tam argues that, since the Babylonian Talmud contains biblical verses

---

6. Ritva, Avoda Zara 19b.
7. Rabbi Yaakov Tam (one of the Tosafists), twelfth century, France/Germany.

as well as citations of tannaitic texts, studying Talmud allows for learning Scipture, Mishna, and Gemara simultaneously.[8]

Rabbi Moshe Taragin[9] argues that Rabbeinu Tam cannot possibly think that studying Gemara, exclusively, can allow us to mathematically cover all three topics (Scripture, Mishna, and Gemara) with the same degree of frequency. After all, some Talmudic tractates contain very few scriptural citations. Rather, explains Rabbi Taragin, the position of Rabbeinu Tam highlights the integrated nature of Torah learning. Instead of viewing Scripture, Mishna, and Gemara as three separate units of study, the Talmud Bavli links all three texts together, thereby emphasizing the organic character of Torah study.[10]

Integrating the Oral and Written Law reminds us of the interpretive history of Torah learning. When we study Torah, we embark on a walking tour of Jewish history, encountering the greatest rabbinic minds, ranging from Moshe to contemporary scholars. Studying the Talmud provides a opportunity to understand the chain of Jewish tradition and become a part of the larger story of Torah study.

Rabbi Aharon Lichtenstein captures this sentiment:

> To open a gemara is to enter their [the rabbinic sages'] overawing presence, to feel the force of their collective personality… to be irradiated and ennobled by them. It is to be exposed, with a sense of intimacy, not only to their discourse, exegesis, aphorisms or anecdotes but to themselves – at once engaging and magisterial, thoroughly human yet overwhelming.[11]

PIRKEI AVOT: LEARNING AND PERSONAL MATURITY

While the aforementioned text in Tractate Kiddushin focuses on dividing study time among various subjects, a passage in Pirkei Avot (Ethics of our Fathers) shifts the dialogue towards the question of which texts

---

8. *Tosafot*, ibid., s.v. *lo tzricha*.
9. Rabbi Moshe Taragin, twenty-first century Israel.
10. Rabbi Moshe Taragin, *Dividing One's Time for Torah Study*, http://etzion.org.il/en/dividing-ones-time-torah-study.
11. Rabbi Aharon Lichtenstein, *Leaves of Faith: The World of Jewish Learning, Volume 1* (Jersey City: Ktav, 2003), 11.

are appropriate for students of different ages.[12] According to this view, from age five until ten, students should focus exclusively on the study of Scripture. From ten to fifteen students should study Mishna. At fifteen, a student begins to study the Gemara.

What is the significance of this division? Why are certain texts more appropriate for specific ages? On the surface, it seems logical that from age five until ten, young students should focus their educational energy on studying Scripture. On a pragmatic level, the text of the Written Law (the Torah) serves as the theological foundation for the Oral Law, and familiarity with the stories of Scripture therefore roots a study in the revelatory experience of Sinai. This view is corroborated by a comment of the *Kedushat Levi*,[13] who argues that by being reminded daily of the Revelation at Sinai, we ensure that our Torah study remains a religious quest and not simply an intellectual exercise.[14] Moreover, heavy emphasis on Scripture during these formative years ensures that a student feels connected to the story of the Jewish people. Beyond the laws and customs that define daily Jewish life, Judaism is the religion of a people connected to a divinely governed historical drama. By studying Scripture exclusively for five years, we ensure that every student feels a profound connection to the history of his people.

After toiling over Scripture for five years and gaining a theological and historical appreciation for our ancestry, Avot directs the pupil to the study of the Mishna. Rabbi Dr. David Weiss Halivni notes that mishnaic law is formulated in an "apodictic" manner, without any explanation for the rationale behind the laws themselves.[15] This method of yes/no adjudicating is particularly appropriate for ten-year-old students who have completed five years of Torah study. While Scripture provides the theological background for Jewish life, the Mishna teaches students the rules by which they can put their spiritual commitments into practice. By solely studying Mishna for five years, the students

12. Avot 5:21.
13. Rabbi Levi Yitzhak (Derbremdiker) of Berdichev, eighteenth century, Galicia.
14. *Kedushat Levi, Parashat Ki Tavo, s.v. vayidaber Moshe.*
15. Rabbi David Weiss Halivni, *Midrash, Mishna, and Gemara: The Jewish Predilection for Justified Law* (Cambridge: Harvard University Press, 1986), 2.

end this part of their academic journey fully equipped to navigate the day-to-day of Jewish life.

At fifteen, students turn to the study of Gemara. Rabbi Yisrael Lifschitz[16] explains that at this age, they are intellectually mature enough to delve into an understanding of the logic (and values) that underlie the law.[17] Dr. Halivni notes that, in contrast to the Mishna, in Gemara, the law is "justified": the Gemara provides the sources and logic that motivate mishnaic rulings.[18] In many ways, Gemara study synthesizes the theology of Scripture with the pragmatic elements of the Mishna. By delving into the ideals behind the law, students ensure that their commitment to Jewish living is not robotic and merely based on a demand that they comply with the dictates of the law. Rather, Gemara study represents a profound opportunity to connect to God and the divine values expressed by the laws.

Professor Robert Cover articulates this idea when he states: "No set of legal institutions or prescriptions exist apart from the narratives that locate it and give it meaning."[19] For Cover, once law is understood in this context, "law becomes not merely a system of rules to be observed, but a world in which we live."[20]

SHAAREI KNESSET HAGEDOLA: STUDY AND THE EXPANDING CANON OF JEWISH BOOKS

While the discussion until now has focused on dividing time among Scripture, Mishna, and Gemara, as well as the relevance of specific texts for students of different ages, a comment of the *Sha'arei Kenesset HaGedola*[21] underscores the challenge of maintaining the traditional educational division in an ever-changing world of book publishing.[22] He notes that the three-part division advocated by earlier authorities applied in a historical reality in which the Jewish canon was limited specifically

---

16. Rabbi Yisrael Lifschitz, eighteenth/nineteenth centuries, Eastern Europe.
17. *Tiferet Yisrael, Avot* 5:21, comment 162.
18. *Midrash, Mishna, and Gemara*, 3-4
19. Robert Cover, "The Supreme Court, 1982 Term – Foreword: Nomos and Narrative," *Harvard Law Review* 97 (1983): 4-5.
20. Ibid.
21. Rabbi Chaim Banbanishti, seventeenth century, Istanbul.
22. Cited in *Hagaot VeHe'arot* on the Tur, Yoreh Deah 246:3.

to these three texts. However, in the post-talmudic era, rabbinic scholars expanded the Jewish canon to include talmudic commentaries, halakhic codes, books of ethics, volumes on Jewish philosophy, and treatises on Jewish mysticism. The *Sha'arei Kenesset HaGedola* argues that with the expansion of the Jewish library, the requirement to focus exclusively on the study of Scripture, Mishna, and Gemara changed as well. After all, these post-talmudic books are also part of the Oral Law, and study of this material is therefore also religiously significant.

This approach reintroduces the personal element in choosing texts to study. A more expansive library means that people will have more books to choose from. Futhermore, by including more modern compilations as viable learning options, the approach of the *Sha'arei Kenesset HaGedola* ensures that students will be free to study material that directly addresses some of their contemporary concerns and challenges.

TALMUD BERAKHOT: BREADTH OR DEPTH?

A fascinating passage in Tractate Berakhot focuses on the derivative question of whether we should prefer breadth or depth in Torah study. The Gemara describes two great scholars, R. Yosef and Rabba, defining R. Yosef as "Sinai" due to his great breadth of knowledge, and defining Rabba as an "uprooter of mountains" because he was an expert in the most precise analysis of the Torah. When it became necessary to choose one of these scholars to assume the leadership of the academy in Babylonia, the scholars there sent a question to the scholars in the Land of Israel, asking which of the two would be the better choice. The Talmud recounts that the response was, "Sinai takes precedence, for all are needful of the matter of wheat [i.e., the one who has gathered many tannaitic teachings]."[23]

Thus, according to this passage, breadth of knowledge is to be preferred over sharp analytical study. Rashi argues that the preference for breadth assumes that someone who has a broad knowledge of material will more likely be able to solve difficult talmudic puzzles, since that person will have more data at hand to analyze the case in question.[24]

---

23. Berakhot 64a.
24. Rashi, Sanhedrin 42a, s.v. *milḥamta shel Torah.*

Someone who relies too heavily on analytical capacities without a parallel breadth of knowledge can easily err because of a limited knowledge of the data.

Rabbi Shlomo Kluger argues that this preference for breadth of knowledge is limited to the talmudic period, when the Oral Law had not yet been committed to writing.[25] In that environment, breadth of knowledge was preferred because the presence of someone who had memorized the Oral Law was essential in order for talmudic discussions to take place. However, once the Oral Law was written down, the need for someone who had mastered tannaitic material was neutralized, since every student had access to a written text. At the present stage of Jewish history, in Rabbi Kluger's view, the "uprooter of mountains" takes precedence. Rabbi Ovadia Yosef[26] disagrees and asserts that even in the post-talmudic period, breadth of knowledge is to be preferred.[27]

Rabbi Yitzchak Blau cites the view of Rabbi Avraham Yitzhak HaKohen Kook, who gives a different rationale for the the talmudic preference for breadth of knowledge: "Sinai is able to teach the masses, but the *oker harim* (one who uproots mountains) cannot, because ordinary Jews find his abstract reasoning incomprehensible."[28] "Sinai" in his view is "the teacher with the ability to speak to the common Jew without the help of an intermediary." Rav Kook's approach reminds Torah students that they have a responsibility not only to study Torah, but to teach Torah as well. While Torah learning can be difficult and abstract, the preference for "Sinai" highlights the need to make Torah accessible to a larger audience.

Rav Kook's interpretation places the experience of Torah study within the larger framework of Jewish continuity. Torah learning can, unfortunately, become a sort of code language understood only by those who are heavily invested in the intricacies of talmudic law. While high-level talmudic discourse is critical and ensures the continued relevance

---

25. Notes on *Peri Megadim*, Orach Chayim 136. Cited also in Responsa *Yabia Omer* Orach Chayim 1 Introduction.
26. Rabbi Ovadia Yosef, twentieth/twenty-first centuries, Israel.
27. *Yabia Omer* Orach Chayim 1 Introduction.
28. Rabbi Yitzchak Blau, *Fresh Fruits and Vintage Wine: The Ethics and Wisdom of the Aggada* (Brooklyn: Ktav, 2009), 76.

and vitality of Torah study, those engaged in the study of Torah need to be mindful of their larger obligation to translate Torah concepts to people of varied backgrounds. Once Torah learning is placed in its proper context, we can appreciate the extent to which every student of Torah is also simultaneously called upon to be a teacher as well.

SUMMARY

Given the centrality of Torah study for rabbinic Judaism, by analyzing the question of how we should divide our study schedule, we gain insight into how the rabbis balanced varied priorities in formulating an educational curriculum. Moreover, this discussion highlights the many spiritual and religious messages that underlie the daily choice of which texts to study. Before embarking on our work day, we Jews are called upon to study Torah and reflect upon these critical messages. In particular, the daily exercise of choosing a text for Torah learning offers a powerful opportunity to reflect on:

- Feeling personally connected to the texts that we study (Talmud Avoda Zara)
- Being a part of a larger educational format (Talmud Kiddushin)
- Finding personal meaning in the context of a fixed system (Ritva)
- Understanding the integrated and organic nature of Torah study (Rabbeinu Tam)
- Choosing texts that mirror our own emotional and developmental growth (*Pirkei Avot*)
- Learning as an exercise in affirming Jewish theology, history, and the law as a value-based system (*Pirkei Avot*)
- Learning in the world of an ever-expanding Jewish library (*Sha'arei Knesset HaGedola*)
- The importance of being familiar with an expansive range of the Jewish tradition (Talmud Berakhot)
- The need to ensure that Torah learning reaches a wide audience (Rav Kook)

Chapter 16

The Weekly Torah Portion

Torah Expertise and the Centrality of the Oral Law

THE OBLIGATION TO BE FAMILIAR WITH
THE WEEKLY TORAH PORTION

As we discussed in the previous chapter, traditional Jewish law allows for a significant degree of autonomy in choosing which text to study when fulfilling the mitzva of daily Torah learning. Despite this flexibility, there is an interesting piece of rabbinic legislation that requires an individual to spend time every week immersed in the study of the weekly Torah portion (*parasha*). According to the *Shulchan Arukh*, we are obligated to review the entire *parasha* that will be read on Shabbat – twice – over the course of the week. Besides reading the verses, we are required to study a traditional rabbinic commentary that provides insights and perspectives on the Torah portion.[1]

On its most basic level, this halakha seems intended to provide a preparatory framework to the experience of hearing the weekly portion. When we arrive at the synagogue with a basic knowledge of the themes and ideas contained in the *parasha*, we will experience a more refined and sophisticated encounter with the public Torah reading.

---

1. *Shulchan Arukh*, Orach Chayim 285:1-2.

Jewish Law as a Journey

Beyond the impact that this regulation has on our experience during the Torah reading on Shabbat, this law also provides meaningful spiritual context for the rest of the week. Tracing the development of this law from its talmudic roots through the modern period will help us understand the religious messages that underlie this rabbinic legislation.

LEVUSH: FACILITATING EXPERTISE WITH THE BIBLICAL TEXT

While this requirement to be familiar with the *parasha* is not mentioned either in the Bible or the Mishna, it is discussed in Tractate Berakhot. In the Talmud, R. Huna bar Yehuda in the name of R. Ami states:

> A person should always complete the Torah portion [of the week] with the congregation, [reading] the Hebrew text twice and the Targum (translation) once.... For whoever completes the Torah portion [of the week] with the congregation [merits] that his days and years are prolonged.[2]

In the original version of the halakha, it is the Targum (Aramaic translation of the Torah) that must be studied along with the parasha text. The Talmud itself gives no reason for the ruling; the *Levush*[3] states that this halakha is intended to create personal familiarity and expertise with the text of the Bible.[4]

Imagine, for example, that we follow this law punctiliously from the age of bar mitzva. This would guarantee that we complete the entire five books of Moshe twice over the course of each year. Over time, we would become intimately aware of both the narrative and legal sections of the Torah. And if this law is observed by the entire Jewish people, it would create a community of learners, an entire people who are deeply educated and well-versed in their most central religious text.

Observance of this requirement would remedy a situation in which many Jews end their formal Jewish education after bar mitzvah,

---

2. Berakhot 8a-b.
3. Rabbi Mordechai Jaffe, sixteenth/seventeenth centuries, Eastern Europe.
4. *Levush*, Orach Chayim 285:1.

146

or after high school, and tend to intellectually outgrow the Jewish paradigm that they were taught as children. Requiring each individual to continuously grapple with biblical texts ensures that we will develop a sophisticated relationship with Torah learning, paralleling our own personal and intellectual growth.

TERUMAT HADESHEN: SETTING THE STAGE FOR A PROPER EXPERIENCE OF HEARING THE TORAH ON SHABBAT

While the *Levush* understands this legislation on a more global level, the *Terumat HaDeshen* notes that, accoding to some authorities, this law is intended to faciliatate a more sophisiticated encounter with the weekly Torah portion.[5] Shabbat is a day designed to facilitate quality family time as well as serious Torah study. When a family or community enters Shabbat with clarity about the content of the weekly portion, the level of the conversation about the messages and themes of the *parasha* is significantly elevated.

Imagine for example, a Shabbat table at which the members of the family are only vaguely familiar with the portion for a given week. Contrast this image with a family in which all adult members have properly followed the dictates of this law and therefore come to the Shabbat table mindful of the substance of the *parasha*.

RAAVAN: CONNECTING THE INDIVIDUAL TO THE COMMUNITY

A different interpretation of this law is suggested by the Raavan. He contends that the law is intended only for someone living in a locale without access to a synagogue for the weekly Torah reading. Instead of going to the synagogue, such a person should read the weekly portion twice, along with a parallel rabbinic interpretation, at the same time that the closest synagogue is reading the Torah.[6]

While this opinion is rejected by the majority of rabbinic authorities, it does highlight the communal significance of the weekly Torah reading and the way in which Jewish law encourages individual Jews to

---

5. Responsa *Terumat HaDeshen, siman* 23.
6. Raavan, *siman* 88, cited in *Beit Yosef*, Orach Chayim 285.

be connected to the larger community. Beyond connecting to the intellectual and spiritual messages of Torah study, reading the weekly Torah portion as a substitute for the reading that takes place in the synagogue reminds people of the communal element of Torah study. Reading the Torah publicly recalls the revelatory moment of Sinai, when the Jewish people stood at the foot of the mountain and listened to the words of God. Linking our own Torah reading to that of the community highlights the Torah's revelatory roots.

THE *MISHNA BERURA*: THE ROLE OF
RABBINIC INTERPRETATION

The positions cited so far explain the significance of the rabbinic insistence that we read the weekly Torah portion twice during the week. Devoting time to studying the *parasha* facilitates increased knowledge of the biblical text, and also connects us to the communal act of public Torah reading. We have not yet examined however, the reasons for the requirement that a rabbinic commentary be studied.

The Talmud, as we saw, requires the reading of the Targum; the *Shulchan Arukh* rules that the biblical commentary of Rashi satisfies this requirement.[7] The *Mishna Berura* explains that Rashi's commentary is particularly helpful, since it regularly references midrashic material rooted in the tradition of the Oral Law.[8]

The requirement to study the weekly portion with a rabbinic commentary thus serves a powerful function, reminding us of the interconnectedness of the Oral and Written Law. We read the Torah publicly every week in order to hear its messages and reenact the revelation on Mount Sinai. Our parallel requirement to individually study a rabbinic commentary prior to our arrival at the synagogue provides us with an understanding of the sources that interpret the biblical text. Linking the Oral Law to the Written Law reminds us of the continued relevance of the values of the Bible and underscores our belief in the interpretations of the sages.

---

7. *Shulchan Arukh* Orach Chayim 285:2.
8. *Mishna Berura*, Orach Chayim 285:6.

SUMMARY

This often overlooked rabbinic law reminds us of the importance of becoming familiar with the biblical text and its rabbinic interpretations. Viewed in the larger context of the requirement to study Torah daily, this obligation allows us to:

- Ensure our continued study of the Torah long beyond our childhood years (*Levush*)
- Become intimately familiar with both the narrative and legal sections of the Torah (*Levush*)
- Experience a more sophisticated encounter with the weekly Torah reading in the synagogue and at home (*Terumat HaDeshen*)
- Connect with the communal Torah reading as a means of emphasizing that the Torah is a divinely revealed document (Raavan)
- Understand the interconnectedness of the Written and Oral Law (*Mishna Berura*)
- Affirm our belief in the integrity of the interpretations of the sages (*Mishna Berura*)

Chapter 17

Washing Hands before Meals

The Power of the Hands and
the World of the Temple

W hile many of the commandments assume the home, the
synagogue, or the house of study as a setting, Jewish law provides other
concrete obligations that are applicable during daily life, irrespective of
locale. For example, before the consumption of bread, Jewish law mandates the ritual washing of hands. This requirement has nothing to do
with hygiene.[1] In fact, in order to ensure that nothing prevents the water
from coming into direct contact with the hands, any residual dirt must
be removed *before* one begins the washing ritual.[2]

At first glance, this practice seems strange. What is the religious
significance of washing already-clean hands? Moreover, why are we
required to wash before the consumption of bread only? If our goal is

---

1. See Rambam, Laws of Blessings 6:1.
2. *Shulchan Arukh*, Orach Chayim 161:1.

to provide a spiritual framework for the physical act of eating, why not mandate a ritualized washing before the consumption of all food?

Despite the apparently mysterious nature of this practice, rabbinic texts provide powerful and meaningful rationales that underlie this obligation. Analyzing the ideals that are at the core of this requirement will a provide meaningful context to appreciate the daily religious opportunities afforded by this mitzva.

WASHING AND THE POWER OF OUR HANDS

In order to gain clarity regarding the logic behind this obligation, it is important to understand some basic facts about the biblical and talmudic laws of purity.

As Rabbi Eliezer Melamed notes, Jewish law views the body as one organic unit.[3] If one part of the body – no matter how small – becomes impure, the entire body follows suit. In order for the body to become purified, one must immerse the entire body in a ritual bath, known as a *mikveh*. Failure to submerge the entire body in the mikveh renders the purification process ineffective.

While Torah law considers the body as one entity, the rabbis issued a special legislative decree regarding the purity status of the hands. According to rabbinic law, all hands are considered to be impure, even if there is no indication that they have come into contact with impurity. The Talmud states that the hands have a special status in the realm of purity laws because hands "are always active," and are therefore likely to become either dirty or impure during the course of a day.[4]

Throughout the period of the First Temple, this legislation was limited to the world of sacrifices. As a result, anyone who was planning to come into physical contact with a sacrifice designated for the Temple was required to ritually wash his hands. During the Second Temple period, the rabbis expanded this legislation and required ritual washing before coming into contact with sacred food designated for the priests (*teruma*). Around the time of the destruction of the Second Temple, the rabbis extended the decree even further and required the

---

3. Rabbi Eliezer Melamed, *Tumat Hayadayim*, http://ph.yhb.org.il/10-02-01/.
4. Shabbat 14a and Rashi ad loc., s.v. *askaniot*.

washing of hands before the consumption of all breads, both sacred and non-sacred.[5]

The Maharal notes that more than any other part of the body, the hands have the greatest potential for mobility. We can move our hands with extraordinary freedom and flexibility. While this feature provides potential for the hands to be used to facilitate acts of goodness, it also highlights the challenges associated with greater freedom. After all, many of the activities for which we use our hands are often religiously neutral, or even sometimes religiously problematic. The risk of sin associated with the hands' mobility caused the rabbis to declare them "impure" by default. Thus, the rabbis required a ritual washing to remove impurity before engaging in sacred actions.[6]

Rabbi Elyakim Krumbein[7] expands on this idea, noting that the location of the hands at the extremities of the body creates maximal distance between the hands on one side of the body and the heart/head on the other. The head and the heart symbolize the more elevated elements of identity. They work in tandem to ensure that the body is used for spiritually positive purposes. The hands, by contrast, are far removed from these core elements of the body and can therefore easily become impure by acting outside the spiritual context of the head and heart.[8] Ritual washing serves as a symbolic reminder that the hands are not independent entities, but rather serve as instruments to actualize the spiritual vision of our more elevated organs.

PRESERVING A CONNECTION TO THE WORLD OF THE PRIESTS

As noted above, the requirement to wash our hands was initially limited to circumstances in which the hands came into contact with sacred foods, such as sacrifices or *teruma*. Since the hands tend to engage in mundane activates during the day, it was logical to mandate a ritual

---

5. See Rabbi Eliezer Melamed, *Tumat Hayadayim*, http://ph.yhb.org.il/10-02-01/.

6. *Netivot Olam, Netiv HaAvoda* 16. See also Rabbi Eliezer Melamed, *Tumat Hayadayim*, http://ph.yhb.org.il/10-02-01/.

7. Rabbi Elyakim Krumbein, twenty-first century, Israel.

8. Rabbi Elyakim Krumbein. *B'Din Netilat Yadayim*, http://www.etzion.org.il/he.

washing to separate the ordinary from the sacred. Moreover, while the Temple still stood, the rabbis wanted to accustom the priests to wash their hands before eating sacred food, and they therefore demanded that priests wash their hands even before the consumption of non-sacred bread.[9] The desire to prevent priests from eating sacred food in an impure state was so great that it motivated the rabbis to legislate that all Jews – even non-priests – wash their hands before the consumption of bread. The goal of this rabbinic legislation was to facilitate a culture in which all Jews wash their hands as a matter of course, thus ensuring that the priests –for whom the legislation was really intended – never mistakenly eat sacred foods in an impure state.[10]

What remains unclear is why the rabbis maintained the hand-washing requirement even after the destruction of the Temple. Why should an ordinary Jew living after the destruction of the Temple be required to ritually wash his hands before the consumption of a bagel? After all, he never comes into contact with sacred foods, and the purity laws are basically suspended in the post-Temple era.

One solution to this question would be to point out that a central component of Jewish theology is the belief in the Messianic Era and the rebuilding of the Temple. As a result, the rabbis consciously decided to maintain the handwashing requirement even after the destruction of the Temple in order to maintain a connection to the world of the Temple and sustain the yearning for its rebuilding. Moreover, the *Mishna Berura* adds, by preserving the legislation after the destruction of the Temple, the rabbis ensured that Jews will be more familiar with ritual purity laws when the Temple is eventually rebuilt.[11]

Additionally, the *Mishna Berura* states that the reason the rabbis required us to wash specifically before the consumption of bread was that the majority of sacred food (*teruma*) separated for the priests was from grain, which is normally eaten as bread.[12] Ritual washing before eating bread thus reminds us of our connection to the Temple and the

---

9. Ḥullin 106a.
10. See *Mishna Berura*, Orach Chayim 158:1.
11. Ibid.
12. Ibid., 2

priestly class, and it helps facilitate a conversation about our relationship to the rebuilding of the Temple in the future.

Again we see the role that Jewish law plays in affirming core issues of Jewish theology through the practical medium of daily ritual. In the context of our daily prayers, we beseech God to speedily rebuild the Temple and reinstitute the sacrificial order. Despite the fact that we recite this prayer three times daily, how many Jews can honestly say that they are fully prepared for a spiritual reality involving the reinstitution of purity laws? Washing our hands before eating bread therefore provides an ongoing reminder that our actions reflect Judaism's larger theological agenda and that we need to strive to develop a sophisticated posture that honestly engages the ideals that the halakha seeks to actualize.

WASHING AND SANCTITY

Beyond establishing a connection to the world of the Temple, ritual handwashing before eating bread helps provide a spiritual framework for the physical act of eating. The Talmud cites the view of Rav, who finds a biblical allusion to the requirement to wash one's hands before eating bread.[13] In the verse cited by Rav, God tells the Israelites to "sanctify [themselves] and be holy,"[14] which Rav claims refers to sanctification through ritual washing before meals. The Maharal explains that eating and drinking are by definition physical activities. By ritually washing our hands before each meal, we remind ourselves that our desire to eat is not merely to satisfy our hunger. Rather, we sustain our physical bodies in order to use our physical strength to enable us to lead a spiritual life.[15]

The Talmud makes a dramatic statement highlighting the religious significance of ritual handwashing before meals, claiming that eating bread without the requisite handwashing is equivalent to having sexual relations with a prostitute![16] Just as the act of marriage provides a framework of sanctity to the physical act of sexual intimacy, the act of

---

13. Berakhot 53b.
14. Lev. 11:44.
15. *Netivot Olam, Netivot HaAvoda* 16.
16. Sota 4b.

washing one's hands places the physical act of eating in the larger context of strengthening our bodies to serve God.

Think about the culture of fast food and eating on the go. Unfortunately, many people shovel food into their mouths without taking the time to meditate properly about the purpose and function of eating. By requiring us to wash our hands before eating, the rabbis compelled us to slow down and reflect on the goals of food consumption.

WASHING IN A POST-TEMPLE WORLD

Until this point, the discussion has been focused on the requirement to wash hands before the consumption of bread. Since the majority of *teruma* given to the priest was from grains, the rabbinic requirement to wash our hands was limited to bread alone. However, the Talmud elsewhere quotes the view of R. Oshaya, who states that "any food that is dipped in a liquid requires washing the hands."[17] R. Oshaya's ruling is premised upon a mishnaic principle that seven specific liquids are susceptible to becoming impure and transmitting that impurity to any food with which they come into contact.[18] Since one's hands are considered impure by rabbinic decree, they must be ritually washed prior to eating any food dipped in liquid to avoid accidental transference of impurity onto the food itself.

Tosafot argue that this requirement differs fundamentally from the obligation to wash our hands before eating bread. Washing before eating bread serves a specific spiritual function – to contextualize the meal within the ethic of sanctity – and it is therefore still applicable even in the post-Temple period. R. Oshaya's mandate, however, is exclusively formal in nature and is only intended to prevent the transfer of impurity. Thus, nowadays, when we assume that all Jews are ritually impure and the purification rituals are no longer operative, this regulation is no longer applicable.[19]

Other scholars, however, disagreed with the approach of the *Tosafot* and understood R. Oshaya's ruling as paralleling the rabbinic

17. Pesachim 115a.
18. Makhshirin 6:4.
19. *Tosafot,* Pesachim 115a, s.v. *kol.*

requirement to wash before eating bread.[20] According to this model, both obligations – washing before eating bread and washing before eating food dipped in liquid – are rooted in an attempt to prevent priests from eating sacred foods with impure hands. Moreover, just as we maintain the rabbinic requirement to wash before bread even in the post-Temple era, the obligation to ritually wash our hands before eating foods dipped in liquid is similarly operative. Both obligations help maintain an appreciation for the world of the Temple and create a perpetual yearning for its ultimate rebuilding.

As a compromise view, the *Shulchan Arukh* rules that we must wash our hands before eating any food dipped in liquid, but without an accompanying blessing.[21] However, despite the clear ruling of the *Shulchan Arukh*, some communities adopted the view of the *Tosafot* and do not require a ritual washing for foods dipped in liquid nowadays. Nevertheless, even those who are lenient about this ruling throughout the course of the year are particularly cautious about observing this ritual at the Passover seder. Since much of the seder experience is intended to create reminders of life during Temple times, observance of this practice helps preserve the themes of the Temple and the priesthood.[22]

WASHING AND RABBINIC AUTHORITY

Beyond the explanations cited so far, the Talmud makes an important observation about the relationship between the required handwashing and the larger mandate to adhere to the words of the sages. Quoting the view of R. Idi bar Avin in the name of R. Yitzchak bar Ashyan, the Talmud states that washing hands for non-sanctified food is required "in order to establish a routine"[23] (for washing before sanctified food). The Talmud adds that we must wash "because it is a mitzva." After questioning the view that there is a biblical commandment to wash hands before eating bread, the Talmud cites the view of Abaye, who asserts

---

20. See *Beit Yosef*, Orach Chayim 158.

21. *Shulchan Arukh*, Orach Chayim 158:4.

22. See the view of the Netziv, quoted in Rabbi Shimon Eider, *Halachos of Pesach* (Jerusalem/New York: Feldheim, 1985), 266, n.69.

23. Chullin 106a.

that the "mitzva" referenced by the Talmud is the obligation to "heed to the directives of the sages."

The Rashba explains that, even without a formal rabbinic directive, it would have been logical to require ritual handwashing before the consumption of bread in order to accustom the priests to wash before eating sacred foods. However, now that ritual washing has been formally decreed by the rabbis, we are certainly obligated to follow their command.[24]

This passage raises interesting questions about the nature of rabbinic authority. After all, not only did the rabbis legislate a ritual handwashing, they also obligated us to recite a blessing before its performance. As the Talmud notes, it seems strange to use the phrase "Who has commanded us" regarding a mitzva that lacks a source in the biblical text.[25] Sensitive to this question, the Talmud cites two verses to biblically substantiate the authority of rabbinically ordained commandments. In the first verse, the Torah states, "You shall not deviate from the word that they [the rabbis] will tell you."[26] In the second verse, Moshe implores the Jewish people, "Remember the days of yore, understand the years of generation after generation; ask your father and he will relate it to you, your elders and they will tell you."[27]

While the topic of rabbinic authority is extraordinarily complex, these verses highlight the fact that the Bible itself set up a system in which rabbinic sages are authorized to continually interpret God's law and apply its values in changing circumstances. The rabbis act as God's agents in ensuring that the Jewish legal system reflects the ideals of the Torah itself.

Prof. Michael Berger offers a helpful analogy, citing the view of legal scholar Ronald Dworkin. According to Prof. Berger, Prof. Dworkin suggests "seeing the history of legal interpretation as the writing of a book, but in a very unique way." More specifically:

24. Rashba, Hullin 106a, s.v. *amar Rav Idi.*
25. Shabbat 23a.
26. Deut. 17:11.
27. Ibid. 32:7.

One author writes one chapter and then passes the book to the next author, who then composes his or her own chapter, only to pass it on to the next author, and so on. Each author is essentially "free" to write a chapter that he or she likes, but each author is also constrained by the chapter already written, for after all, this is a book, and the chapters need to be sufficiently integrated to ensure overall coherence. The preceding chapters constrain each author presently writing so that they cannot begin an entirely new plot, utterly ignoring the facts and characters introduced in previous chapters. To have the book make sense, the themes introduced by the previous author(s) have to be continued or finished off; they cannot all be left hanging.[28]

Washing our hands before eating bread provides a powerful meditative moment to appreciate the role that the rabbinic sages play in keeping the ongoing conversation of Torah values alive. Affirming our commitment to rabbinic precepts helps create an attitude of reverence and appreciation for rabbinic creativity. Moreover, by affirming our commitment to rabbinic authority, we solidify our trust in the integrity of rabbinic scholars and the larger interpretive venture of rabbinic legislation.

SUMMARY

The obligation to wash our hands before eating bread is a powerful example of rabbinic legislation that is operative throughout the day irrespective of locale. Whether at home, at the office, or at a sporting event, we are always required to ritually wash our hands before consuming bread. Taking a moment before we wash our hands to reflect on the values that underlie the mitzva allows us to think about:

- The activities that we have used our hands for in the context of our day (Maharal)
- The extent to which our hands are utilized to actualize a more elevated vision for our lives (Rabbi Krumbein)

---

28. Michael S. Berger, *Rabbinic Authority* (New York/Oxford: Oxford University Press, 1998), 123.

- Our yearning for the rebuilding of the Temple and our connection to the world of the priesthood
- Our meals being contextualized through an ethic of sanctity (Talmud)
- Washing in an exilic reality in which purity laws are unfortunately no longer operative (Talmud, Tosafot)
- The central role of rabbinic interpretation in our continuing to apply the values of the Torah in changing circumstances (Talmud)

Chapter 18

Birkat Hamazon

History, Dependency, and the Centrality of the Land of Israel

W hile Jewish law provides a preparatory introduction to the experience of eating a meal by mandating ritual handwashing, it creates a parallel obligation at the end of the meal by requiring the recitation of a blessing. Furthermore, if we snack during the day, there is a legal requirement to recite a blessing before the consumption of even the smallest morsel of food.

We have seen the reasons to bless God *before* we partake in the act of eating, while ritually washing our hands. However, the source of the legal obligation to thank God *after* we have completed our meal seems more mysterious. What religious message is the Torah conveying to us by requiring us to bless God when we are already satiated? The question becomes even more interesting in light of the fact that, while blessing God before eating is a rabbinic obligation, reciting *Birkat HaMazon* (Grace after Meals) after a meal fulfills a biblical imperative. Moreover, the text of *Birkat HaMazon* is a series of long passages containing diverse themes that extend far beyond the act of eating, itself.

What is the connection, for example, between eating and the centrality of Jerusalem, a theme that is included in the text of *Birkat HaMazon*?

Over the course of a busy day, it may be fairly easy to recite a blessing before eating; but reciting *Birkat HaMazon* requires much more time and focus. Reflecting on and analyzing sources that address the obligation to recite *Birkat HaMazon* with an eye towards understanding its broader set of values will help ensure that the legal obligation to praise God after a meal is experienced as a profoundly spiritual fulfillment of God's word.

BIBLICAL SOURCE: THE CHALLENGE OF PROSPERITY

The biblical source of the obligation to recite *Birkat HaMazon* is a verse from the book of Deuteronomy: "You will eat and you will be satisfied, and bless Hashem, your God, for the good Land that he gave you."[1] What is particularly striking about this verse is the insistence that we are obligated to bless God specifically after having eaten our food. Why this reminder to thank God when we are satiated?

The Ramban answers this question by noting that the act of thanking God after eating a meal places our material success in context and reminds us of the Jewish people's more humble beginnings.[2] After all, throughout their time in Egyptian servitude, the Jews regularly experienced hunger and were dependent on their Egyptian slave-masters for sustenance. After we eat, there is a natural inclination to lose perspective on the economic blessings that God has bestowed upon us and forget the more complicated earlier stages of Jewish history. *Birkat HaMazon* is, thus, more than an opportunity to express gratitude. Its recitation allows the Jewish people to re-experience the drama of Jewish history and appreciate God's hand in guiding the Israelites from slavery to a place of freedom and economic prosperity.

The *Meshekh Chokhma* offers a slightly different approach, noting that there is a natural tendency for people to forget God's kindness especially after achieving material success. When we are desperate, we instinctively turn to God for help. However, after our situation improves, we can erroneously attribute our good fortunes exclusively to our own

---

1. Deut. 8:10.
2. Ramban, Deuteronomy 8:10.

hard work and forget to thank God for our successes. Similarly, when we are hungry and finally receive food, we naturally thank God for what we have received. However, after we are satiated, we may no longer feel the need of divine assistance, and therefore neglect to express the requisite thanks. For this reason, it is specifically in these moments that we are obligated to overcome our natural inclination, and thank God for the meal that we have consumed.[3]

If we take these suggestions seriously, the act of reciting *Birkat HaMazon* provides unique religious and theological opportunities beyond affirming our commitment to the halakhic system. This prayer allows us to reflect on the gift of food and remember times in both our personal as well as national life when we did not have such easy access to daily sustenance. Moreover, *Birkat HaMazon* reminds us of possible challenges of economic and material success. Reciting this prayer specifically when we are satiated reminds us of our dependency on God even when our successes can seemingly be traced to our own hard work.

THE BIBLICAL DIRECTIVE: EXPANDING
THE THEMATIC REQUIREMENTS

While the Ramban and the *Meshekh Chokhma* focus on thanking God specifically when we are satiated, other commentators discuss the thematic requirements of *Birkat HaMazon*. The *Kesef Mishneh* quotes the view of the Ramban, who maintains that according to biblical law, no formal text is required when reciting *Birkat HaMazon*.

Nonetheless, according to Torah, the after-meal prayer must make reference to God's providing nourishment, the Land of Israel, and the centrality of Jerusalem. While the exact text is not specified in the Torah, referencing these three themes is crucial to fulfill the mitzva even on a biblical level. [4]

On the surface, the view of the Ramban is difficult to understand. Why should the Bible mention these specific themes? What is the relationship between these topics and the act of thanking God after eating

---

3. *Meshekh Hokhma*, Deuteronomy 8:10.
4. *Kesef Mishneh*, Laws of Blessings 2:1. The original source of the Ramban is his commentary to Rambam Sefer Hamitzvoth 1.

food? What religious message is the halakha trying to convey by including these ideas in the recitation of *Birkat HaMazon*?

BIRKAT HAZAN ET HAKOL: HIGHLIGHTING
OUR DEPENDENCE

Early rabbinic sources grapple with these questions. In fact, the Midrash Tanchuma claims that until the Jewish people entered the Land of Israel, the only blessing that was recited after a meal was the blessing for nourishment.[5] This particular blessing thanks God, "Who in His goodness feeds the whole world."[6] According to the Talmud, this blessing was composed by Moshe specifically in the desert when the manna fell from heaven.[7]

Rabbi Eliezer Melamed notes that life in the desert was exceptionally difficult.[8] Lacking basic resources, these early Israelites needed extraordinary faith in God in order to maintain hope for the future. The manna was a test of faith for the Jewish people. Since they were not allowed to store manna from one day to the next, faith that God would provide sustenance from day to day was an essential component of Jewish identity during those years in the desert.

In fact, this represented a critical stage in the theological development of the Jewish people. By providing them with their daily food supply, God taught the Jewish people that, ultimately, it is God who is in control of their destiny. Regardless of any material success they may enjoy in the future, they must always remember the source of their prosperity.

If we reflect on this blessing, it becomes clear that the introductory passage of *Birkat HaMazon* is intended to bring us back to the time when God was overtly the source of the Jewish people's daily nourishment. While we do not personally experience this today, remembering that earlier time in Jewish history connects us with our national roots and reaffirms our theological commitment to viewing our own successes as gifts from God.

5. Midrash Tanhuma (Buber), *Parashat Masei* 5.
6. Rabbi Jonathan Sacks, *The Koren Siddur with Introduction, Translation, and Commentary by Rabbi Jonathan Sacks* (Jerusalem: Koren, 2009), 978.
7. Berakhot 48b.
8. Rabbi Eliezer Melamed, *Mashmaut Birkat Hazan*, http://ph.yhb.org.il/10-04-03/.

BIRKAT HAARETZ: REFLECTING
ON THE LAND OF ISRAEL

While, conceptually, it makes sense to mention nourishment from God after the completion of a meal, the second blessing of *Birkat HaMazon* seems thematically out of place. The Talmud tells us that this blessing, known as the *Birkat HaAretz* (blessing of the land), was composed by Joshua upon entering the Land of Israel.[9] Describing the uniqueness of the Land of Israel, this blessing thanks God "for having granted as a heritage to our ancestors a desirable, good, and spacious land."[10]

The Talmud cites two other additional themes that must be mentioned in the context of this blessing. According to the sage Nachum the Elder, one must mention "the covenant [of circumcision] in the blessing for the land." Rashi explains that by referring to circumcision, we remember the fact that the Land of Israel was promised to Avraham as part of the circumcision covenant.[11] The Talmud continues to quote the view of R. Yosi, who asserts that one must also mention the Torah in this blessing. Explaining the rationale for this addition, Rashi[12] cites a verse that states that it was through the merit of Torah observance that our ancestors received the Land of Israel.[13] The obligation to mention both circumcision and the Torah in this blessing is codified in the *Shulchan Arukh*.[14]

Rabbi Eliezer Melamed contends that this blessing is a natural extension of the "blessing of nourishment." The Land of Israel represents a shift in the collective religious posture of the Jewish people. During their time in the desert, the Israelites were dependent on God for physical survival. While this was a critical stage in the Jewish people's theological development, it was intended to be temporary. After all, the ideal Jewish view is that man is to partner with God in perfecting the world. By working the fields in the Land of Israel, the Jewish people

---

9. Berakhot 48b.
10. Rabbi Jonathan Sacks, *The Koren Siddur with Introduction, Translation, and Commentary by Rabbi Jonathan Sacks* (Jerusalem: Koren, 2009), 978.
11. Rashi, ibid., s.v. *tzarikh sheyizkor berit.*
12. Rashi, ibid., s.v. *tzarikh sheyizkor Torah.*
13. Deuteronomy 8:1.
14. *Shulchan Arukh*, Orach Chayim 187:3.

began to mature and to take responsibility for their own destiny, while still affirming God's providential role.[15]

Moreover, by referring to Torah and circumcision, we place our experience of receiving the Land of Israel in the proper context. Returning to the Land of Israel represents the fulfillment of a divine covenant, linking us to our ancestors. However, this ancestral bond with the Land of Israel is not simply a fulfillment of a national vision; rather, we are connected to our forefathers based on a shared commitment to living a life dedicated to Torah ideals. As Rabbi Haggai London notes, returning to the Land of Israel allows us to manifest divine values even outside the framework of codified halakha. By having, for example, an army, government, and political system rooted in Torah principles, we affirm the all-encompassing nature of God's theological system.[16]

BLESSING FOR JERUSALEM: APPRECIATING JEWISH SOVEREIGNTY

After we have thanked God for nourishment as well as the Land of Israel, *Birkat HaMazon* brings us to the "blessing for Jerusalem." According to the Talmud, this blessing was composed together by David and Solomon. At the beginning of the blessing, we find the passage written by King David. Since David conquered Jerusalem, it is appropriate that he compose the prayer asking God to have mercy "on Israel Your people and on Jerusalem Your city."[17] As the one who built the Temple, it is King Solomon who wrote the line describing "the great and holy House."

Jerusalem and the Temple represent Jewish sovereignty. Moreover, the Temple represents a unique affirmation of Jewish theology. As Prof. Yehezkel Kaufman notes:

> Pagan sanctity is rooted in nature and may therefore be found
> everywhere. Israelite sanctity is the creation of the will of

---

15. Rabbi Eliezer Melamed, *Merkaziyuta Shel Birachat Haaretz*, http://ph.yhb.org.il/10-04-04/.

16. Rabbi Haggai London, *Look Under Judaism: Theoretical Thinking About Basic Concepts in Judaism*, (Yediot Achronot, 2015), 28.

17. Berakhot 48b, translated in *The Koren Siddur with Introduction, Translation, and Commentary by Rabbi Jonathan Sacks* (Jerusalem: Koren, 2009), 982.

God; it originates always in a historical election, a revelation of God's word …. The Deuteronomic Temple of the future is diametrically opposed to the pagan temple, whose sanctity is prehistoric, mythological … . [The Jewish Temple is] to be established only after Israel arrives at "the rest of the inheritance." [The Temple] will be entirely new, its sanctity created *ex nihilo*, unrelated to any ancient holiness. This historical-eschatological conception of the Temple is the ultimate negation of pagan ideas of sanctity.[18]

While the prayer originally composed by David and Solomon asked God to maintain a continued tranquil state of life in the Land of Israel, the text was eventually amended slightly after the destruction of the Temple and subsequent Jewish exile.[19] Awareness of these slight liturgical changes reminds us of our ultimate messianic goal of returning to the Land of Israel, rebuilding the Temple, and establishing Jewish sovereignty. Meditating on these themes allows us to experience the continuous drama of Jewish history. Moreover, it prevents us from feeling content with the status quo. Material success and even returning to the land are means, and certainly not ends. Our ultimate national dream is to build a Jewish society affirming God's vision for the world in the Land of Israel.

BLESSING OF GOD'S GOODNESS: TOWARDS A POSTURE OF HOPE

While the first three blessings of *Birkat HaMazon* are rooted in the Bible, rabbinic consensus maintains that the fourth blessing is a rabbinic enactment. According to the Talmud, this blessing, which references God's goodness, was composed by the sages of Yavneh following the failed rebellion of Bar Kochba in gratitude for God's kindness to the bodies of the Jews killed in Betar.[20]

18. Yehezkel Kaufman, *The Religion of Israel: From Its Beginnings to the Babylonian Exile*, translated and abridged by Moshe Greenberg (Chicago: The University of Chicago Press, 1960), 289-290.
19. Rashba, Berakhot 48b, s.v. ha.
20. Berakhot 48b.

After defeating the Jews, the Romans had continued to massacre the Jews of Betar, and had then denied the survivors the right to bury their murdered brethren. Many years later, after the Jews finally received permission to bury their dead, they discovered that a miracle had occurred and the bodies had not decayed. The blessing therefore refers to God as one "Who is good and confers good." The Talmud states that the phrase "Who is good" alludes to the fact that "the bodies did not decay," while the phrase "Who confers good" thanks God for the fact that the bodies were ultimately "afforded burial."

Rabbi Jonathan Sacks notes that the failure of the Bar Kokhba rebellion was one of the low points in Jewish history.[21] The fact that "the sages were able to salvage a fragment of consolation from the fact that the dead were not denied the dignity of burial is testimony to an extraordinary ability to survive catastrophe and preserve the lineaments of hope." This last blessing thus acknowledges our current state of exile and provides a way of preserving hope despite any delay in the arrival of the Messianic Era. It encourages a religious posture of optimism whereby a person can always look for positive expressions of God's benevolence even in more troubling times.

SUMMARY

As we demonstrated in this chapter, *Birkat HaMazon* is significantly more than just an additional opportunity to offer thanks to God. The specific texts mandated by halakha provide an opportunity to reflect on central components of Jewish theology in the context of our day. Internalization of these messages is a critical element of proper recitation of *Birkat HaMazon*.

In particular, reciting *Birkat HaMazon* daily allows us to:

- Place our prosperity in context and appreciate the Jewish people's more humble beginnings (Ramban)
- Overcome our natural inclination to forget God after achieving economic success (*Meshekh Chokhma*)

---

21. Rabbi Jonathan Sacks, *The Koren Siddur with Introduction, Translation, and Commentary by Rabbi Jonathan Sacks* (Jerusalem: Koren, 2009), 986-987.

- Remember the Jewish people's sojourn in the desert and understand its intended role to inculcate a posture highlighting our dependency on God (Talmud, Rabbi Eliezer Melamed)
- Affirm our ultimate goal of partnering with God in perfecting the world, as symbolized by our working in the Land of Israel (Rabbi Eliezer Melamed)
- Remember the Land of Israel's ability to actualize divine ideals even outside the context of codified law (Rabbi Haggai London)
- Understand the profound connection between the Land of Israel, the covenant of circumcision, and the centrality of Torah observance as precursors to entering the land (Talmud, Rashi)
- Affirm the centrality of Jerusalem as a symbol of Jewish sovereignty, as well as the unique theological message of the Temple (Talmud, Prof. Kaufman)
- Experience the ever-unfolding drama of Jewish history and maintain a continued posture of hope and optimism during our Exile (Talmud, Rabbi Sacks)

Chapter 19

Keeping Kosher
Self-Discipline and Jewish Distinctiveness

I n addition to providing religious context to the experience of eating by mandating specific blessings before and after the consumption of food, Jewish law also contextualizes the act of eating by placing restrictions on the types of foods Jews may eat. Indeed, the laws of *kashrut* that govern traditional Jewish eating patterns are extremely complex and comprise a significant component of the curriculum in traditional rabbinical schools.

Beyond ensuring that we eat only kosher animals sanctioned by Jewish law, maintaining a kosher kitchen requires intricate knowledge of a large section of Jewish law dealing with the separation of meat and milk. Outside the home, observance of *kashrut* limits the choices of restaurants where we may eat. By frequenting only kosher establishments, we ensure that the food we eat is prepared according to strict *kashrut* standards, but these kosher restaurants also serve as a cultural oasis in which the overall environment is Jewish, often in the heart of a predominantly non-Jewish city or town.

The constant encounter we have with the laws of *kashrut* offers a unique opportunity to regularly reflect on their underlying messages. What is keeping kosher ultimately about? Is there one overarching

theory that explains all the details of *kashrut*, or do the varied components of *kashrut* observance reflect a multiplicity of ideals inherent in its
observance? Analyzing traditional sources dealing with this topic will
provide a spiritual framework for ongoing reflection about the nature
and meaning of the institution of *kashrut*. [1]

KASHRUT AND HEALTH

A theory held by some medieval Jewish thinkers is that *kashrut* prohibitions
stem from health concerns. *Sefer HaChinukh*, for example, argues that the
animals prohibited by the Torah for Jews to eat are harmful to the human
body.[2] Since the body is a physical vehicle for a person to actualize the more
elevated vision of the soul, any substance that would adversely affect the
body is prohibited. This theory, while popular among many medieval thinkers, was rejected by other rabbinic scholars. Abrabanel, for example, argues
strongly against linking *kashrut* laws to physical health, and instead argues
that foods prohibited by the Torah can have an adverse impact on the soul.[3]

Regardless of whether or not one accepts the theory that *kashrut*
is linked to health, this approach challenges us to reflect before eating
and ask ourselves whether or not the food on our plate is consistent with
the larger vision of healthy living outlined in the Torah. It also provides
an opportunity to affirm our belief in the body as a physical conduit
for spiritual living, ensuring that our food consumption maximizes our
chances to live a long life dedicated to this elevated ideal.

YOU ARE WHAT YOU EAT: KASHRUT AS A SYMBOL

Another theory used by medieval and modern thinkers to understand
kashrut restrictions links the prohibited foods symbolically to problematic character traits. Representative of this school of thought is the view
of Rabbi Samson Raphael Hirsch.[4] Rabbi Hirsch explains that one of

---

1. Many academic and rabbinic articles have been written about the meaning and
   significance of *kashrut*. For an excellent survey, see Rabbi Meir Soloveichik, *Locusts,
   Giraffes, and the Meaning of Kashrut,* http://azure.org.il/include/print.php?id=151.
2. *Sefer HaHinukh, mitzva* 154.
3. Lev. 11, s.v. *Issur Ha'maachalim.*
4. See for example, Rabbi Samson Raphael Hirsch, *Horeb,* trans. Isidor Grunfeld (New
   York: Soncino, 1962), par. 454.

the Bible's goals is to create a passive bodily identity. According to Rabbi Hirsch, "the more passive and submissive the body is, the more it will yield to the dictates of the soul as man's higher nature."[5] *Kashrut* laws are a biblical attempt to inculcate this ethic of passivity. As a result, all vegetables and fruits are permitted, since they are fundamentally passive foods. Animals, by contrast, are permissible only if they represent this specific trait. Aggressive animals are off-limits, since permitting their consumption would be giving a stamp of approval to their aggressive behavior.

While this explanation is appealing, it is open to question. As Rabbi Meir Soloveichik observes, "Are all the permitted animals indeed more passive than the forbidden ones? Is the deer, for instance, truly more passive than the rabbit?"[6] Despite its limitations, this approach, like that of the *Sefer HaChinukh*, reminds us of the ultimate purpose of our bodily existence. Eating is ultimately a physical exercise intended to fortify the body to maximize its spiritual potential. Being mindful of the food we eat reminds us of the problematic character traits from which we are required to distance ourselves.

KASHRUT AND SELF-DISCIPLINE

While the two explanations discussed so far focus on the specific foods prohibited by the Torah, a third approach focuses on the role of self-discipline in the context of eating. An early midrashic precursor to this idea discusses the question of why God forbade Adam and Eve to eat the fruits of one tree while permitting the consumption of fruits from others. According to the Midrash, this edict was enacted in order that "he [Adam] may remember his Creator each time he looks at this tree, submit to the divine authority, and beware of pride."[7] This idea is further developed by the *Akedat Yitzhak*,[8] which locates the rationale behind the laws of *kashrut* as ensuring that "man... live a life of discipline and

5. Rabbi Yaakov Beasly in "Kashrut and Understanding: Part Two," http://etzion.org.il/en/kashrut-and-understanding-part-two.
6. Rabbi Meir Soloveitchik, "Locusts, Giraffes, and the Meaning of Kashrut," http://azure.org.il/include/print.php?id=151.
7. Midrash Tadsheh, ch. 6, cited in Nechama Leibowitz, *New Studies in Vayikra* (Jerusalem: Haomanim Press, 1996), 155.
8. Rabbi Yitzchak b. Moshe Arama, fifteenth century, Spain.

abstinence and accept the yoke of Heaven by depriving himself of many things that his soul desires and which other people regard as normal, because it is a divine precept."[9]

This approach does not look for meaning in the fact that specific animals are prohibited. Rather, the meaning of *kashrut* lies in its ability to generate self-discipline in an area of life in which physical desires are particularly potent. Rabbi Joseph Soloveitchik expands on this theme, noting that "the Torah is of the opinion...that it is impossible to hallow and inspire the spirit without disciplining the body."[10] *Kashrut* laws, he argues, "belong to the category of discipline of the body and its sanctification."[11] As a result, "what is forbidden here is overindulgence in satisfying human corporeal needs and drives."[12]

This explanation reminds us of the risks of being overly indulgent in the context of eating. By refraining from eating certain foods, we sanctify ourselves by disciplining our bodies to avoid satisfying every physical urge that we experience. This abstinence, in turn, encourages a posture of humility, reminding us again that our physical existence is ultimately about serving a spiritual being greater than ourselves.

FOOD AND JEWISH DISTINCTIVENESS

Another theory that similarly moves the conversation away from the meaning of prohibiting certain animals while permitting others is found in the writings of Shadal.[13] Rejecting the aforementioned view that *kashrut* laws are linked to health concerns, he argues that observance of *kashrut* is intended to "separate the Jews from [gentile] nations and

---

9. *Akeidat Yitzhak*, Lev. 18:24, cited in Nechama Leibowitz, *New Studies in Vayikra* (Jerualem: Haomanim Press, 1996), 153.

10. Rabbi Joseph B. Soloveitchik, cited in Rabbi David Etengoff, Parashat Shemini, 5776, 2016, "Kashrut and Kedushah of the Body and Soul," http://www.reparashathashavuah.org/blog-rabbi-david-etengoff-parashat-hashavuah/parashat-shemini-5776-2016kashrut-and-kedushah-of-the-body-and-soul.

11. Rabbi Joseph B. Soloveitchik, *Festival of Freedom: Essays on Pesach and the Haggadah*, eds. Joel B. Wolowesly and Reuven Ziegler (Jersey City: Ktav, 2006), 137.

12. Ibid.

13. Shmuel David Luzzato, nineteenth century, Italy.

also to elevate the soul."[14] Shadal notes that, just as the priestly class has its own statutes that create distinctions between the priests and the rest of Israel, so, too, many of the Torah's food regulations are intended to distance the Israelites from their non-Jewish surroundings and fortify their own national and religious identity.[15]

Early Christians argued for abrogating the Jewish dietary laws, and Prof. Jacob Milgrom notes that in so doing, they demonstrated that they understood a "central aspect of Jewish observance." After all, according to this approach, the laws of *kashrut* are intended to serve as a daily reminder to Jews to remain distinct from the non-Jewish world. *Kashrut* serves as a symbolic medium to highlight the distinction between Jew and gentile. The founders of Christianity wanted "to end once and for all the notion that God had covenanted himself with a certain people who would keep itself apart from all of the other nations."[16] Abrogating *kashrut* regulations served as the perfect method to affirm their new theological orientation.

This suggestion, which views the primary value of *kashrut* as its ability to counter national assimilation, seems to have support in the Bible as well. Describing the requirement to observe *kashrut*, the Torah states:

> You shall separate between the clean animal and the unclean
> and between the clean bird and the unclean; and you shall not
> render your souls abominable through such animals and birds
> and through anything that creeps on the ground which I have
> separated for you to render unclean.[17]

Immediately following this description, we are told that, "You shall be holy for Me, for I Hashem am holy; and have separated you from the

---

14. Shadal, Commentary on the Torah, Leviticus 11:1 (Jerusalem: Chorev Publishers Third Printing 1993), 407.

15. Ibid., n. 1.

16. Jacob Milgrom, *The Anchor Bible: A New Translation with Introduction and Commentary* (New York: Doubleday, 1991), 726. Cited in Rabbi Meir Soloveitchik, *Locusts, Giraffes, and the Meaning of Kashrut*, http://azure.org.il/include/print.php?id=151.

17. Lev. 20:25.

nations to be mine."[18] The word "separate" is used three times in two verses in order to emphasize the link between the separation of kosher and non-kosher animals, on the one hand, and the separation of Jews and gentiles, on the other. Rabbi Joseph Soloveitchik further notes the unique power of *kashrut* regulations to preserve Jewish identity;

> We have existed for almost two thousand years without a sanctuary [*Beit HaMikdash*], and the absence of its service has not affected the integrity of our people. If a Jewish community would reject *kashrut*, however, it would become assimilated in a few generations.[19]

MISHNAIC ATTEMPTS TO PRESERVE THE BIBLICAL ETHIC OF DISTINCTIVENESS

In the rabbinic period, the sages extended the *kashrut* regulations with the goal of maintaining the biblical ethic of cultural and religious uniqueness. For example, in the Mishna we find a list of rabbinically prohibited foods.[20] Commenting on this Mishna, the Rambam claims that the majority of food items forbidden on this list are prohibited in order to further distance the Jew from the gentile world and minimize cultural crossover that would result from excessive social mingling.[21]

While the sages did not totally prohibit socializing with gentiles, rabbinical food regulations provided Jews with constant reminders of their religious and cultural uniqueness. Prof. Ephraim Urbach notes:

> The laws which demanded that Jews maintain a social distance from gentiles and from their customs and modes of behavior were applied in all their stringency even by those sages who tended to leniency with regard to idolatry itself... . While there was no fear that their contemporaries would serve other gods

---

18. Ibid. 20:26.
19. Rabbi Joseph B. Soloveitchik, cited in Rabbi David Etengoff, Parashat Shemini, 5776, 2016:"Kashrut and Kedushah of the Body and Soul", http://www.reparashathashavuah.org/blog-rabbi-david-etengoff-parashat-hashavuah/parashat-shemini-5776-2016kashrut-and-kedushah-of-the-body-and-soul
20. Avoda Zara 2:6.
21. Rambam, ibid.

or participate in heathen cults, the sages were very aware of the
danger of national assimilation and moral degeneration and of
abandoning the Torah and its commandments because of social
contact with the gentiles.[22]

In other words, the sages were particularly stringent about food regulations due to their sensitivity to the role of food in facilitating levels of
social comfort that could easily lead to assimilation.

AMORAIC ATTEMPTS TO PRESERVE BIBLICAL VALUES

A fascinating passage in the Talmud highlights the desire of the rabbis
to maintain the biblical ideal of separateness in changing circumstances.[23]
The Talmud begins by asking, "Why did [the rabbis] prohibit the beer
of idol worshipers?" One answer assumes that the rabbis prohibited the
beer of non-Jews in order to discourage intermarriage. Rashi explains
that if beer were permissible, Jews would become accustomed to having parties at the homes of gentiles, thus significantly increasing the
likelihood of falling in love with a non-Jewish woman.[24] The Talmud
goes on to state that since beer was prohibited because of a concern of
intermarriage, under certain circumstances it would be permissible to
drink it. For example, "R. Pappa would bring [the beer of a non-Jew] out
to the door [of the non-Jew's] shop and he would drink it [there]. For
R. Achai, they would bring the beer to his house and he would drink it
[there]." Moving the food in question to a culturally safe space, such as
the home of a Jew, neutralized the prohibition.

   Tosafot note that this prohibition of consuming the beer of non-
Jews is not found anywhere in the tannaitic literature, yet the Talmud
takes it as a given that it is forbidden.[25] *Tosafot* argue that this prohibition was actualized only during the time of the Amoraim and did not
exist before then. Similarly, the Rashba argues that there was never a

---

22. Prof. Ephraim Urbach, cited in Christine Elizabeth Hayes, *Between the Babylonian
    and Palestinian Talmuds: Accounting for Halakhic Difference in Selected Sugyot from
    Tractate Avoda Zara* (New York/Oxford: Oxford University Press, 1997), 166.
23. Avoda Zara 31b.
24. Rashi, Avoda Zara 31b, s.v. *mishum chatnut.*
25. *Tosafot,* Avoda Zara 31b, s.v. *mipnei ma asru.*

formal decree prohibiting the beer of gentiles; rather, it was a pietistic practice observed by individuals to further distance themselves from non-Jewish parties.[26]

This talmudic passage and the commentaries of the traditional commentators highlights the role that food can play in helping to forge a uniquely Jewish identity. The desire of the Amoraim to expand the prohibitions cited in the Mishna to include the beer of a gentile represents a rabbinic awareness of the possible negative effects that alcohol can have in breaking down cultural barriers. This legislation thus further substantiates the claim that food prohibitions in rabbinic sources are at least partially intended to preserve Jewish uniqueness.

SUMMARY

Theories regarding the rationale behind *kashrut* regulations are many. While the source material covered in this chapter is by no means exhaustive, it represents some of the major trends in both medieval and modern rabbinic thinking. Given the centrality of food in our daily lives, it is especially critical to develop a confident philosophical understanding of the underlying ideals and values of *kashrut*. In particular, appreciating the rabbinic attempt to legislate in a way that enhances and preserves *kashrut*'s fundamental religious messages allows us to feel a part of the ever-unfolding story of the development of Jewish law. Meditating for a few moments before we begin our daily encounter with *kashrut* principles allows us to:

- Reflect on the biblical ideal of healthy living and eating (*Sefer HaChinukh*)
- Understand the religious value of consuming food that will maximize our chances for long-term survival so that we can actualize our spiritual mission in the physical world (*Sefer HaChinukh*)
- Appreciate the spiritual symbolism of certain kosher foods and try to distance ourselves from the negative religious traits associated with non-kosher food (Rabbi Hirsch)

---

26. See *Beit Yosef,* YD 114.

- Reflect upon the spiritual self-discipline fostered by *kashrut* (*Akedat Yitzchak*, Rav Soloveitchik)
- Understand the role of food legislation in preserving the distinctiveness of the Jewish people's culture and religion (Bible, the Shadal, Prof. Milgrom)
- Feel a part of the ongoing rabbinic goal to preserve the values of Jewish uniqueness in constantly changing historical circumstances (Talmud, *Tosafot*, the Rashba)

Chapter 20

One Hundred Blessings

An Opportunity to Continuously Dialogue With God

Traditional Jewish law provides endless opportunities for spiritual moments even outside the framework of synagogue life. In this section of the book, we will shift the conversation away from the synagogue and move the dialogue into the "real world." The goal is to analyze some of the mitzvot that we encounter during the work day, as well as some other mitzvot that are intended to provide perpetual guidance for a life devoted to the ideals of Jewish law.

One example of this category of mitzvot is the requirement to recite blessings before the consumption of food. This requirement extends beyond the synagogue or study hall and requires a Jew to recite a blessing regardless of his locale. One could be at a basketball game, studying for a physics midterm, or at an important business meeting – the obligation to recite blessings would still apply.

While many Jews are familiar with the text of traditional Jewish blessings, the scope of the obligation to recite daily blessings is often not well known even to Jews who are committed to a life of Jewish ritual. According to Jewish law, one is required to recite one hundred blessings daily![1] In fact, while the Talmud states this requirement as one hundred blessings,[2] the *Shulchan Arukh* clarifies that this number is a *minimum* requirement, and certainly not a maximal number.[3] This raises interesting questions about the nature of blessings in the Jewish tradition and the unique obligation to recite a fixed number of blessings daily.

What is the purpose of reciting blessings before eating food, viewing a rainbow, or performing a mitzva? Are the blessings merely intended to contextualize our experiences, or do they serve some additional metaphysical purpose? Moreover, why does the number of blessings we recite daily matter? Is there something specific about the recitation of *one hundred* blessings that facilitates a deeply religious encounter with God? Analyzing these questions will help us understand the purpose of blessings in traditional Judaism, as well as the medium through which blessing God during our day facilitates a heightened awareness of His presence.

RASHBA: GOD IS THE SOURCE OF ALL BLESSINGS

There are various perspectives in Jewish tradition regarding the purpose and nature of reciting blessings.[4]

The Rashba argues that the goal of blessing God is to recognize that He is the source of all blessing.[5] Our blessings acknowledge God's role as ruler of the universe and the source of everything that exists. The Rashba explains that the Hebrew word *berakha* is linguistically connected to the phrase *bereikhot mayim* (reservoir of water), thus metaphorically highlighting God as the sustainer of life. In this philosophical model, reciting blessings throughout the day provides a constant reminder of God and His providential role. Blessings provide a context for a person to internalize and understand God's constant role in human affairs and recognize that divinity is the source of our daily experience.

---

1. *Shulchan Arukh,* Orach Chayim 46:3.
2. Menachot 43b.
3. *Shulchan Arukh,* Orach Chayim 46:3.
4. For additional perspectives on this topic, see: "The Concept and Practice of Brachot," https://www.morashasyllabus.com/class/Brachot.pdf.
5. Responsa Rashba 1:423.

The Gaon of Vilna explains that the specific textual formulation mandated by the halakha relates to two dimensions of God's providence.[6] When we mention God as "Ruler of the Universe" (*Melekh Ha'Olam*), we relate to his providential sovereignty over all of humanity. However, by mentioning God as "our God" (*Elo-heinu*), we highlight God's unique role in caring for and guiding the fate of the Jewish people. The requirement to bless God using a specifically mandated rabbinic formula, therefore, prompts us to recall these two dimensions of divine providence.

MIDRASH/RAMBAM: *BERAKHA* AND GOD-CONSCIOUSNESS

The Midrash offers a slightly different philosophical perspective. In the Rashba's conception, reciting a *berakha* affirms an awareness of God specifically as the source of all blessing. The Midrash, by contrast, asserts that by reciting blessings, we create a consciousness that is more God-centered.[7] Citing the view of Rav, the Midrash insists that any blessing that does not use the formulation of "Blessed are You, Hashem, our God" (*Barukh ata Hashem Elo-heinu*) does not have the status of a halakhically valid blessing. As a proof for this position, the Midrash cites a verse from Psalms: "I have set Hashem before me always; because He is at my right hand, I shall not falter."[8] In this conceptual framework, reciting a blessing that makes reference to God Himself affirms a state of mind in which we are constantly aware of the Divine.

A similar approach is suggested by the Rambam. The Rambam begins by noting that there are three different types of blessings in the Jewish tradition. The first relates to blessings recited before experiencing some form of physical benefit, such as eating food. The second category relates to blessings that are said before the performance of mitzvot. The third involves giving thanks after experiencing something that activates feelings of wonder, such as hearing thunder or seeing lightning. The Rambam states that the purpose of establishing the last

---

6. *Aderet Eliyahu*, Deuteronomy 1:6, cited in "The Concept and Practice of Brachot," https://www.morashasyllabus.com/class/Brachot.pdf.
7. *Midrash Tehillim* (Buber) 16:8.
8. Ps. 16:8.

category of blessings – despite there being no mitzva performance or benefit experienced – is to maximize one's opportunities to remember God and activate a fear of heaven.[9]

The daily recital of blessings, thus, serves as a way of maintaining a sensitivity to the miraculous nature of the physical world. We often take for granted majestic moments, such as seeing a rainbow or hearing powerful thunder. By requiring the recitation of a blessing, Jewish law ensures that we cultivate an attitude of wonder towards the miracles of God's creation.

RABBI BACHYA: *BERAKHOT* AS ACTIVATORS OF DIVINE BLESSING

Rabbi Bachya ben Asher[10] adds another layer to the conversation, interpreting the purpose of traditional blessings using both rational as well as mystical explanations.[11] He begins by noting that the recitation of blessings is intended to affect the person reciting the *berakha*, and not God, Himself. After all, Rabbi Bachya notes, even blessing God all day would not begin to capture the nature of His infiniteness. Rather, whenever we utter a blessing, we testify to God's providential involvement in the world. The regular act of affirming God's role in human affairs helps us develop a more sophisticated relationship with one of the most foundational theological tenets of Judaism.

Rabbi Bachya adds an additional explanation based on Jewish mystical tradition. According to this approach, the word *berakha* refers to God's endless abundance. To substantiate this, he cites a Torah verse that states we are to "worship Hashem … and He will bless your bread and your water … and I [Hashem] shall remove illness from your midst."[12] The word used in this verse to refer to God's providing for the Jewish people is *barekh*, which has the same root as *berakha*. Whenever we bless God, Rabbi Bachya explains, we increase the Divine Presence in the world, and our blessings thus cause additional blessing to flow from God onto the world. In this mystical model, our blessings not only provide an opportunity

9. Laws of Blessings 1:2-4.
10. Rabbi Bachya b. Asher, thirteenth/fourteenth centuries, Spain.
11. Rabbi Bachya, Deuteronomy 8:10.
12. Exodus 23:25.

for us to develop a more refined religious personality, but can also have an impact on the cosmos.

R. LEVI: BLESSINGS AS TRANSFER OF OWNERSHIP

The Talmud emphasizes the severity of failing to recite a blessing before deriving any physical benefit from something: "It is forbidden for a person to derive benefit from the world without [first reciting] a blessing."[13] Moreover, if we do derive benefit without reciting the accompanying blessing, we have, in effect, made unauthorized use of God's property. The Talmud bases this view on R. Levi, who contrasts two seemingly contradictory verses. One verse states, "To Hashem belongs the earth and its fullness,"[14] which implies that the entire earth "belongs" to God. The second verse states, "The heavens are Hashem's, but the earth He has given to mankind,"[15] suggesting that man can utilize the earth as he sees fit. R. Levi harmonizes these verses by stating that the first verse, which portrays the world as God's property, describes the state of existence before a blessing is made. In that context, the world truly does belong to God. However, the second verse, which allows man to govern, refers to the situation after the blessing has already been made. Thus the blessing transfers ownership of the physical from God to man.

RABBI SAMSON RAPHAEL HIRSCH: BLESSINGS AS CONTEXTUALIZING MITZVOT

Rabbi Samson Raphael Hirsch[16] deepens R. Levi's view. He explains that by reciting a blessing before eating, we affirm that any added strength we receive from the food will be utilized in the service of God. It is only through committing ourselves to utilize the physical world in service of God that we are permitted to benefit from God's creation.[17]

Rabbi Hirsch adds another layer as well, referring to the requirement to recite a blessing before the performance of mitzvot. According

---

13. Berakhot 35a.
14. Ps. 24:1.
15. Ibid. 115:16.
16. Rabbi Samson Raphael Hirsch, nineteenth century, Germany.
17. Rabbi Hirsch, Deuteronomy 8:10.

to Rabbi Hirsch, the purpose of reciting a blessing before performing a mitzva is to provide the proper preparatory context to be religiously effected by the mitzva. By reciting a blessing that includes the phrase, "Who has sanctified us through His commandments (*asher kidishanu bemitzvotav*)," we remind ourselves that mitzvot are not ends in themselves. Rather, they are intended to sanctify us and make us more refined religious personalities. It is for this reason, Rabbi Hirsch explains, that blessings are recited before those rituals whose sole purpose is to sanctify us religiously. Without the divine command, there is no reason to wear ritual fringes or to blow the shofar. The *berakha* recited on these mitzvot reminds us that these commandments are entry points to the development of a more refined religious identity. By contrast, mitzvot such as restoring lost property or giving charity require no formal blessing, since they serve a clearly functional and tangible purpose, which is accomplished by performing the action in question even without a formal blessing.[18]

A similar observation is made in the *Sefer HaChinukh*,[19], where it is noted that blessings recited before the performance of a mitzva allow us to thank God for the spiritual potential provided by performing the mitzva.[20] According to this view, a *berakha* contextualizes the performance of a mitzva by reminding us that mitzvot represent profound opportunities to connect with God, and they should not be experienced as a burden. By reciting the blessing, we not only provide the proper framework for the mitzva, but we affirm our positive attitude to mitzvot as a whole.

KLI YAKAR: ONE HUNDRED BLESSINGS A DAY AS RECAPTURING DIVINE INTIMACY

Having explained various models to better understand the purpose of reciting blessings, we can now reflect on the the talmudic requirement to recite one hundred blessings each day. The source of this ruling is a

---

18. Ibid., cf. the chapter about Blessings on Interpersonal Commandments.
19. Attributed to Rabbi Aharon Ha-Levi of Barcelona, thirteenth century.
20. *Sefer HaHinukh*, mitzva 430.

statement by R. Meir, [21] who bases this halakha on a verse in Deuteronomy, which asks, "Now Israel, what does Hashem, your God, ask of you?" and replies "Only to fear Him. Hashem, your God, to go in all His ways, and to love Him, and to serve Hashem … with all your heart and all your soul."[22]

On the surface, this biblical imperative seems overwhelming. We are asked not only to fear and love God, but also to serve Him with all our heart and soul! The *Kli Yakar* explains that, while this request seems nearly impossible to properly observe, it was not an unreasonable demand to place upon the ancient Israelites, who witnessed first-hand the miracles performed by God for the Jewish people.[23]

According to this explanation, R. Meir instituted the obligation to recite one hundred blessings daily in order to facilitate a continuous divine awareness that somewhat parallels the intimacy that the Jews experienced with God during a time of overt divine providence. Reciting the required one hundred blessings daily serves to inculcate a profound sense of fear and awe. The Jewish nation experienced God's power and might through God's miraculous involvement throughout their sojourn in the desert. Today, we lack these overt signs of divine involvement. Reciting blessings provides a much more subtle and quiet entry point for God into our lives.

By shifting responsibility for divine encounter to individual Jews, the halakha offers a powerful means for contemporary Jews to take ownership of their religious lives. Achieving a deep relationship with God is certainly possible. The onus is on the individual to recite one hundred blessings with an eye to achieving this goal.

RASHI: ONE HUNDRED BLESSINGS AND SELF-TRANSCENDENCE

Rashi provides another rationale for the requirement to recite one hundred blessings each day.[24] Commenting on the verse in Deuteronomy cited by R. Meir, Rashi notes that the Talmud cites the same verse as the

---

21. Menachot 43b.
22. Deut. 10:12.
23. *Kli Yakar*, Deuteronomy 10:12.
24. Rashi, Deuteronomy 10:12, s.v. *ki*.

source for the philosophical concept that "everything is in the hands of heaven except for the fear of heaven."[25] According to Rashi's approach, the requirement to recite one hundred blessings is a rabbinic attempt to help us cultivate a sense of fear of God.

As Rabbi Shlomo Wolbe[26] explains, fear of God is bound up with a full awareness of the existence of something beyond ourselves. [27] This awareness allows us to be humbled by the limits of our own power and to recognize that there are many things that are simply beyond our control. The blessings, then, serve as frequent reminders, helping us to maintain awareness and fear of God. By consciously referencing God throughout the day, we achieve a state of self-transcendence, acknowledging and being humbled by the limits of our own power.

TANYA: PERSONALIZING OUR RELATIONSHIP WITH GOD

We have not yet clarified the significance of the number one hundred. What is so significant about reciting a fixed number of blessings daily?[28] Moreover, why does the *Shulchan Arukh* insist that the number one hundred is the minimum number of blessings to be recited daily? The Talmud records an exchange between Bar Hei Hei and Hillel on this topic:

> Bar Hei Hei said to [Hillel]: What is [the meaning] of that which is written, "You will return and see the difference between a righteous person and a wicked person, between one who serves God and one who does not serve Him"? [The verse appears to be repeating itself.] A "righteous person" is the same as one who serves God, and "a wicked person" is the same as one who does not serve Him! He [Hillel] answered: One who serves [God] and one who does not serve Him are both completely righteous. Nevertheless, there is no comparison between one who [reviews his studies] one hundred times and one who [reviews his studies] one hundred and one times. He [Ben Hei Hei] said

---

25. Berakhot 33b.
26. Rabbi Shlomo Wolbe, twentieth century, Israel.
27. *Alei Shur Volume 1* (Jerusalem: Beit Hamussar, תשמה), 95.
28. See Tur Orach Chayim 46 for an additional perspective.

to him [Hillel]: And because [he failed to review his studies] one [extra] time he is called "one who does not serve God"?! He [Hillel] responded to him: Yes! Go out and learn this from the market of donkey drivers, [for a journey of] ten parsahs [costs] one *zuz*, [but a journey of] eleven parsahs [costs] two *zuzim*.[29]

Rabbi Shneur Zalman of Liadi explains that in the talmudic period, it was the norm for a student to review his studies one hundred times. This constant review enabled the student to master the material and internalize the messages inherent in the texts. Still, it was only a formal requirement, and the student who reviewed one hundred times was considered to be just doing what was expected. The one hundred and first time, by contrast, represented the moment when the student took responsibility for his own religious identity, thus personalizing his religious experience.[30] By reviewing for the one hundred and first time, the student affirmed his passion and love for his studies and demonstrated that his constant review of the material was a matter of choice and not performed out of coercion.

If we apply this construct to the case of reciting one hundred blessings daily, it becomes clear that the recitation of one hundred *berakhot* represents the standard requirement mandated by halakha in order to ensure that an ordinary Jew experiences an elevated sense of divinity throughout his day. The one hundred and first blessing, by contrast, affirms that the practitioner of Jewish law truly desires to develop an acute sense of Godliness and *chooses* to invest in the ritual of one hundred daily blessings based on an awareness that this is an effective way to assume ownership of his religious identity. This is why the *Shulchan Arukh* asserts that one hundred daily blessings represents a minimum and not a maximum. It is exactly at the moment when we exceed the required one hundred blessings that we declare our personal commitment to a life motivated by a constant awareness of God.

---

29. Hagiga 9b.
30. *Tanya*, ch. 15.

SUMMARY

Reciting at least one hundred blessings daily represents an opportunity to connect to God and develop a more refined sense of divinity. Going about our day while mindfully reciting a minimum of one hundred blessings allows us to:

- Affirm that God is the source of all blessing (Rashba)
- Develop a more acute and sophisticated God-consciousness (Midrash Tehillim, Rambam)
- Reflect upon the cosmic impact of reciting blessings (Rabbi Bachya)
- Understand that our physical desires are intended to help facilitate spirituality (Rabbi Hirsch)
- Contextualize the performance of mitzvot by affirming their ability to affect us spiritually (Rabbi Hirsch)
- View *berakhot* as a means of recapturing a sense of divine intimacy (*Kli Yakar*)
- Understand how blessings inculcate an increased sense of the fear of God, and by extension, a more self-transcendent religious posture (Rashi, Rabbi Wolbe)
- Personalize our relationship with God (*Tanya*)

Chapter 21

Blessings on Interpersonal Mitzvot

Jewish Uniqueness, Intuitive
Commandments, and the
Challenges of Coercion

Ⅰn the previous chapter, we discussed the values that underlie the
halakhic requirement to recite at least one-hundred blessings a day.
Practically, how do we achieve this religious goal daily? Are there more
than one hundred opportunities to recite a blessing during anyone's day?[1]

On the surface, one of the easiest ways to accomplish this would be
to legislate the recitation of blessings before the performance of interpersonal commandments. For example, Jewish law could mandate that before
comforting mourners, honoring parents, or giving charity, we would be
required to recite a blessing. While this approach is advocated by a minority

---

1. For practical suggestions for how to reach the required 100 daily blessings, see Rabbi
   Shraga Simmons, "100 Blessings Each Day," http://www.aish.com/jl/jewish-law/
   blessings/43-100-Blessings-Each-Day.html.

of Jewish sages, the majority position (as well as the accepted practice) is not to recite blessings on interpersonal commandments. Rather, we limit the requirement to those commandments that are between man and God.

In the preceding chapter we saw how blessings provide a Godly framework for the action being performed. Then why not require an individual to recite a blessing before performing interpersonal commandments as well? Analyzing traditional sources that deal with these questions will help us to better appreciate how even the smallest details of Jewish law are replete with meaning and purpose.

RABBI YITZHAK ISAAC SAFRIN OF KOMARNO: THE MINORITY VOICE

While the overwhelming majority of classical sages reject any formal requirement to recite a blessing over the performance of interpersonal mitzvot, there are minority voices in the tradition that do affirm such an obligation. Rabbi Dr. Daniel Sperber cites the view of Rabbi Yitzhak Isaac Safrin of Komarno,[2] who requires the recitation of a blessing before performing any mitzva, including interpersonal ones. Rabbi Safrin states:

> Over all mitzvot, one must make a [full] blessing *beshem umalkhut* [including God's name and mention of His Kingship]: over honoring our parents, paying wages on time, charity, and good deeds, for there is a general principle: "Over all mitzvot one makes a blessing…." And all who make more such blessings than are mandated will be blessed by the Lord a hundred holy blessings; so one should make blessings over every mitzva, great or small.[3]

While this view represents a minority voice and is not accepted in the realm of practical halakha, Rabbi Safrin's perspective highlights the tension that exists in determining which actions require introductory blessings and which do not.

---

2. Rabbi Yitzhak Isaac Safrin, nineteenth century, Galicia.
3. Cited in *On the Relationship of Mitzvot between Man and his Neighbor and Man and his Maker* by Dr. Daniel Sperber, (Jerusalem/New York: Urim Publications, 2014), 35.

At least intuitively, this minority opinion has significant conceptual merit. With regard to interpersonal commandments, there is always the risk that we will associate these actions with natural morality, divorced from any divine imperative. It is easy to remember that God desires us to pray, wear tzitzit, or observe the Sabbat. The challenge is to acknowledge that God also demands that we give charity and visit the sick. These actions are no less divine than rituals usually categorized as commandments "between man and God." The blessing, according to the approach of Rabbi Safrin, reminds us that actions that are intuitive even without a divine command are nonetheless divine.

RASHBA: SENSITIZING US TO THE
POWER OF RECITING GOD'S NAME

Unlike Rabbi Safrin, the Rashba accepts the majority opinion that one does not recite blessings on interpersonal commandments. The Rashba's explanation for this rule is based on the Talmud's statement that "anyone who utters an unnecessary blessing transgresses the prohibition 'You shall not take the name of Hashem, your God, in vain.'"[4] This view is codified by the Rambam: "Whoever recites a blessing for which he is not obligated is considered to have taken God's name in vain. He is considered as one who took a false oath, and it is forbidden to answer Amen after his blessing."[5]

Given the severity of the prohibition of reciting God's name in vain, before reciting any blessing, a Jew needs to pause briefly and ascertain that the blessing being recited is in fact legally mandated.

In the realm of commandments between man and God, the risk of uttering a blessing in vain is minimal. If a person recites a blessing before shaking a lulav, for example, the chances are slim that he would somehow misplace the lulav in question, thus causing his blessing to have been made in vain. However, the Rashba notes, with regard to interpersonal commandments, the risks are much greater. Since the action in question is dependent on two people, there is a risk that one person will

---

4. Ex. 20:7, cited in Berakhot 33a.
5. Rambam, Laws of Blessings 1:15, translated at http://www.chabad.org/library/article_cdo/aid/927667/jewish/Berachot-Chapter-One.htm.

not want the mitzva to be performed, and any blessing recited would then become unnecessary. The Rashba states that this is the reason that blessings are not recited on interpersonal commandments.[6]

Conceptually, the Rashba agrees with Rabbi Safrin that we should, ideally, recite a blessing before the performance of any mitzva. However, he argues that the risk of possibly reciting a blessing in vain outweighs the potential gain of prefacing interpersonal commandments with a preparatory blessing. The Rashba thus reminds us of the religious responsibility associated with uttering God's name.

In the framework of our religious lives, we often take for granted the fact that we refer to God in the second person when reciting blessings. This allowance generates a sense of personal intimacy between the practitioner of Jewish law and God. However, there is a risk that this permissive stance could desensitize an individual to the religious significance of uttering God's name. In an extreme scenario, excessive comfort with this legal allowance could cause us to accidently utter God's name in vain. By limiting blessings to mitzvot between man and God, Jewish law reminds us of our responsibility to maintain a sense of awe and reverence when referring to God during our daily blessings.

OR ZARUA: BERAKHOT AND PERPETUAL MITZVOT

Rabbi Yitzchak ben Rabbi Moshe of Vienna[7] (*Or Zarua*) offers an alternative way to understand the lack of blessings recited before performing interpersonal commandments. According to his view, blessings are recited on only ritual obligations that have a specifically fixed time. For example, the mitzva of sitting in the sukka requires a blessing because the mitzva is obligatory only throughout the seven-day Sukkot festival. During the rest of the year, this mitzva is not operative. Since these mitzvot are practiced at specific times, the blessing allows us to momentarily reflect on the mitzva at hand and achieve a more elevated state of consciousness when performing the mitzva.

Interpersonal mitzvot, by contrast, have no fixed time for their performance. A person is *always* obligated to visit the sick, give charity,

---

6. Responsa Rashba 1:18.
7. Twelfth/thirteenth centuries, Ashkenaz.

or comfort mourners, for example. Since the obligation to perform these commandments is perpetual, there is no parallel requirement to recite a blessing before their performance.[8]

This approach emphasizes the role that the blessing plays in making the transition from secular consciousness to a focus on religious obligation. Mitzvot that lack a set time can often "show up" spontaneously in our lives. Anyone who has experienced the Jewish calendar cycle can appreciate the feeling of shock upon the arrival of the High Holiday season. The goal of the blessing is to shift our awareness and create some distance between our default mindset and our mental state when performing a time-sensitive, obligatory, religious ritual.

Conversely, the absence of blessings before interpersonal commandments reminds us that we should *always* be in a mental state of awareness, ready to help a fellow human being when called upon. Reciting a blessing before visiting the sick, for example, would imply that we are not fully prepared for this mitzvah, and the blessing would thus serve as an intermediary for proper preparation. By not reciting any blessing, we affirm our commitment to a state of consciousness that is always ready and willing to help another person in need.

TORAH TEMIMA: BERAKHOT AND JEWISH UNIQUENESS

The *Torah Temima*[9] offers a third reason to explain why blessings are not recited on interpersonal commandments, challenging us to reflect upon the ways in which Jewish uniqueness manifests itself. Jews are obligated to act ethically and in a dignified manner in their relations with other people, but interpersonal commandments are not specific to the Jewish people. Gentiles also visit the sick, give charity to the poor, and comfort mourners. By contrast, commandments that are between man and God are obligatory exclusively for Jews. Non-Jews have no parallel obligation to observe Shabbat, wear tefillin, or sit in a sukka. Therefore, the unique covenantal bond between God and the Jewish people is at least *externally* manifested through those commandments that are limited to Jews alone.

---

8. *Or Zarua,* Laws of the Blessing of *Hamotzi* 1:140.
9. Rabbi Baruch Halevi Epstein, nineteenth/twentieth centuries, Lithuania.

The *Torah Temima* notes that in the blessing that we recite before performing commandments, we thank God as the one who "sanctifies us through His commandments." The Jewish concept of sanctity reflects the way in which the Torah distinguishes the Jewish people from their gentile neighbors. Commandments between man and God are unique to the Jewish people and highlight their separateness. It is for this reason that we recite a blessing, since the phrase "sanctifies us" is uniquely relevant to this genre of mitzvot. Regarding interpersonal mitzvot, however, with their more universal element, using the words "sanctifies us" would be inappropriate.[10]

The *Arukh HaShulchan* provides a slightly different explanation for the absence of a requirement to recite blessings for interpersonal commandments. He begins by noting that Jewish people are obligated to perform even those mitzvot that could have been intuited without the divine command. True, the source of the obligation to perform even rational mitzvot is the Revelation at Sinai, not human logic. Nonetheless, the sanctity and uniqueness of the Jewish people expresses itself to the outside world through the revealed commandments, rather than those we could have figured out on our own. In other words, the source of Jewish uniqueness is the Revelation at Sinai, highlighted by mitzvot between man and God. Interpersonal commandments were also commanded at Sinai, but since they could have been intuited without the divine command, they do not underscore the Sinaitic bond in the same way and therefore lack a parallel blessing that refers to Jewish uniqueness.[11]

The perspectives of the *Torah Temima* and the *Arukh HaShulchan* emphasize the way in which reciting blessings throughout our day serves as a perpetual reminder of the uniqueness of the Jewish people. Moreover, an awareness that we do *not* recite blessings on interpersonal mitzvot because they do not sufficiently underscore Jewish distinctiveness and its Sinaitic roots provides another opportunity to reflect on the chosen status of the Jewish nation.

---

10. *Torah Temima*, Exodus 24, footnote 30.
11. *Arukh HaShulchan*, Choshen Mishpat 427:10.

THE *SERIDEI EISH*: MITZVOT AS AN
END AND NOT A MEANS

The *Seridei Eish*[12] adds an additional perspective regarding the larger question of performing religious rituals from a place of obligation versus from a spirit of volunteerism.

The *Seridei Eish's* comments appear in a responsum in which he addresses the question of why we do not recite a blessing on the mitzva of *mishloach manot*. This rabbinic commandment requires every Jew to provide a small package of food to at least two friends during the holiday of Purim. Traditional commentators explain that since the book of Esther (*Megillat Ester*) describes the Jewish people as fractured and divided, the rabbis legislated the mitzva of *mishloach manot* to create a sense of fraternity and help facilitate Jewish unity. Explaining the rationale behind the lack of blessing for this mitzva, Rabbi Weinberg refers to a talmudic principle that it is preferable to perform a religious ritual out of a sense of obligation rather than from a place of volunteerism.[13] He argues that while this talmudic dictum is true in most cases, with regard to *mishloach manot*, performing this ritual out of a sense of obligation would actually undermine the mitzva itself, since the purpose of the mitzva is to facilitate feelings of closeness between two people. How can *mishloach manot* generate a sense of unity if those receiving the gift feel as though they are being given the present only because of the obligation? Reciting a blessing would link the action to the obligation and effectively transform the receiver of the gift from a subject to an object.

The *Seridei Eish* suggests that this is similarly the reason why we do not recite a blessing on interpersonal mitzvot such as giving charity or honoring our parents. Charity, for example, is supposed to be given from a place of care and sympathy for a poor person. Reciting a blessing beforehand would imply that giving the charity is simply to fulfill a religious duty.[14]

According to the *Seridei Eish*, blessings recited before performing ritual commandments connect the action in question to the domain

---

12. Rabbi Yechiel Yaakov Weinberg, nineteenth/twentieth centuries, Russia/Switzerland.
13. Bava Kamma 87a.
14. Responsa *Seridei Eish* 1:61.

of obligation. Mitzvot between man and God require a blessing before their performance because they affirm the practitioner's relationship with the Commander Himself and highlight the talmudic preference for acting from a place of being commanded. However, with regard to interpersonal commandments, the requirement to recite a blessing would actually provide a mistaken context for the performance of these commandments. While God is the source of these obligations as well, He *prefers* that we engage in these commandments without referencing the obligation itself.

Paradoxically, Jewish law teaches us that, in order to maximize God's presence in certain actions, we must remove any overt reference to His role as the Commander. Following this approach prevents us from viewing others as objects of our religious duties.

SUMMARY

The various explanations offered for the absence of any blessings recited before interpersonal commandments provide insight into the scope of Jewish law, emphasizing meaning and value. Not only do the blessings contain a wellspring of ideas and ideals, but even the *absence* of blessings for certain actions reflects a conscious attempt on the part of halakha to impart powerful religious lessons. Reciting blessings before certain rituals, while actively avoiding making blessings before performing interpersonal commandments, allows us to:

- Appreciate the (rejected) minority voices in Jewish tradition that require blessings to be recited even before performing interpersonal commandments (Rabbi Yitzchak Isaac Safrin of Komarno)
- Reflect on the religious significance of reciting a blessing in vain (Rashba)
- Understand the idea of "perpetual" mitzvot and reflect on our perpetual readiness to be willing and able to engage in this obligation (*Or Zarua*)
- Reflect on traditional conceptions of Jewish uniqueness (*Torah Temima*)

- Think carefully about our relationship to revealed laws versus rationally intuitive legislation (*Arukh HaShulchan*)
- Reflect on the traditional notion of "being commanded" and its parameters (*Seridei Eish*)
- Ensure that we never cause people to feel like objects in our attempt to fulfill the divine will (*Seridei Eish*)

Chapter 22

Ethical Living

Finding God Outside the Context
of Formalized Ritual

The central focus of this book is the expansive power of Jewish law to facilitate profound divine encounters during the course of the day. Unfortunately, many people mistakenly assume that Jewish law is interested *only* in ritualistic behavior and does not pay much attention to issues that are not codified by traditional decisors of halakha.

For example, let's begin by briefly discussing the role of ethics in traditional Jewish life. Ethical living is the cornerstone of a Jew's halakhic identity. In fact, the Gaon of Vilna maintains that the totality of divine worship is predicated upon our ability to refine our character.[1] Regrettably, this element of Jewish observance is sometimes lost in contemporary halakhic discourse. People often seek religious guidance and counsel regarding ritual law, and view the mitzvot that are encountered each day as the exclusive entry points for a powerful dialogue with God. However, traditional Jewish sources provide a much more

---

1. *Even Shelema* 1:1.

nuanced approach to the role of character development and its legal and religious ramifications.

Imagine an ordinary day at the office. Jewish law demands that we recite blessings before eating food, recite the afternoon service, and wash our hands before eating bread. It also demands that we avoid any behavior associated with theft or deceit. Moreover, there are some quite specific rules on ordinary speech, concerning avoidance of harmful or idle speech, such as malicious gossip, insult, shaming, etc. (which are beyond the scope of this book). Other than these clearly articulated laws, does Jewish law have something to say about the way we interact with our colleagues? What about the broader postures of compassion and mercy? How should observant Jews incorporate these virtues into their daily living? Are there passages in classical codes that provide guidance and clarity? If not, what does that say about the nature of Jewish law? Could the absence of neatly articulated regulations on these issues be an intentional attempt by the codifiers to impart a message about the relationship between the ritual and ethical?

Studying traditional Jewish texts about these questions will help us expand the conversation of Jewish ritual and better understand the endless opportunities that an ordinary day provides for authentic divine encounters.

RIGHTEOUSNESS AND JUSTICE AS A RELIGIOUS POSTURE

The central source dealing with these issues is a verse from Deuteronomy. Describing the proper behavior that will facilitate divine protection, the Torah encourages the Jewish people to "observe this entire commandment and I command you, to perform it, to love Hashem, your God, to walk in all His ways and to cleave to Him."[2] Beyond traditional rituals such as tefillin, tzitzit, and sacrifices, the Torah addresses a broader obligation to "love God, walk in God's ways, and cleave to Him."

While we will discuss the biblical imperative to love God in the next chapter, the exact substance of the requirement to "walk in God's ways and cleave to Him" remains unclear. Seforno,[3] for example, understands this

---

2. Deut. 11:22.
3. Ovadia b. Yaakov Seforno, fifteenth/sixteenth centuries, Italy.

verse to be legislating two parallel commitments. The first requires one to emulate God by modelling our own behavior after God. Just as God governs the universe through an uncompromising commitment to justice and righteousness, so too should those virtues be at the center of our identities.[4]

This interpretation of the Seforno is supported by a verse in Genesis that tells us God chose Avraham to be the father of the Jewish nation because of his commitment to transmit the divine ethics of justice and righteousness to his children.[5] As Rabbi Dr. Meir Y. Soloveichik notes:

> Throughout the Bible, God declares that when Israel imitates its ancestor Avraham and pursues righteousness, such as during the reigns of David, Hezekiah, and Josiah, God will bless and strengthen Israel. When Israel fails to live up to Abraham's legacy, such as during the reigns of Jeroboam and Manasseh, then a betrayed God will punish Israel.[6]

A commitment to these values is intended to be the religious posture of the observant Jew. In addition to observing the commandments, the Torah demands that our general attitude and worldview be governed by these broader ideals.

The Seforno goes on to note that the second part of the verse mandating that we "cleave to God" means that all of our actions should be dedicated to the fulfillment of the divine will. He quotes a verse from Proverbs demanding that we should know God "in all of our ways."[7] While this directive has a rich interpretive history, its primary function is to remind us that before engaging in any activity, we need to reflect and seek counsel in God's word. Not every action that one encounters throughout the day is legally legislated in the classical codes. Nonetheless, this verse expands the halakhic conversation and reminds us that Torah has a perspective even regarding those issues for which formal legislation is not explicitly

---

4. Seforno, Deuteronomy 11:22.
5. Gen. 18:19.
6. Rabbi Meir Y. Soloveichik, "God's Beloved: A Defense of Closeness," http://azure.org.il/article.php?id=201.
7. Prov. 3:6.

provided. Having this verse in our thoughts throughout the day reminds us that, as long as our minds are properly focused on living according to the values of the Torah, the potential for divine encounter is endless.

COMPASSION, MERCY, AND GOD'S NAME

The *Sifrei* offers a slightly different approach, which also understands the requirement to emulate God as being about adopting a religious attitude. According to the *Sifrei*, God is biblically associated with the attributes of mercy, grace, righteousness, and piety. Based on a close reading of various biblical verses, the *Sifrei* argues that, just as God is associated with these virtuous qualities, the Jewish people must also strive to become intimately connected to these virtues. In fact, the *Sifrei* argues, identifying with these attributes is the way in which the Jewish people are able to connect to the name of God. When we call someone's name, we aim to get their attention. In this case, the *Sifrei* asserts, by developing a posture whereby we instinctively respond when called upon to perform acts of mercy, grace, righteousness, and piety, we affirm the biblical imperative "to walk in God's ways."[8]

Consider for a moment how this source challenges us in a work setting. Whenever a human being thinks of a particular person – a boss or a co-worker, for example –certain adjectives immediately come to mind. We may define certain co-workers as nice, hard-working, mean-spirited, or even rude, for instance. But the Torah mandates that we Jews behave in such a way that – whenever someone thinks of us – the first adjectives that come to mind are the divine attributes listed in the Torah.

DEVELOPING A GODLY POSTURE: THE ROLE OF ACTION

While the sources cited thus far delineate the importance of developing a godly religious identity, other texts provide more detailed guidance about the practical means for achieving this goal. The Talmud, for example, notes that we develop a reputation connected to divine values by constantly behaving in a way that reflects these ideals.[9] According to the Talmud, God clothes the naked, visits the sick, comforts mourners, and

---

8. *Sifrei, Parashat Ekev* 49.
9. Sota 14a.

buries the dead. These activities are not simply good deeds or practices reserved for exceptionally pious individuals. Rather, they are reflections of divine virtues, and we are required to engage in them as expressions of our commitment to the biblical ideal of "following in God's ways."

Rabbi Samson Raphael Hirsch and the *Or HaChayim*[10] expand on these themes, adding two other divine qualities that we should strive to emulate.[11] Rabbi Hirsch claims that being easily forgiving is also a godly practice, while the *Or HaChayim* notes that practicing what we preach affirms God's commitment to truth and justice.

All these interpreters agree that while formalized and codified rituals represent one critical component in our aspiration to be godly, there is also a broader obligation to ensure that all our actions and behaviors are rooted in divine values. Our goal is to follow in God's ways as best we can. In the words of the Rambam, "a person is obligated to accustom himself to these [virtuous] paths and to resemble Him to the extent of his ability."[12]

BEING GODLY BY ENGAGING IN
MEANINGFUL FRIENDSHIPS

All of the actions, virtues, and attributes discussed so far seem to be natural expressions of the Divine. Visiting the sick and acting with mercy, for example, are inherently meaningful, and it is therefore not surprising that the Torah and Talmud associate these behaviors with God Himself. But what about more neutral activities? Is there an element of "walking in God's ways" when socializing with friends, engaging in sports, or going on a family vacation?

While giving a formal "yes/no" answer to these questions can be difficult, traditional sources do provide some practical guidance. For example, the Gemara[13] argues that surrounding ourselves with scholars and their students represents a fulfillment of the biblical verse requiring us to "cling to God." The Rambam codifies this principle: "It is a positive

---

10. Rabbi Chayim ben Moshe ibn Attar, seventeenth/eighteenth centuries, Morocco.
11. Commentaries on Deuteronomy 11:22.
12. Laws of Character Traits 1:6, translated at http://www.chabad.org/library/article_cdo/aid/910340/jewish/Deot-Chapter-One.htm.
13. Ketubot 111b.

commandment to cleave unto the wise and their disciples in order to learn from their deeds, as stated in Deuteronomy 10:20: 'And you will cling to Him.'"[14] Surrounding ourselves with scholars is religiously advantageous because we learn from their ethical traits and thereby develop behavioral patterns that are linked to God himself. Rabbi Shlomo Levi explains that the friendship of scholars is normally for the sake of Heaven and not for some ulterior motive. By exposing ourselves to people of great stature, we learn the true meaning of companionship.[15]

If we expand upon these sources, it becomes clear that choosing the right social circle can have significant religious ramifications. After all, as the Rambam notes, "a man's character and actions are influenced by his friends and associates, and he should follow the local norms of behavior."[16] As a result, when we surround ourselves with people of stature and learn from their positive attributes, we interact with the Divine on some level.

BEING GODLY BY HAVING A SENSE OF HUMOR

Rabbi Joseph B. Soloveitchik adds an additional perspective, noting the role of humor in attempting to imitate the ways of God. According to an aggadic passage in the Talmud, God divides his day as follows:

> [During the] first three hours [of each day, God] sits and involves Himself with Torah [study]. [During the] second [three-hour period], He sits and judges the entire world.... [During the] third [three-hour period], He sits and provides [nourishment] for the entire world. [During the] fourth [three-hour period], He sits and amuses [Himself] with the Leviathan [a gigantic sea creature].[17]

According to Rav Soloveitchik, the Talmud describes God spending a portion of His day in amusement with the Leviathan in order to teach

---

14. Laws of Character Traits 6:2, translated at http://www.chabad.org/library/article_cdo/aid/910346/jewish/Deot-Chapter-Six.htm.
15. *Biur Hada Maspik* Laws of Character Traits 6:1.
16. Laws of Character Traits 6:1, translated at http://www.chabad.org/library/article_cdo/aid/910346/jewish/Deot-Chapter-Six.htm.
17. Avoda Zara 3b.

us that an observant Jew need not be in a perpetually serious and heavy head space.[18]

Rabbi Daniel Feldman explains that humor has the ability to place various elements of our lives in proper perspective: "It seems that the intent [of Rav Soloveitchik] was to highlight humor (or, in this case, playfulness) as an indication of one's awareness of the relative importance, or lack of same, contained in various elements of life."[19] Through laughter and developing a posture of appropriate playfulness, one affirms a model of balance that, according to the Talmud, is rooted in divine ideals.

This more expansive explanation of "walking in His ways" again demonstrates the extent to which we have the opportunity to confront God during every day. Jokes are often told in social and professional settings. Similarly, opportunities for playfulness with our children abound. How do we relate to these activities? Do we see them as religiously neutral and consider them only from the perspective of "Am I violating a formal prohibition?" Or do we understand that these moments represent a wonderful opportunity to affirm Judaism's positive approach to a religiously appropriate, while simultaneously meaningful, holistic worldview? If we opt for the latter, then the opportunities that we have to encounter God and His values increase exponentially.

EMULATING GOD BY ENGAGING IN
MEANINGFUL ACTIVITIES

While Rabbi Soloveitchik speaks specifically about the virtues of humor and playfulness, Leviticus Rabba states that the act of planting trees in Israel is a fulfillment of the biblical directive to "cleave to God."[20]

Rabbi Aharon Lichtenstein explains the significance of planting trees by citing a midrashic critique of Noah upon exiting the ark.[21] The Bible notes that after being saved from the flood, Noah immediately

18. Rabbi Tzvi Schachter, *Nefesh HaRav* (Jerusalem: Reishit Yerushalayim, 1995), 69.
19. Rabbi Daniel Feldman, "Does God Have a Sense of Humor?" https://www.ou.org/jewish_action/05/2013/does-god-have-a-sense-of-humor/.
20. Leviticus Rabba (Vilna), *Kedoshim* 25:3.
21. Rabbi Aharon Lichtenstein, *These Are the Generations of Noach*, http://etzion.org.il/en/these-are-generations-noach.

planted a vineyard.[22] The world had basically been destroyed, yet Noah decided to plant something excessive and certainly not critical for its rebuilding.[23] Unlike God, who constantly plants trees with the goal of building a better world, Noah was self-absorbed, failing to understand the underlying responsibility entailed in planting.

In other words, planting represents an affirmation of the obligation "to cleave to God" because we are commanded to act responsibly and ensure that our actions are always linked to divine values. Planting a vineyard after the world's destruction, in contrast, lacks all sense of purpose and meaning.

If we take this approach seriously, then the Midrash is asking us to be like God and ensure that all of our actions are rooted in values and contribute to the larger goal of building a more elevated world. Defining the exact parameters of such a requirement is difficult. However, if we regard ourselves as called upon to struggle with this question, then we maximize our chances of behaving in a value-based way that reflects the ideals of God Himself.

THE LEGAL SIGNIFICANCE OF THESE INTERPRETATIONS

It could be argued that all of these recommendations by the Talmud and its interpreters are merely homilies lacking any legal consequence. However, the Rambam explicitly states that emulating God, following His ways, and living by His virtues is a biblical requirement.[24] The truth remains, however, that even according to the Rambam, defining the legal contours of these virtues is much more complex than identifying the halakhic requirements of a sukka, for example. Traditional ritual is codified in an exacting way, leaving little room for confusion. The values discussed with regard to the mitzva to walk in God's ways and cleave to Him are much more loosely defined.

For example, there is no section in the *Shulchan Arukh* that discusses the exact way to cultivate the ethic of compassion or mercy. The Talmud and subsequent codes do not regulate such matters as character

---

22. Bereishit 9:20.
23. See Rashi comments to Bereishit 9:20, s.v. *Vayachel*.
24. *Sefer HaMitzvot*, positive commandment 8.

growth or the proper measures of anger, humility, and other attributes. The Rambam, indeed, spends significant time in *Hilkhot Deot* (Laws of Character Traits) discussing the need to follow the "Golden Mean" and not go to the extreme when striving to refine our character. However, even the Rambam does not define the exact details of these rules with traditional precision.

The *Or Sameach* explains the lack of formal Torah legislation in the realm of character traits by noting that the Torah can legislate only those issues that share a uniform baseline. Every Jew wears the same basic tefillin, for example, and the Torah legislates accordingly. Character development, however, is deeply subjective; the proper balance between various attributes can vary from person to person.[25] The suggestion of the *Or Sameach* does not mitigate the Torah's concern for personal refinement. On the contrary, by providing the larger directive to "walk in God's ways" without legislating detailed regulations for achieving this goal, the Torah places the onus on individual Jews to constantly question and reflect on whether we are honestly behaving according to the Torah's ideal.

Rabbi Avraham Yitzhak Kook offers yet another model for understanding the absence of formal commandments dealing with certain ethical issues.[26] Rav Kook notes that, although in general, Jewish law maintains that "greater is one who is commanded than one who acts from the spirit of volunteerism,"[27] this principle applies only to ritual laws. With regard to the ethical realm, it is preferable that ethical behavior be a natural outgrowth of an awareness of right and wrong, rather than based on a divine command. Imagine if someone visits the sick, helps the needy, or comforts mourners simply because God commanded him to do so. What type of religious personality would this create? In such a scenario, a person would be transforming subjects into objects by engaging in ethical behavior merely to score additional "mitzva points." Ironically, it is when we act ethically, based on a profound respect for our fellow man – and not based on a divine

25. *Or Same'aḥ*, Laws of Torah Study 1:2.
26. *Iggerot HaRe'aya* 1:89.
27. Bava Kamma 87a.

command – that we actually experience an authentic interaction with God and His ideals.

SUMMARY

The mitzva of walking in God's ways and clinging to Him serves as a perfect example of how studying halakha with an eye towards appreciating its underlying values presents a rich and holistic vision of Jewish law. In particular, this commandment provides us with opportunities to engage in a divine encounter even outside of formalized rituals. Reflecting on this mitzva allows us to:

- Appreciate the central role of righteousness and justice in the Jewish tradition (Seforno)
- Develop a reputation that is defined by divine virtues (*Sifrei*)
- Invest heavily in actions that help mold a more divinely-centered character (Talmud Sota)
- Appreciate the religious significance of choosing friends that help us develop a refined character (*Sifrei*, Rambam)
- Understand the role of non-intrinsically religious activities, such as humor, in developing a balanced and holistic Judaic worldview (Rav Soloveitchik, Rabbi Feldman)
- Ensure that our actions are value-based in fulfillment of the biblical ethic of following God's way (Leviticus Rabba)

Chapter 23

Loving God

Reason, Experience, and Shared Responsibility

While most halakhic regulations relate to actions that are clearly defined, Jewish law also places demands on certain emotional experiences that provide a framework for the entire enterprise of halakhic observance. For example, we are commanded to "love Hashem, your God, with all your heart, with all your soul, and with all your resources."[1]

The commandment to love God is so central to Jewish thought that Ibn Ezra describes it as the "root of all of the commandments."[2] Rabbi J.H. Hertz[3] provides historical perspective on the significance of this directive, noting that "this is the first instance in human history that the love of God was demanded by any religion." Moreover, "if the

---

1. Deut. 6:5.
2. Ibn Ezra, Exodus 31:18.
3. Rabbi Dr. J.H. Hertz, twentieth century, England.

unity of God is the basis of the Jewish creed, the love of God is to be the basis of Jewish life."[4]

Commandments that place demands on our hearts are difficult to categorize. What does "love" mean according to Jewish tradition? Is there a uniform way to love God, or are there different mediums for different people? By analyzing sources dealing with these questions, we shall come to understand the significance of this mitzva and the way in which it offers a spiritual context for the entire corpus of halakha.

RABBI TZADOK AND *SEFER HACHINUKH*: LOVE AS PROVIDING CONTEXT

Both Rabbi Tzadok HaKohen[5] and the *Sefer HaChinukh* point out that the requirement to love God is more expansive than most Jewish rituals. The majority of mitzvot are localized in their application. When a Jews observes Shabbat, it has little conceptual impact on their observance of *kashrut*, for example. Loving God, however, gives meaning to mitzvot as a whole. The *Sefer HaChinukh* articulates this point by noting that mitzvot can be performed properly *only* if an individual has a well-developed sense of love for the Commander-in-Chief Himself.[6] Loving God provides the proper context for mitzva observance by constantly reminding the us that Jewish rituals are not an arbitrary set of rules. Rather, they represent spiritual entry points, enabling us to connect with God.

Rabbi Tzadok expands on this approach and explains that while Jew is required to love God, the Torah, and the Jewish people, loving God is unique in that it is the *source* of the requirement for a Jew to love the Jewish people and God's Torah. Rabbi Tzadok maintains that, if a person loves the Torah without loving God, he runs the risk of loving the intellectual aspect of Torah learning while ignoring its divine source. The mitzva to love God contextualizes the experience of learning by highlighting the divine nature of the Torah's wisdom. Moreover, he argues, if a person loves the Jewish people without having a parallel

---

4. Rabbi Dr. J.H. Hertz, *The Pentateuch and Haftorahs: Hebrew Text English Translation and Commentary: Second Edition* (London: The Soncino Press, 1972), 770.
5. Rabbi Tzadok HaKohen of Lublin, nineteenth century, Poland.
6. *Sefer HaHinukh*, mitzva 418.

love for God, his love of the Jewish people may simply be an expression of love for companionship and fraternity, and not based on an awareness of the metaphysical uniqueness of the Jewish people.[7]

SIFREI/RAMBAM: LOVE AS A SOURCE OF RESPONSIBILITY

While Rabbi Tzadok and the *Sefer HaChinukh* focus on the love of God as the framework for mitzva observance, other sources provide more practical advice on fulfilling the mitzva of loving God. The *Sifrei*, for example, refers to Avraham as the paradigm of proper performance of the commandment to love God. According to the *Sifrei*, the mitzva of loving God requires us to actively enable *other* people to be positively affected by God and the Torah. The *Sifrei* describes Avraham as someone who converted people to a monotheistic way of life and brought them closer to God.[8]

The Rambam also expresses this idea, noting that the mitzva of loving God requires us to reach out to other people and demonstrate the power of a Jewish way of life. He argues that this requirement is a natural extension of the obligation to love God. After all, when a person loves something, he will naturally speak about it often and seek to share his passion with others. The Rambam claims that if we truly love God, we will "without a doubt" seek out non-believers and try to convince them of the truth that we holds so dear. Referencing the passage in the *Sifrei*, the Rambam says that Avraham's love for God was expressed by his outreach to others.[9]

This perspective challenges us to reflect on the nature of our love for God and the extent to which we feel a sense of obligation to reach out to others and share our Jewish passion with them.

This is particularly relevant in a framework in which we are interacting with Jews who lack exposure to the profundity of the traditional Jewish canon. We frequently become excited when our favorite sports team wins a big game or when a candidate we support is elected to a

---

7. *Tzidkat HaTzadik* 196.
8. *Sifrei*, Deuteronomy 32, s.v. *davar acher*.
9. *Book of Mitzvot*, positive commandment 3.

high office. The excitement we feel is often palpable to those around us, and we are usually eager to talk about these events with friends and colleagues. Do we experience the same excitement and passion for the world of Jewish learning and living? If so, to what extent are we eager to share our passion with other Jews whom we encounter? The mitzva to love God serves as a perpetual reminder to reflect on the extent of our passion for our Jewish commitments.

TALMUD: LOVE BY EXAMPLE

The Talmud offers another suggestion for contemplating practical mediums to affirm our love for God.[10] Similar to the approach of the *Sifrei*, the Talmud suggests that the observant Jew's love of God should result in others being attracted to a Torah-based way of life. However, unlike the *Sifrei*, which requires a person who truly loves God to actively reach out to others, the Talmud sees the outreach component as a natural extension of proper behavior performed by observant Jews. The Talmud cites a *beraita* which states:

> You shall love Hashem your God: [Which can be interpreted as commanding] that the name of Heaven become beloved through you. [This means] that one should read [Scripture], learn [Mishna], and serve Torah scholars, and his dealings with people should be [conducted] in a pleasant manner. What do people say about him? Fortunate is his teacher who taught him Torah! Woe unto those who do not learn Torah! This person who is learning Torah – see how pleasant are his ways, how refined are his deeds!

Thus the biblical requirement to love God requires each person to see himself as a vehicle to demonstrate how a life of commitment to Torah is associated with ethical and moral perfection. When we truly love God, we recognize that Jewish law aims to shape our collective character by infusing it with God-conscious. This heightened awareness generates added responsibility and obligates us to act in a way that is fitting for someone who represents God Himself. Once ritual observance is automatically

---

10. Yoma 86a.

associated with people who act with impeccable ethics, God and His laws become "beloved" even to those who are not ritually observant.

According to this approach, the perpetual obligation to love God obligates Jews who are committed to halakhic observance to constantly reflect on how their behavior is perceived by others. Aside from the broader moral imperative to act in an ethically refined manner, the mitzva to love God reminds us that, as practitioners of Jewish law, we are the representatives of God's word in the world. Therefore, we have an added responsibility to ensure that our behavior also meets the standard demanded by God Himself.

RAMBAM AND *SIFREI*: LOVE BASED ON INTELLECTUAL REFLECTION

An alternative suggestion of the Rambam focuses on the intellect as the instrument to facilitate love of Hashem. The Rambam refers to this intellectually based experience of love in the Laws of Repentance:

> One can only love God [as an outgrowth] of the knowledge with which he knows Him. The nature of one's love depends on the nature of one's knowledge. A small [amount of knowledge arouses] a lesser love. A greater amount of knowledge arouses a greater love.[11]

This approach assumes that philosophical reflection will allow us to gain a more profound understanding of God's essence, and that this more developed intellectual perspective will then activate feelings of love. While Maimonidean scholars debate the parameters of the Rambam's position, it is clear that the Rambam's model underscores the role that the mind plays in facilitating emotional experiences. Just we love our spouses the more we get to know them, so too our love of God is affected by the extent to which we understand Him.

The intellectual love of God may also be based on contemplation of God's commandments. The *Sifrei* for example, claims that Torah study

---

11. Laws of Repentance 10:6, translated at http://www.chabad.org/dailystudy/rambam. asp?tdate=5/9/2036&rambamChapters=3.

and a more sophisticated understanding of God's mitzvot provide the most effective means to fulfill the directive of loving God.[12] The Rambam in the *Book of Mitzvot* also advocates this position, bidding us to "meditate upon and closely examine His mitzvot, His commandments." [13]

In the same passage, the Rambam also states that the contemplation of God's *works* is part of the foundation for an intellectual love of God.[14] He also states this in his great code, *Mishne Torah:*

> When a person contemplates His wondrous and great deeds and creations and appreciates His infinite wisdom that surpasses all comparison, he will immediately love, praise, and glorify Him, yearning with tremendous desire to know His great name.[15]

By articulating the values that underlie the observance of mitzvot, we emphasize the eternal ideals that represent God's unchanging will. By focusing on God's works and deeds, we develop a sense of God's involvement with humanity and gain some degree of perspective on God's unique relationship with the Jewish people. While studying the mitzvot allows us to reflect on divine values, intellectual reflection on God's role in history underscores his care and compassion for humanity. Both of these channels can help us to cultivate the love of God.

TALMUD: LOVE BASED ON SELF-SACRIFICE

In the Talmud, the discussion is expanded beyond the intellectual realm and hones in on the role of sacrifice in developing a refined love for God. Any healthy relationship involves some degree of give and take. One way of affirming love is by demonstrating willingness to sacrifice something for the person or object that one loves. Advocating this approach, the Talmud cites a *beraita,* which states:

---

12. *Sifrei,* Deuteronomy 33, s.v. *vehayu.*
13. *Book of Mitzvot,* positive commandment 3, translated at http://www.chabad.org/library/article_cdo/aid/940228/jewish/Positive-Commandment-3.htm.
14. Ibid.
15. Laws of the Foundations of the Torah 2:2, translated at http://www.chabad.org/library/article_cdo/aid/904962/jewish/Yesodei-haTorah-Chapter-Two.htm.

R. Eliezer said: If it is stated, "with all your soul," why [was it necessary] to state, "with all your resources?" and if it stated, "with all your resources," why [was it necessary] to state, "with all your soul?" Rather, [the reason for this is so that] if you have a person whose body is more precious to him than his money, for this [person], it was said, "with all your soul," [so that he should be prepared to give up for the love of God, i.e., to avoid idolatry, that which is most precious to him]. And if you have a person whose money is more precious to him than his body, then for this [person], it was said, "with all your resources" [so that he, too, will be prepared to give up for the love of God that which is most precious to him]. R. Akiva says, "With all your soul." [This teaches that you should love Him] even if He takes your soul.[16]

This passage underscores both the physical and economic burdens that a life committed to ritual observance can be. At the same time, it shifts the dialogue away from the language of burden towards that of opportunity. Committing our monetary resources to God allows us to affirm our profound love for God and His mitzvot. Moreover, the halakhic requirement to give up one's life to avoid certain halakhic violations highlights our love for God's ultimate virtues. By stressing the role of sacrifice in affirming our love for God, the Talmud reminds us that our economic and personal priorities are good indications of where our love truly resides.

LOVE AND EXPERIENCE

Thus far, we have attempted to provide philosophical and practical guidance for the best way to fulfill the mitzva of loving God. The Rambam goes further, delineating the extent of the biblical requirement. According to the Rambam, the mitzva to love God is not a one-time exercise; rather, loving God is about maintaining the love of God as a perpetual state: "A person should love God with a very great and exceeding love,

16. Berakhot 61b.

until his soul is bound up in the love of God. Thus, he will always be obsessed with this love as if he is lovesick."[17]

This directive can seem overwhelming and almost impossible to ever fully observe, as it demands a constant state of love with God. *Netivot Shalom*[18] quotes from the Baal Shem Tov,[19] whose approach provides another way to think about the contours of the requirement to love God. According to this interpretation, the mitzva of loving God obligates a Jew to constantly contemplate ways to activate this love. Loving God is thus the natural consequence of a religious orientation that regularly attempts to awaken feelings of love for God.[20] In this model, we are not required to be in a perpetual state of love. Rather, our responsibility is to constantly engage in activities that will facilitate this emotional state.

This broadening of the conversation requires us to constantly think about effective ways to activate experiences of divine love. For some, this may be achieved by studying a complex passage from the Talmud or from the world of Jewish philosophy. Others may take a more experiential approach and seek to actualize the emotion of love by going on a hike in nature or spending extensive quality time with their families. Whatever way we choose, this perspective reminds us that God's presence can always be found wherever His transcendent values are manifest. Traditional Judaism asks us to appreciate the endless opportunities for divine encounters and to utilize them as occasions for fulfilling the mitzva of loving God.

SUMMARY

The variety of source material focusing on the topic of loving God highlights the complex nature of defining the exact parameters of this mitzva. The varied perspectives provide different approaches to incorporate profound love of God into our daily religious lives. Reflecting on values highlighted by these sources allows us to:

---

17. Laws of Repentance 10:3, translated at http://www.chabad.org/library/article_cdo/aid/911914/jewish/Teshuvah-Chapter-Ten.htm.
18. Rabbi Shalom Noah Berezovsky, twentiety century, Eastern Europe/Israel.
19. Rabbi Israel b. Eliezer, eighteenth century, Eastern Europe.
20. *Netivot Shalom*, Va'etchanan, 33.

- Realize that loving God is the source of our mitzva observance (Ibn Ezra)
- Understand the historical uniqueness of the Jewish obligation to love God (Rabbi Hertz)
- Recognize how loving God contextualizes our love for Torah and the Jewish people (Rabbi Tzadok HaKohen)
- Reflect on our own love of God and our responsibility to share our love with others (*Sifrei*, Rambam)
- Think about our ethical behavior and contemplate whether or not our conduct inculcates a larger love for God and the Torah in others (Talmud)
- Appreciate the mystery of the universe and view philosophy, metaphysics, and study of natural sciences as means of knowing God and cultivating feelings of love (Rambam)
- Utilize the divine values that underlie the mitzvot and God's unique providential role as springboards to activate feelings of love (*Sifrei*, Rambam)
- Understand the role of sacrifice in developing a profound love of God (Talmud)
- Constantly seek ways to activate latent feelings of love (Baal Shem Tov)

Chapter 24

The Mezuza

Jewish Theology and the
Promise of Longevity

The mitzva of mezuza is meant to remind us to observe Jewish law with an awareness of its broader religious agenda. During the course of a day, however, we may walk past a mezuza numerous times as we go in and out of the home or walk from room to room, and we easily become desensitized to the spiritual goals of the mezuza.

Routine observance of the mitzva of mezuza has the potential to compromise its entire purpose. As the *Chizkuni*[1] notes, according to the Torah, we should be inspired by the religious messages of the mezuza each time we leave and enter a room.[2] The mezuza is intended to provide a religious framework to our daily experience by reminding us that all of our actions should be devoted to Torah ideals.

Beyond this more general goal of providing spiritual context, what specific religious messages does the mezuza teach us? Reflecting on sources

---

1. Rabbi Hezekia b. Manoch, thirteenth century, France.
2. *Chizkuni*, Deuteronomy 6:9.

that address the religious vision of the mitzva of mezuza will help facilitate a more mindful observance of this mitzva. In addition, understanding the eternal values represented by the mezuza will help neutralize any risk that the mezuza will become a mindless and rote part of our daily routine.

DIVINITY CAN BE FOUND ANYWHERE

A mezuza is a piece of parchment placed on the right side of the doorpost. Written on the mezuza are two sets of verses from the book of Deuteronomy. The first set is from Deuteronomy chapter 6 (verses 4-9), and the primary topic is the acceptance of divine sovereignty. These verses are also contained in the boxes of tefillin, and they are recited as part of the *Shema*, and they focus on the idea that the values of the Torah are intended to permeate every aspect of our lives, "when you sit in your home and when you are travelling on the way; when you lie down and when you rise."[3] The second group of verses, from Deuteronomy chapter 11 (verses 13-21), is also found in the tefillin and as part of the *Shema*, and it has to do with central concepts of Jewish theology, such as the importance of ritual observance and the rewards and punishments that are associated with a life of commitment.

Why were these specific sets of verses chosen to be placed in the mezuza? Beyond the fact that the commandment to affix a mezuza on one's doorpost is found in the passages,[4] Rabbi Bachya argues that these verses highlight fundamental themes of Jewish theology. By glancing at the mezuza and reflecting on the passages it contains, we are encouraged to think about the importance of Torah study, God's oneness, and the Exodus from Egypt. The mezuza thus serves as a daily reminder of Judaism's larger theologic agenda.[5]

Beyond its focus on central concepts of Jewish thought, the mezuza's unique religious message can be better appreciated when we understand the Torah's directive in contrast to ancient Egyptian practices. As Dr. Jeffrey Tigay notes, ancient Egyptians had the practice of "writing instructions at the entrance of temples, enumerating moral and cultic prerequisites for entering the temple." This custom was limited

---

3. Deut. 6:7.
4. See *Beit Yosef*, Yoreh Deah 285:1.
5. Deut. 6:9.

specifically to Egyptian temples. The Torah "differs in that it is not stating prerequisites for entering the sanctuary, but seeking to make people aware of God's instructions at all times and places."[6] This is a critical distinction and highlights why these specific verses from Deuteronomy were chosen. The religious vision of the Torah requires its ideals to be manifest in every area of our lives. Religious life is by no means limited to the synagogue.

The verses from Deuteronomy remind us of God's all-encompassing spiritual agenda. Every time we walk past a mezuza, we should be reminded of this message, and our behavior should be directly affected as a resut. Placing the mezuza on the doorpost of our homes reminds us that our private lives need to be guided by the values that the mezuza represents.

Moreover, in Israel, where mezuzot are placed in public buildings (albeit without the accompanying blessing), the public domain is religiously contextualized by the spiritual messages of the mezuza. As a result, we are reminded that God's word has a say in every area of our lives and we should seek its guidance "when we sit in our homes and when we travel on the way; when we lie down and when we rise."

GOD IS THE SOURCE OF ALL POWER

Beyond the sets of verses that we are required to write on the parchment of the mezuza, the Rambam notes a custom to write the letters "*shin*," "*daled*," and "*yud*," spelling God's name, on the outside of the parchment.[7] The Rambam writes that there is no legal problem with adding these letters (beyond what the Torah legislated), since the writing of God's name is on the outside of the parchment, separated from the required verses from Deuteronomy. This practice is codified as well by the *Shulchan Arukh*.[8]

Dr. Martin Gordon provides some interesting background information that may help explain the rationale behind this practice. He notes:

---

6. Jefferey Tigay, *The JPS Torah Commentary: Deuteronomy* (Phidelphia/New York: The Jewish Publication Society, 1996), 444.
7. Rambam, Laws of Tefillin, Mezuzot, and Torah Scrolls 5:4.
8. *Shulchan Arukh*, Yoreh Deah 288:15.

> Among the ancients, divine names were considered a source of supernatural power, which, if activated by the skilled magical practitioner, could control and coerce even the gods themselves, and were thought to be reliant for their strength on these secret name formulae.[9]

The Torah fundamentally rejects this conception of divine names having independent power. Instead, "God Himself is the exclusive source of all power, and His name(s) is in no way possessed of independent potency." What, then, is the purpose of the divine names according to the Torah? As Dr. Gordon writes, "Divine names merely designate God and serve to convey to the worshiper a sense of His closeness."[10]

In light of these observations, the practice of writing God's name on the outside of a mezuza serves a specific religious function. Contemporary observance of mezuza involves rolling up the parchment and placing it in a protective cover before affixing it to the doorpost. While we do not see the actual texts from the book of Deuteronomy written on the parchment, God's name, "Sha-dai," by contrast, can usually be seen by anyone who walks and glances at the mezuza. When we look at God's name, we are supposed to be reminded of God's nearness and the unique opportunities that we have to experience divine intimacy throughout the day. Moreover, beyond providing a sense of religious closeness, the mezuza also reminds us about Judaism's unique theological worldview. Judaism's commitment to monotheism affirms the principle that God's might and power are His alone and cannot be manipulated by appeals to magic and witchcraft.

Moreover, as the second set of verses from Deuteronomy placed in the mezuza attest, God's power has a practical effect on our daily affairs, as we are rewarded or punished based on our adherence to His laws. Rabbi Bachya substantiates this claim, noting the beliefs of other religions that the material success that one experiences in the home is a function of manipulation of the stars.[11] Judaism, by contrast, affirms the

---

9. Dr. Martin Gordon, "Mezuza: Protective Amulet or Religious Symbol," *Tradition* 16:4 (Summer 1977), 10.
10. Ibid.
11. Deut. 6:9.

idea that God is the sole source of all blessing. By placing God's name on the outside of the mezuza, we uphold our commitment to Judaism's unique theological message.

This custom is particularly significant because it links the practical observance of the mitzva of mezuza with Judaism's larger theological vision. God demands specific behavioral patterns, and these rituals are applications of broader divine values. However, in addition to the spiritual significance of the mitzvot themselves, Judaism has a profoundly distinct theological vision, and the mitzvot also serve as a practical medium to affirm our commitment to Judaism's unique worldview.

MEZUZA AND THE CENTRALITY
OF THE LAND OF ISRAEL

In addition to the religious messages imbedded in the texts found inside and outside of the mezuza, many of the laws related to mezuza speak to the larger virtues that the mitzva represents. For example, the Talmud notes that there are halakhic differences with regard to the obligation to place a mezuza on a house that one is renting, depending on whether the house in question is located inside or outside the Land of Israel:

> One who… rents a house outside of the land [of Israel] is exempt from [affixing] a mezuza [to the doorpost for] a full thirty days. From then on, he is obligated. However, one who rents a house in the Land of Israel must [affix] a mezuza immediately, on account of [the mitzva of] settling the Land of Israel.[12]

This talmudic distinction is codified by the *Shulchan Arukh*.[13]

On the surface, it is difficult to understand the logic of the talmudic position. In contrast to the mitzva of the seven-year sabbatical cycle, for example, mezuza is not inherently connected to the Land of Israel. Why does the halakha seem to indicate otherwise? Rashi addresses this question by citing a talmudic position that forbids us from ever removing the mezuzot from our doorposts, once they have

---

12. Menahot 44a.
13. *Shulchan Arukh*, YD 286:22.

been affixed.[14] In requiring us to place mezuzot in our homes in Israel immediately upon the start of the rental agreement, the rabbis made it less likely that we would move out of the house in the Land of Israel, since leaving our homes would mean losing all the mezuzot affixed to the doorposts of the house, a considerable financial loss. Moreover, even if a renter decides to leave, it will be easier for the landlord to find a new occupant, since the new renter will benefit from a home that already has mezuzot.[15]

Rabbi Avraham Yitzhak HaKohen Kook offers another explanation of the talmudic distinction between rentals inside and outside the Land of Israel. According to many halakhic authorities, the mitzva of mezuza is activated only when we live in a home with a sense of permanence.[16] Until thirty days have passed, a renter is still assumed to be a temporary dweller. However, Rav Kook explains, this is true only during the first thirty days in a rental *outside* the Land of Israel. The act of dwelling in the Land of Israel – even for a short time – represents the fulfillment of the biblical precept to settle the land. The ideal place for a Jew to live is in the Land of Israel. As a result, Jewish law considers even a temporary rented apartment in the land to be a permanent dwelling, and this is reflected in the requirement to place mezuzot immediately on the doorpost of a rented home in the Land of Israel.[17]

The intimate connection between mezuza and the Land of Israel is implied in the biblical verses found in the mezuza as well. In the Torah, the verse immediately following the commandment to affix mezuzot to the doorposts of our homes, notes that commitment to this law will allow "your days and the days of your children [to endure] *in the land* that the Lord swore to your fathers."[18] As Rashi notes, ritual observance of halakha is qualitatively different in the Land of Israel.[19] The mezuza reminds us that, while living a vibrant Jewish life in the Diaspora is certainly possible, our ideal place to dwell is in the Land of Israel. Ultimately,

---

14. Bava Metzia 102a.
15. Rashi, Menaḥot 44a, s.v *mishum yishuv.*
16. See for example, the ruling of Rabbi Mordecai Yoffe, *Levush*, Yoreh Deah 286:22.
17. Responsa *Daʾat Kohen* 179.
18. Deut. 11:21.
19. Rashi, Deuteronomy 11:18.

we strive to actualize the values that the mezuza represents as a nation in our homeland.

MEZUZA AND LONGEVITY

In addition to emphasizing the connection between the mitzva of mezuza and the Land of Israel, the verses from Deuteronomy also underscore the link between observance of this mitzva and the blessing of a long life. In fact, the *Shulchan Arukh* opens the discussion concerning the laws of mezuza by stating that those who observe this precept properly will be blessed (along with their children) with long life. By contrast, people who neglect to perform this mitzva properly will have shortened lives.[20] This statement of the *Shulchan Arukh* is rooted in a passage in the Talmud that notes the juxtaposition of the biblical verse legislating the mitzva of mezuza (Deuteronomy 11:20) with a passage promising a long life for an individual and his children (Deuteronomy 11:21).[21]

As a classical code of Jewish law, the *Shulchan Arukh* rarely cites homiletic interpretations of the law without also stating legal consequences. What, then, are the legal implications of the *Shulchan Arukh*'s statement? Interestingly, the fact that observance of the mezuza precept is linked to the promise of long life is cited by classical legal interpreters to explain various *halakhot* related to the mitzva of mezuza itself. For example, the *Shulchan Arukh* rules that women are equally obligated in observing the mitzva of mezuza.[22] In general, Jewish law exempts women from positive commandments that are bound to a specific time frame. Thus, women are formally exempt from shaking a lulav, wearing tefillin, and sitting in the sukka. The *Shakh*[23] explains that since the obligation to affix a mezuza to our doorposts transcends any time restrictions, women are equally obligated to perform this mitzva. However, the *Shakh* adds another explanation as well. He notes that the Torah promises a long life to anyone who punctiliously observes the precept of mezuza, and since women desire and deserve a prolonged physical

---

20. *Shulchan Arukh*, Yoreh Deah 285:1.
21. Shabbat 32b.
22. *Shulchan Arukh*, Yoreh Deah 291:3.
23. Rabbi Shabbetai b. Meir HaKohen, seventeenth century, Lithuania.

existence to the same degree as men, the Torah's promise of a long life cannot distinguish between different genders. Therefore, the mitzva of mezuza (which is one means by which one achieves long life) must be applicable to women as well.[24]

The *Taz* uses this biblical linkage of the mezuza to the promise of longevity to explain another detail of the laws concerning the mezuza. According to the *Shulchan Arukh*, two people sharing a home are obligated to affix a mezuza to the doorposts of their house.[25] However, the *Rema* adds the important qualification that this rule is applicable only if the people in question are both Jews.[26] A Jew who shares a home with a gentile, is exempt from the mitzva of mezuza. The *Shakh* offers an explanation for this rule, explaining that the Torah obligation to affix a mezuza is intended only for homes that are owned by Jews, and since part of the house, in this case, is owned by a non-Jew, there is no obligation to place a mezuza on the doorpost.[27] However, the *Taz* suggests a different explanation. He notes that the requirement for two people living in a home to affix a mezuza is derived from the fact that the verse promising a long life for the fulfillment of the mezuza precept is written in the plural. The promise made by the Torah is dependent on observance of the law and is limited to the Jewish people, whom God obligated to follow his statutes. Gentiles, by contrast, are not obligated to place mezuzot on their doorposts, and the promise of longevity, in this context, is therefore not relevant to them. Since the precept of mezuza is so intimately connected to the promise of longevity, the obligation is activated only when all the people living in the house in question share this unique metaphysical assurance. As a result, a Jew sharing a home with a non-Jew is exempt from the mitzva of mezuza.[28]

These rulings highlight mezuza's significance as an example of a law whose theological underpinnings actually affect the details of the law itself. Reflecting on this aspect of the mitzva of mezuza reminds us

---

24. *Shakh*, Yoreh Deah 291:4.
25. *Shulchan Arukh*, Yoreh Deah 286:1.
26. Ibid.
27. *Shakh*, Yoreh Deah 286:6.
28. *Taz*, Yoreh Deah 286:2.

of the interplay between our observance of God's word and the larger promises made by the Bible as a reward for proper observance.

SUMMARY

Given the frequency with which we encounter the mitzva of mezuza during our day, it is particularly critical to have a thorough understanding of the spiritual goals and ideals underlying this mitzva. By requiring us to affix mezuzot to our doorposts, the Torah gives us the privilege of meditating and reflecting on its eternal values every time we enter or leave a room in our home. In particular, the mitzva of mezuza compels us to:

- Reflect on central claims of Jewish theology, such as the importance of Torah study, God's oneness, and the Exodus from Egypt (Rabbi Bachya)
- Ensure that our behavior is influenced by the values and ideals that mezuza symbolizes (Chizkuni)
- Appreciate the Torah's claim that God's statutes are equally applicable in the home and in the synagogue (Dr. Tigay)
- Affirm our commitment to the idea that God is the source of all power, and, ultimately, the material blessings that we receive are from Him (Dr. Gordon, Rabbi Bachya)
- Be aware of the legal consequences of the centrality of the Land of Israel in Jewish thought (Talmud, Rashi, Rav Kook)
- Reflect on the connection between the mitzva of mezuza and the Torah's promise of longevity for those who observe this precept (*Shulchan Arukh, Shakh, Taz*)

Chapter 25

The Bedtime Shema

Transitioning from One Day to the Next

T he journey of the halakhic day ends with the arrival of bedtime. As demonstrated throughout this book, Jewish law encompasses much more than merely a list of prescribed rituals that we are commanded to observe. Understanding the eternal ideals that underlie the halakhot that we practice allows us to be profoundly transformed by the wisdom of Jewish law. However, since consciousness and awareness are such critical components of any authentic religious experience of halakha, the act of sleep poses a particular challenge. What is the attitude of Jewish law towards the act of sleeping? Is there some prayer or ritual that can transform the unconsciousness of sleep into a "Jewish" sleep experience?

Jewish law requires us to recite the *Shema* with an accompanying blessing right before going to bed. This obligation is particularly mysterious, since we are required to say *Shema* in *Maariv,* the evening prayer service, thus rendering the bedtime *Shema* seemingly superfluous. What is the rationale behind this ritual? Moreover, what religious statement is evidenced by the halakhic requirement that the recital of the *Shema* be the final ritual of the day? Exploring sources that deal with these questions will help us understand the spiritual messages that underlie this practice. It will also provide an opportunity to reflect on the essential religious message that we get from Jewish law to carry us into our next day.

THE BEDTIME *SHEMA* AS A SPIRITUAL REFLECTION

The primary source of the obligation to recite *Shema* before going to bed is a passage in Tractate Berakhot. Quoting the view of R. Shimon ben Levi, the Talmud states that even though we have already recited the *Shema* during evening prayers in the synagogue, we must nonetheless recite the *Shema* again before going to bed.[1] Seeking scriptural support for this position, the arbiters of the Talmud quote a verse from Psalms that states: "Tremble and sin not; reflect in your hearts [while] on your beds, and be utterly silent [Selah]."[2] Rabbi Samson Raphael Hirsch explains that the verse requires us, when in bed, to reflect on "God's ever-present omnipotence and greatness." Moreover, we are required to think about "how insignificant mortal man really is."[3]

As *Metzudat David*[4] notes, the moments before going to bed is a particularly reflective time.[5] The busy day has ended and we have quiet time to think about what we accomplished during the past day and what we hope to accomplish throughout the upcoming day. This model seems to view the *Shema* as a type of spiritual evaluation. After all, the first paragraph of the *Shema* highlights our obligation to affirm our commitment to Torah study in all facets of our lives. We are commanded to speak words of Torah "when you sit at home, and when you travel on the way; when you lie down, and when you rise."[6] The basic message of this paragraph is to ensure that all of our daily activities are infused with the values of the Torah. Reciting these verses places our life in context and reminds us of the transcendent ideals that highlight what life is truly about.

---

1. Berakhot 4b-5a.
2. Ps. 4:5.
3. Rabbi Samson Raphael Hirsch, *The Psalms: Translation and Commentary by Rabbi Samson Raphael Hirsch* (Jerusalem/New York: Feldheim Publishers, 1978), 22.
4. Rabbi David Altschuler, seventeenth/eighteenth centuries, Eastern Europe.
5. *Metzudat David*, Psalms 4:5.
6. Deut. 6:7.

BEDTIME *SHEMA* AND PROPER RELIGIOUS THOUGHT

The Talmud Yerushalmi makes an interesting observation that adds another layer to the conversation. According to the Yerushalmi, R. Ze'ira had the practice of reciting *Shema* multiple times before bed, until he was physically overcome by sleep.[7] Based on this custom, *Haggahot Maimoniyyot*[8] argues that *Shema* must be the last prayer that we recite before bed.[9] Along these same lines, the *Rema* adds that we should not eat or drink after the recitation of the *Shema*.[10]

What is the significance of these rulings, and how do they affect the larger religious message of the bedtime *Shema*? Another passage in Berakhot states that anyone who recites *Shema* before bed is considered "as though he holds a double-edged sword in his hand," which protects him from evil spirits.[11] While the interpretative history of demons in rabbinic literature is quite complex, the Meiri provides a more rational approach that may have particular appeal to the modern ear.[12] The Meiri argues that these negative spirits are actually foreign thoughts that can enter our heads when we have extended time to think by ourselves. When the mind wanders, it is theoretically possible for us to think about anything, including religiously problematic ideas. Saying *Shema* before bed with proper intention protects us from these invasive thoughts, since it focuses our minds on the ideals of the *Shema*, which then leads to more value-oriented thoughts when trying to go to sleep.

This suggestion is supported by another passage in the Talmud in which R. Nachman claims that a Torah scholar is not required to recite the bedtime *Shema*.[13] The Maharsha explains that the Torah this scholar has learned during the day has the power to protect him, presumably because he will be continuously reviewing the material in his head while going to sleep.[14]

---

7. Cited in *Haggahot Maimoniyot*, Laws of Prayer and the Priests' Blessing 7:3.
8. Rabbi Meir b. R. Yekutiel HaKohen, thirteenth century, Europe.
9. *Haggahot Maimoniyot*, Laws of Prayer and the Priests' Blessing 7:3.
10. *Rema*, Orach Chayim 239:1.
11. Berakhot 5a and Rashi, s.v. *ki'ilu*.
12. Meiri, Berakhot 4b.
13. Berakhot 5a.
14. Maharsha, *Chiddushei Aggadot* 5a, s.v. *af*; see also Rashi, Berakhot 5a, s.v. *ve'im talmid chakham*.

This view challenges us to think about the thoughts that occupy our minds when we have extended time to ourselves. It is likely that the thoughts that enter our heads are indications of our innermost commitments and priorities. By reciting the *Shema* before going to bed, we contextualize our sleep experience by reminding ourselves that as much as our actions are formally governed by halakha, Jewish law expects our thoughts to reflect Torah values as well.

BEDTIME *SHEMA*: A REAFFIRMATION OF JEWISH THEOLOGY

A third perspective on the bedtime *Shema* is quoted by the *Kolbo*, who cites an opinion that the recitation of the *Shema* before sleep is a formal re-acceptance of the yoke of heaven and a reaffirmation of divine sovereignty.[15] This view seems to be supported by the position of Rabbi Chananel.[16] While most authorities assume that we are required to recite only the first paragraph of the *Shema* before bed,[17] Rabbi Chananel maintains that the second paragraph must be recited as well. Rabbi Eliyahu Lipschitz[18] notes that the second paragraph of the *Shema* comprises the theme of commitment to a life of mitzvot. Since the goal of reciting *Shema* before bed (according to Rabbi Chananel), is a re-acceptance of divine sovereignty, it is crucial not only that we acknowledge God's oneness in the abstract, but also that we recite the second paragraph of the *Shema* to reaffirm our belief that God's authority fosters daily religious obligations.[19]

According to this approach, the goal of the bedtime *Shema* seems very similar to some of the spiritual goals that we accomplish when we recite *Shema* during the evening service. However, this apparent redundancy is not accidental. Given the centrality of these themes in traditional Jewish thought, it is not surprising that Jewish law would have us affirm these concepts as the last line that we recite before going to bed.

---

15. *Kolbo*, siman 29.
16. Rabbi Chananel, tenth century, Italy, cited in Rosh, Berakhot 9:23.
17. See *Shulchan Arukh*, OH 239:1.
18. Twenty-first century, Israel.
19. Rabbi Eliyahu Lipschitz, Sugya 22: Kriyat Shema al Hamita, http://www.toralishma. org/wp-content/uploads/2014/01/כב-הראיה-ברכות.pdf.

BIRKAT HAMAPPIL: PLACING SLEEP IN CONTEXT

Besides the recitation of the *Shema*, the Talmud also requires the recitation of a long blessing before going to bed.[20] The text of this blessing[21] is as follows:

> Blessed [are you Hashem our God, King of the universe] who casts the bonds of sleep upon my eyes and slumber upon my eyelids and who illuminates the pupils of the eye. May it be Your will, Hashem my God that You lay me down to sleep toward peace and grant me my share in Your Torah and accustom me [to submit] to the authority of [Your] commandments, but do not accustom me [to submit] to the authority of a transgression. Do not bring me into the grasp of an error or into the grasp of a sin, or into the grasp of a challenge, or into the grasp of scorn. Let the good inclination dominate me, but let not the evil inclination dominate me. Rescue me from an evil mishap and from terrible diseases. May I not be confounded by bad dreams or bad notions. May my offspring be perfect before You and may You illuminate my eyes lest I die in sleep. Blessed are You Hashem, who illuminates the entire world with His glory.

This long blessing is thematically quite complex and touches upon some of the most central aspects of Jewish theology. One of the most striking aspects of the prayer is the line in which we beseech God and ask Him to "lay me down to sleep toward peace and grant me my share in Your Torah." This request is particularly mysterious, as the act of Torah study requires total focus of the mind, which is impossible to accomplish while in a state of sleep. In general, Jewish law requires us to be proactive and fill our days with meaningful activities that both better us as human beings, as well as the world as a whole. Wasting time is a concept that is antithetical to traditional Judaism. The term "*bittul Torah*," used regularly

---

20. Berakhot 60b.
21. Some traditional prayer books do contain this specific formulation while others utilize a shortened version. For example, see *The Koren Siddur: Edited by Rabbi David Fuchs, Nusach Sepharad* (Jerusalem: Koren, 2010), 166, where this text is used.

in yeshiva parlance, assumes that all actions must be evaluated in light of their potential enhancement of, or detraction from, the Torah's larger vision. On the surface, sleep seems to be a curious activity to fit into a model that demands constant striving for betterment. After all, how are we bettering the world when we sleep? Moreover, excessive sleep can fall into the category of *"bittul Torah,"* turning an essential human experience into a potentially religiously problematic activity.

The *Tzelach*[22] addresses this question, explaining that this part of the blessing serves to affirm the fact that our sleeping is not an attempt to shirk our responsibilities. We ask God to "grant me my share in Your Torah" even while we sleep, since proper sleep is critical for physical and mental health. Having a healthy body and mind are essential elements enabling us to make our contribution to the world of Torah.[23]

The position of the *Tzelach* reminds us that halakha's vision is so all-encompassing that even our sleep should be rooted in a larger divine context. Reciting the *Shema* before bed ensures that our bedtime thoughts are Torah thoughts. The *HaMappil* blessing reminds us that sleep itself is a profound opportunity to properly take care of our bodies and ensure that we are fully energized to begin the next day with the requisite vigor and excitement to implement the values of Jewish law during our day.

SUMMARY

The bedtime *Shema* marks the end of our halakhic day. Assuming we sleep throughout the entire night, the *Shema* and its accompanying blessing are the last mitzva that accompany us into the next day. Reflecting on the ideals that underlie this mitzva allows us the unique opportunity to:

- Evaluate our accomplishments during the past day and examine the extent to which our actions reflected the values of the Torah (*Metzudat David*)

---

22. Rabbi Yehezkel b. Yehuda Landau, eighteenth century, Poland.
23. *Tzelah*, Berakhot 60b.

- Ensure that the thoughts we have while preparing for bed are consistent with the Torah's ideas and ideals (Yerushalmi, Meiri)
- Reaffirm our commitment to the acceptance of divine sovereignty as well as a life committed to Jewish law (*Kolbo*, Rabbi Chananel)
- Ensure that we regard sleeping as a religiously meaningful attempt to strengthen our bodies to allow maximal fulfillment of God's law (Talmud, *Tzelach*)

Chapter 26

Concluding Thoughts and Daily Meditations

This book attempts to articulate the transcendent religious messages that underlie many of the mitzvot that we encounter in a day committed to halakha. Although punctiliously observing the detailed prescriptions of the law is a central focus of halakhic observance, halakha is also intended to inspire religious development through awareness of the values inculcated by Jewish law. Rabbi Yehuda Amital captures this sentiment by noting that "Mitzvot need to be performed physically, but that does not mean that they should be performed mechanically."[1] In order to facilitate a more concrete awareness of messages discussed in this book, below are daily meditations that will hopefully inspire a more focused and mindful observance of halakha.

---

1. Rabbi Yehuda Amital, *Ya'akov Was Reciting the Shema*, adapted by Dov Karoll, http://etzion.org.il/en/yaakov-was-reciting-shema.

REFLECTIONS WHILE RECITING *MODEH ANI*:

- Have I fully internalized the meaning of central Jewish beliefs, such as the belief in God's ultimate redemption and resurrection of the dead? (Talmud, Lamentations Rabba)
- Do I appreciate God's hand in facilitating the miracle of waking up each morning? (Rabbi Sacks, *Mishna Berura*)
- Have I cultivated an appreciation for each day as its own unit of time? (Rabbi Nagen)
- Do I view each day as a unique opportunity to actualize my personal religious mission? (Rav Soloveitchik)
- Am I able to develop a heightened consciousness and appreciate the power of the moment? (Rabbi Nagen)
- Do I feel emotionally connected to God in a way that transcends philosophical inquiry? (Rabbi Schneerson)

REFLECTIONS WHILE WASHING HANDS IN THE MORNING:

- Do I fully appreciate the importance of proper preparation before engaging in sacred acts? (Biblical account of the priest washing his hands daily)
- Have I internalized the need to spiritually reflect every day and not be content with yesterday's spiritual accomplishments? (Rabbi Nagen's understanding of the priestly washing)
- Do I fully understand the religious and spiritual challenges of compromised consciousness? (Zohar with the explanation of Rabbi Melamed)
- Am I able to affirm my commitment to the Abrahamic covenant? (Ramban)
- Do I view my ten fingers as tools to transform the world, paralleling the ten *Sefirot*, through which God engages the world of the cosmos? (*Sefer Yetzira*)
- Am I prepared to accept divine sovereignty through daily prayer? (Rosh)
- Do I fully understand the importance of spiritual cleansing before encountering the Divine? (Malbim)

- Did I fully express my thanks to God upon waking up anew? (Rashba)
- Have I fully internalized the responsibilities of the Jewish people as a nation of priests? (Rashba)

REFLECTIONS WHILE DONNING THE *KIPPA*:

- Have I reflected on the ethic of humility by being reminded that God rests "above" me? (Malbim, Talmud Shabbat, Kiddushin)
- Have I meditated on what it means to fear God? (Talmud Shabbat)
- Does wearing a *kippa* help me avoid issues of arrogance and entitlement? (Maharal)
- Does the *kippa* help safeguard my identity against the evil inclination? (Talmud Shabbat)
- Do I proudly assert my distinct Jewish identity by wearing a *kippa* daily? (Mahari Bruna)
- Am I able to ensure my own religious distinctiveness and avoid imitating gentile norms? (*Taz*)
- Does the *kippa* help me avoid desecration of God's name by ensuring that my behavior is consonant with the values associated with the *kippa*? (Rabbi Moshe Feinstein)
- Does the *kippa* help me assert with pride my commitment towards a life of observance? (Rabbi Ovadia Yosef, Rabbi Eliezer Melamed)

REFLECTIONS WHILE WEARING TZITZIT:

- Do the tzitzit help me avoid religiously problematic behavior? Do they serve as a perpetual reminder of the choice between compliance and non-compliance to God's commandments? (Rashi)
- Do the tzitzit allow me to transform my evil inclination into a tool for positive religious growth? (Rabbi Nagen)
- Have I internalized the fact that the tzitzit serve as the uniform for the "kingdom of priests?" (Prof. Milgrom)
- Do the tzitzit help affirm my pride in my religious identity? (Rabbi Melamed)

- Are the tzitzit serving their function as an aid to reflection on Jewish theology – in particular, our relationship to God's role in history (the Exodus from Egypt) and our covenantal bond with Him (the covenant at Sinai)? (Ritva)
- Have I reflected upon the dynamic of worshiping God out of fear versus the more elevated worship from a place of love (sea symbolizing fear while the sky symbolizes love)? (*Kli Yakar*)
- Am I fully aware of the complex legal question regarding whether or not I am required to purchase a four-cornered garment and to obligate myself in the mitzva of tzitzit? (Abrabanel versus the *Shulchan Arukh*)
- Have I fully internalized the value of "opting-in" to commandments that are not formally required? (Tosafot, Rambam, Rosh)
- Am I able to affirm mitzvot as opportunities for connection, as opposed to obligations I may try to circumvent? (Rambam, Rabbi Yonah)
- Can I fully appreciate the status of tzitzit as the collective uniform of those who have "opted-in" to a life of commitment? (Rabbi Moshe Feinstein)
- Am I able to reflect on tzitzit as signifying a divine servitude based on love and devotion and not fear and coercion? (Rabbi Asher Weiss)

REFLECTIONS WHEN GETTING DRESSED IN THE MORNING:

- Have I fully internalized the power of clothing to help prevent cultural assimilation? (Midrash, *Meshekh Chokhma*)
- Do I understand the way in which clothing helps affirm the nationalist component of Judaism committed to a uniquely Jewish cultural ideal? (Rabbi Akiva Yosef Schlesinger)
- Am I able to reflect upon the Torah's modesty ethic and how clothing affirms our commitment to this value? (Maharik, Rabbi Moshe Isserles)
- Am I fully aware of the extent to which I choose my clothing based on a desire to culturally assimilate? (Midrash)

- Am I mindful of the unique forms of Jewish identity as expressed before and after the giving of the Torah? (Rabbi Moshe Feinstein)
- Am I aware of the power of Jewish customs to affirm Torah values and serve as a medium for sanctifying God's name? (Talmud Sanhedrin)

REFLECTIONS WHEN RECITING *BIRKAT HATORAH*:

- Do I understand Torah study as an entry point to developing a relationship with God and understanding His essence? (Talmud, Rabbi Sacks)
- Am I able to reflect upon the obligation to study Torah daily? (Shmuel)
- Can I appreciate how *Birkat HaTorah* highlights my own unique relationship with Torah? (R. Yochanan)
- Can I appreciate how *Birkat HaTorah* highlights the Torah as the national treasure of the Jewish people? (R. Hamnuna)
- Do I appreciate how Torah study is a multi-faceted mitzva containing a fixed obligation, a strong individualist component, and a communal/national element? (R. Pappa)
- Do I understand our intrinsic and profound connection to Torah study and the latent awareness it creates? (*Tosafot*, Rav Soloveitchik)
- Do I view Torah study as contextualizing our entire religious life? (*Shibbolei HaLeket*)
- Do I recognize the daily opportunities to reflect and engage in conversations about Torah? (*Shibbolei HaLeket*)

REFLECTIONS WHEN WEARING TEFILLIN:

- Do I appreciate the educational role of tefillin, especially when contrasted with ancient amulets? (Dr. Tigay)
- Am I able to affirm the theological assumptions inherent in the biblical passages in the tefillin? (Rabbi Melamed)
- Do I understand the model of Torah study symbolized by tefillin? (Tractate Tefillin, Rabbi Nagen)

- Am I aware of the challenges of the perpetual divine awareness demanded by tefillin? (*Shulchan Arukh*)
- Do the tefillin prompt me to reflect on Jewish pride? Moreover, am I aware how the internalizing of the Torah's values helps generate an added appreciation for God and His commandments among both Jews and gentiles? (Talmud, Margaliot HaShas)

REFLECTIONS BEFORE PRAYER:

- Do I experience prayer as a direct divine encounter? (Rav Soloveitchik)
- Am I aware of prayer's ability to create a more refined character? (Rabbi Albo)
- Do I fully appreciate how, by changing myself, I make it possible for my prayers to be answered? (Rabbi Albo, Mishna Avot)
- Am I able to think about the substance of my desires and ask myself if my will truly aligns with the will of God? (Rav Soloveitchik)
- Do I appreciate humanity's limited power and appreciate our ultimate dependence on God? (Rav Soloveitchik)
- Am I able to neutralize my own ego by acknowledging the often trivial nature of my requests? (Rabbi Dov Ber)
- Do I appreciate the ability of prayer to facilitate a God-centric life? (Rabbi Heschel)

REFLECTIONS WHEN PRAYING WITH A
MINYAN AND/OR IN THE SYNAGOGUE:

- Do I acknowledge the centralizing power of the synagogue in creating a shared sacred space for the community? (*Chafetz Chayim*)
- Do I appreciate the cosmic efficacy of communal prayer? (Talmud, Rambam)
- Am I able to fully experience prayers related to the sanctity of God that are recited only in the presence of a *minyan*? (Talmud)
- Do I recognize the impact of mitzvot performed by a group versus those performed by individuals? (*Chafetz Chayim*)

- Am I able to fully reflect on my own spiritual shortcomings and how we need others to complement us in our experience of prayer? (*Kuzari*)
- Can I fully appreciate prayer as an experience of self-transcendence, in which thinking of others is an essential part of what it means to pray? (Talmud, Rav Kook)
- Do I understand the power of collectively sanctifying God's name by affirming our shared theology in a group setting? (Talmud, Rosh)
- Am I able to affirm my own confidence in the efficacay of prayer? (Rabbi Moshe Feinstein)

REFLECTIONS BEFORE PRAYING FROM A SIDDUR:

- Am I able to connect to God during moments of crisis, thus acknowledging my dependence on the Divine? (Rambam, Ramban)
- Do I appreciate prayer from the prayer book as an exercise in religious consistency? (Rabban Gamliel)
- Am I able to focus on prayer as a spontaneous encounter with God? (R. Eliezer)
- Does the siddur allow me to locate personal meaning in the context of my daily routine? (R. Yehoshua)
- Can I effectively ensure that my prayer experience is supplicatory and not burdensome? (Rabbi Yosef Karo)
- Does the siddur allow me to existentially reflect on my current religious state and identify aspects of my life that are not addressed by the formal liturgy? (Mar, the son of Ravina)

REFLECTIONS BEFORE PRAYING IN HEBREW:

- Do I view the prayer experience as an appeal to divine mercy? (Talmud)
- Do I consciously try to maximize the chances for my prayers to be heard? (Rif)
- Am I aware of prayer and the role of angelic intermediaries? (Rif)

- Am I mindful of the importance of utilizing precise language in my daily prayer? (Rosh)
- Am I conscious of the primacy of proper intent when praying? (*Sefer Hasidim*)
- Have I internalized the unique metaphysical status of the Hebrew language? (*Hafetz Hayim*)
- Am I aware of the challenges of properly translating the Hebrew text? (*Mishna Berura*, Rabbi Moshe Sofer)
- Can I fully appreciate prayer and its role in unifying Jews internationally? (Rabbi Eliezar b. David Fleckeles)
- Am I mindful of the role of Hebrew in preserving communal identity? (Rabbi Weinberg)
- Am I aware of personal prayer in the vernacular as a means of facilitating fluid conversation with the Divine? (Rabbi Nachman of Breslov)

REFLECTIONS BEFORE RECITING THE *SHEMA*:

- Do I appreciate the way in which *Shema* affirms Torah study as a religious experience and not just an intellectual exercise? (Rav Soloveitchik)
- Do I appreciate how *Shema* allows me to reflect daily on central theological concepts such as God's oneness, divine providence, reward and punishment, and the Exodus from Egypt? (verses in Deuteronomy and Numbers)
- Am I mindful of the centrality of Jewish theology and the way that it provides the proper context for authentic Jewish observance? (Mishna Berakhot)
- Do I fully understand the *Shema*'s unique role in defending traditional Jewish theology from external threats? (Dr. Tigay)
- Do I feel a profound connection to the millions of Jews who lived before me and who affirmed their faith by reciting the *Shema*? (Rav Soloveitchik)
- Do I appreciate how *Shema* allows me to affirm a commitment to trying my best to pass on the tradition of my forefathers to my children? (Tractate Pesachim)

- Do I have the requisite intent and fully accept God's sovereignty and oneness? (*Shulchan Arukh*)
- Am I able to appreciate Judaism's unique theology and its national, philosophical, and eschatological significance? (Rashi, Rambam, Rashbam)

REFLECTIONS BEFORE TORAH STUDY:

- Am I aware of the primacy of Torah study in the rabbinic tradition?
- Do I appreciate the potential metaphysical impact of Torah study? (Rashbi)
- Am I mindful of the challenges of balancing time between the physical and the spiritual? (R. Yishmael, Rabbi Moshe Feinstein)
- Am I aware that Torah study has the power to highlight the unique qualities of each individual? (*Or Sameach*)
- Am I able to ensure that Torah study is a permanent feature of my day? (*Mishna Berura*)
- Does my Torah study generate a sense of responsibility for sharing Torah with others? (*Avot DeRebbe Natan*)

REFLECTIONS BEFORE CHOOSING A TEXT TO STUDY:

- Do I feel personally connected to the texts that I study? (Tractate Avoda Zara)
- Am I aware of the rabbis' larger educational vision? (Tractate Kiddushin)
- Am I able to find personal meaning in the context of the fixed rabbinic system? (Ritva)
- Can I fully appreciate the integrated and organic nature of Torah study? (Rabbeinu Tam)
- Am I aware of the rabbinic insistence on choosing texts to study that mirror personal emotional and developmental growth? (Mishna Avot)
- Do I appreciate Torah learning as an exercise in affirming Jewish theology, history, and the law as a value-based system? (Mishna Avot)

- Am I mindful of Torah study in the world of an ever-expanding Jewish library? (*Shaarei Knesset HaGedola*)
- Am I aware of the importance of being familiar with the expansive scope of Jewish tradition? (Tractate Berakhot)
- Do I fully identify with the need to ensure that Torah study reaches a wide audience? (Rav Kook)

REFLECTIONS ON WASHING HANDS BEFORE MEALS:

- Am I fully cognizant of the activities that I use my hands for in the context of my day? (Maharal)
- Am I mindful of the extent to which my hands are utilized to actualize a more elevated vision for my life? (Rabbi Krumbein)
- Does this ritual washing put me in touch with my yearning for the rebuilding of the Temple and my connection to the world of the priesthood?
- Does washing my hands help contextualize my eating experience with an ethic of sanctity? (Talmud)
- Am I aware of the way in which washing in an exilic reality allows me to meditate on the purity laws that are unfortunately no longer operative? (Talmud, *Tosafot*)
- Am I mindful of the central role of rabbinic interpretation in continuing to apply the values of the Torah in changing circumstances? (Talmud)

REFLECTIONS BEFORE RECITING *BIRKAT HAMAZON*:

- Do I fully understand how reciting *Birkat HaMazon* reminds us to place our prosperity in context and appreciate the humble beginnings of the Jewish People? (Ramban)
- Does reciting *Birkat HaMazon* help me overcome my natural inclination to forget God after achieving economic success? (*Meshekh Chokhma*)
- Do I remember the Jewish People's time in the desert and understand it as highlighting our dependency on God? (Talmud, Rabbi Melamed)

- Am I able to affirm our ultimate goal of partnering with God in perfecting the world as symbolized by our working of the Land of Israel? (Rabbi Melamed)
- Am I mindful of the role that the Land of Israel plays in actualizing divine ideals, even outside the context of codified law? (Rabbi Haggai London)
- Do I understand the profound connection between the Land of Israel, the covenant of circumcision, and the centrality of Torah observance as precursors to entering the Land? (Talmud, Rashi)
- Am I able to affirm the centrality of Jerusalem, and the unique theological message of the Temple, as symbols of Jewish sovereignty? (Talmud, Prof. Kaufman)
- Do I feel the ever-unfolding drama of Jewish history and maintain a continued posture of hope and optimism during the period of exile? (Talmud, Rabbi Sacks)

REFLECTIONS WHILE OBSERVING THE LAWS OF *KASHRUT*:

- Am I able to reflect on the biblical ideal of healthy living and eating? (*Sefer HaChinukh*)
- Do I fully understand the religious value of consuming food that will maximize my chances for long-term survival so that I can actualize my spiritual mission in the physical world? (*Sefer HaChinukh*)
- Am I able to appreciate the spiritual symbolism of certain kosher foods and try to distance myself from the negative religious traits associated with non-kosher food? (Rabbi Hirsch)
- Am I able to meditate upon the spiritual self-discipline that committing to a life of *kashrut* observance facilitates? (*Akedat Yitzchak*, Rav Soloveitchik)
- Do I understand the role of food legislation in preserving the distinctive cultural and religious qualities of the Jewish People? (Bible, Shadal, Prof. Milgrom)
- Do I feel a part of the ongoing rabbinic objective to preserve the values of Jewish uniqueness in constantly changing historical circumstances? (Talmud, *Tosafot*, Rashba)

REFLECTIONS WHILE AIMING TO RECITE
ONE HUNDRED BLESSINGS PER DAY:

- Am I able to affirm that God is the source of all blessings? (Rashba)
- Does reciting blessings allow me to develop a more acute and sophisticated God-consciousness? (Midrash Tehillim, Rambam)
- Does reciting blessings help me understand that our physical desires are intended to help facilitate spirituality? (Rabbi Hirsch)
- Do blessings recited before the performance of mitzvot contextualize the performance of mitzvot by affirming their ability to religiously impact the person performing them? (Rabbi Hirsch)
- Do I view the recitation of blessings as a way of recapturing a sense of divine intimacy? (*Kli Yakar*)
- Am I aware that blessings are meant to facilitate an increased sense of fear of Hashem and a more self-transcendent religious posture? (Rashi, Rabbi Wolbe)
- Am I mindful of the way in which reciting more than the required one-hundred blessings per day personalizes my relationship with God? (*Tanya*)

REFLECTIONS WHEN REFRAINING FROM RECITING
BLESSINGS ON INTERPERSONAL COMMANDMENTS:

- Do I fully appreciate the (rejected) minority voices in the Jewish tradition that require blessings to be recited even before performing interpersonal commandments? (Rabbi Yitzchak Isaac Safrin of Komarno)
- Am I aware of the religious significance of reciting a blessing in vain? (Rashba)
- Do I fully understand the idea of "perpetual mitzvot?" Am I able to reflect on my readiness to be constantly willing and able to engage these obligations? (*Or Zarua*)
- Do I fully affirm traditional conceptions of Jewish uniqueness? (*Torah Temima*)
- Am I able to think carefully about my relationship to revealed laws versus rationally intuitive legislation? (*Arukh HaShulchan*)

- Am I fully mindful of traditional notions of "commandedness" and its parameters? (*Seridei Eish*)
- Am I able to ensure that I never make people feel like "objects" in my attempt to fulfill the will of the Divine? (*Seridei Eish*)

REFLECTIONS WHILE ATTEMPTING TO OBSERVE THE MITZVA OF "WALKING IN GOD'S WAYS":

- Do I fully appreciate the central role of righteousness and justice in the Jewish tradition? (Seforno)
- Am I able to develop a reputation that is defined by divine virtues? (*Sifrei*)
- Am I able to invest heavily in actions that help mold a more divinely centered character? (Talmud Sota)
- Do I appreciate the religious significance of choosing groups of friends that help to develop a more refined character? (*Sifrei,* Rambam)
- Do I fully understand the role of activities that are not specifically religious, such as humor, in developing a balanced and holistic Judaic worldview? (Rav Soloveitchik, Rabbi Feldman)
- Am I fully mindful of the fact that ensuring all of our actions are value-based is a fulfillment of the biblical ethic of following in God's ways? (Leviticus Rabba)

REFLECTIONS WHILE BEING MINDFUL OF THE MITZVA TO LOVE GOD:

- Do I realize that loving God is the source of our mitzva observance? (Ibn Ezra)
- Do I understand the historic impact of the Jewish obligation to love God? (Rabbi Hertz)
- Do I recognize how loving God contextualizes our love for Torah and the Jewish people? (Rabbi Tzadok)
- Am I able to reflect on my own love of God and my responsibility to share my love with others? (*Sifrei,* Rambam)
- Am I able to reflect on my ethical behavior and ask if my conduct inspires others to love of God and the Torah? (Talmud)

- Do I appreciate the mystery of the universe and see philosophy, metaphysics, and study of natural sciences as means to know God and engender feelings of love? (Rambam)
- Do I utilize the divine values that underlie the mitzvot, as well as God's providential role in human affairs, as springboards to inspire feelings of love? (*Sifrei*, Rambam)
- Am I constantly trying to look for ways to kindle latent feeling of divine love? (Baal Shem Tov)

REFLECTIONS UPON SEEING THE MEZUZA:

- Am I fully mindful of central claims of Jewish theology, such as the importance of Torah study, God's oneness, and the Exodus from Egypt? (Rabbi Bachya)
- Do I always try to behave according to the values and ideals symbolized by the mezuza? (*Chizkuni*)
- Do I appreciate the Torah's claim that God's statutes are equally as applicable in the home as they are in the synagogue? (Dr. Tigay)
- Am I able to affirm my commitment to the idea that God is the source of all power and that, ultimately, the material blessings we receive are rooted in Him? (Dr. Gordon, Rabbi Bachya)
- Am I aware of the how the centrality of the Land of Israel is reflected in the laws of the mezuza? (Talmud, Rashi, Rav Kook)
- Am I able to reflect on the connection between the mitzva of mezuza and the Torah's promise of longevity for those who observe this precept? (*Shulchan Arukh, Shakh, Taz*)

REFLECTIONS BEFORE RECITING THE BEDTIME *SHEMA*:

- Do I appreciate how this mitzva allows me to evaluate my accomplishments during the past day and examine the extent to which my actions reflected the values of the Torah? (*Metzudat David*)
- Am I able to ensure that the thoughts that I have while going to bed are consistent with the Torah's ideas and ideals? (Yerushalmi, Meiri)

- Am I able to reaffirm my acceptance of divine sovereignty, as well as a life committed to Jewish law? (Kolbo)
- Can I regard sleeping as a religiously meaningful attempt to strengthen my body to allow maximal fulfillment of God's laws? (Talmud, *Tzelach*)

Bibliography

Adler, Eli. *Tefillat Yesharim: Iyun Emuni BeYesodot HaTefilla*. Kiryat Arba: M'Emek Hevron, 2003.

Amital, Yehudah. "Ya'akov Was Reciting the Shema," adapted by Dov Karoll. http://etzion.org.il/en/yaakov-was-reciting-shema.

Beasly, Yaakov. "Kashrut and Understanding: Part Two." http://etzion.org.il/en/kashrut-and-understanding-part-two.

Benovitz, Moshe. *Talmud HaIggud: Meaimatay Korein at Shema*. Jerusalem: HaIggud LeParshanut HaTalmud, 2006.

Berger, Michael. *Rabbinic Authority*. New York/Oxford: Oxford University Press, 1998.

Blau, Yitzchak. *Fresh Fruits and Vintage Wine: The Ethics and Wisdom of the Aggada*. Brooklyn: Ktav, 2009.

——— "Flexibility with a Firm Foundation: On Maintaining Jewish Dogma." *The Torah U-Madda Journal* 12 (2004): 179-191.

Blidstein, Gerald. "Kaddish and Other Accidents." *Tradition* 14:3 (Spring 1974): 80-85.

Brofsky, David. "Washing Hands Upon Waking and Before Prayer." http://etzion.org.il/en/washing-hands-upon-waking-and-prayer.

Cover, Robert. "The Supreme Court, 1982 Term – Foreword: Nomos and Narrative." *Harvard Law Review* 97 (1983): 4-68.

Eider, Shimon. *Halachos of Pesach*. Jerusalem/New York: Feldheim, 1985.

Feldman, Daniel. *Does God Have a Sense of Humor?*. https://www.ou.org/jewish_action/05/2013/does-god-have-a-sense-of-humor/.

Gilat, Yitzchak. *Perakim BeHishtalshelut HaHalakha*. Ramat Gan: Bar Ilan University, 1992.

Gordon, Martin. "Mezuza: Protective Amulet or Religious Symbol." *Tradition* 16:4 (Summer 1977): 7-40.

Halivni, David Weiss. *Midrash, Mishna, and Gemara: The Jewish Predilection for Justified Law.* Cambridge: Harvard University Press, 1986.

Hartman, David. "Prayer and Religious Consciousness: An Analysis of Jewish Prayer in the Works of Joseph B. Soloveitchik, Yeshayahu Leibowitz and Abraham Joshua Heschel," *Modern Judaism* 23:2 (2003): 105-125.

Hayes, Christine. *Between the Babylonian and Palestinian Talmuds: Accounting for Halakhic Difference in Selected Sugyot from Tractate Avoda Zara.* New York/ Oxford: Oxford University Press, 1997.

Hertz, J.H., ed. *The Pentateuch and Haftorahs: Hebrew Text English Translation and Commentary: Second Edition.* London: The Soncino Press, 1972.

Heschel, Abraham Joshua. *Moral Granduer and Spiritual Audacity: Essays.* Edited by Susannah Heschel. New York: Farrar, Straus and Giroux, 1996.

Held, Shai. *Abraham Joshua Heschel: The Call of Transcendence.* Bloomington/ Indianapolis: Indiana University Press, 2013.

Kaufman, Yehezkel. *The Religion of Israel: From Its Beginnings to the Babylonian Exile.* Translated and abridged by Moshe Greenberg. Chicago: The University of Chicago Press, 1960.

Kook, Avraham Yitzchak Hakohen. *Talelei Orot with Commentary from Haggai London,* Eli: Machon Binyan Hatorah, 2011.

———. "Chacham Adif M'navi." In *Orot.* Jerusalem: Mossad HaRav Kook, 2005.

Krumbeim, Elyakim. *Mussar For Moderns.* Jersey City: Ktav, 2004.

———. "B'Din Netilat Yadayim." http://www.etzion.org.il/he/.

Korobkin, N. Daniel. *The Kuzari: In Defense of a Despised Faith.* Jerusalem/New York: Feldheim, 2009.

Lamm, Norman. *The Shema: Spirituality and Law in Judaism.* Philadelphia/Jerusalem: Jewish Publication Society, 2000.

Leibowitz, Nechama. *New Studies in Vayikra.* Jerusalem: Haomanim Press, 1996.

Lichtenstein, Aharon. *Leaves of Faith: The World of Jewish Learning Volume 1.* Jersey City: Ktav, 2003.

———. "Make Your Torah Permanent: The Centrality of Torah Study," adapted by Rabbi Reuven Ziegler. http://etzion.org.il/en/make-your-torah-permanent-centrality-torah-study.

———. "These Are the Generations of Noach." http://etzion.org.il/en/these-are-generations-noach.

Lichstenstein, Mayer. "Hadevarim Haeleh: The Connection Between Keriat Shema and Torah Study." *Mishlav* 31 (1997): 35-44.

London, Haggai. "Look Under Judaism: Theoretical Thinking About Basic Concepts in Judaism." *Yediot Achronot*, 2015.

Melamed, Eliezer. *Peninei Halakha Likutim 1*. Israel: Machon Har Beracha, 2006.

———. "Hichlot Netilat Yadim Shel Schacharit." http://www.yeshiva.org.il/midrash/1946.

———. "Tumat Hayadayim." http://ph.yhb.org.il/10-02-01/.

———. "Mashmaut Birkat Hazan." http://ph.yhb.org.il/10-04-03/.

———. "Merkaziyuta Shel Birachat Haaretz." http://ph.yhb.org.il/10-04-04/.

Milgrom, Jacob. *The JPS Torah Commentary Numbers*. Philadelphia/New York: Jewish Publications Society, 1990.

Nagen, Yakov. *Waking Up to a New Day*. Jerusalem: Koren, 2013.

———. "Todah Al HaTorah." https://yakovn.wordpress.com/tag/.

———. "Tefilatam Shel Tannaim: Bein Keva L'zerima." http://www.daat.ac.il/chazal/maamar.asp?id=139.

———. "Netilat Yadim Shel Boker: Yeud Mechadash." https://yakovn.wordpress.com/2006/11/10/.

Naor, Betzalel. "Two Types of Prayer." *Tradition* 25:3 (Spring 1991): 26-34.

Rackefet, Aaron Rothkoff. *The Rav: The World of Rabbi Joseph Soloveitchik, Volume Two*. New Jersey: Ktav, 1999.

Sacks, Jonathan, ed. *The Koren Siddur with Introduction, Translation, and Commentary by Rabbi Jonathan Sacks*. Jerusalem: Koren, 2009.

Sacks, Yonason. *Orchot Yamim: Insights into the Laws of Kriyat Shema and Prayer*. Passaic: Rabbi Yonason Sacks, 2007.

Schachter, Tzvi., *Nefesh HaRav*. Jerusalem: Reishit Yerushalayim, 1995.

Schneerson, Menachem Mendel. *On the Essence of Chassidus*. Brooklyn: Kehot Publication Society, 1986.

Silber, Michael. "The Emergence of Ultra-Orthodoxy: The Invention of a Tradition." In *The Uses of Tradition: Jewish Continuity Since Emancipation*, edited by Jack Wertheimer. New York: JTS, distributed by Harvard University Press, 1992.

Soloveitchik, Meir. *Locusts, Giraffes, and the Meaning of Kashrut*. http://azure.org.il/include/print.php?id=151.

———. "God's Beloved: A Defense of Chosenness." http://azure.org.il/article.php?id=201.

Soloveitchik, Joseph B. *Yemei Zikkaron*, edited by Moshe Krone. Jerualem: World Zionist Organization, 1986.

———— *Worship of the Heart: Essays on Jewish Prayer*, edited by Shalom Carmy. Jersey City: Ktav, 2003.

————*Shiurei HaRav*: "On the Love of Torah: Impromptu Remarks at a Siyyum", prepared by M. Kasdan. In *A Conspectus of the Public Lectures of Joseph D. Soloveitchik*, 181-186. Hoboken: Ktav, 1974.

———— *The Lonely Man of Faith*. New York: Doubleday, 1992.

———— "Redemption, Prayer and Talmud Torah," *Tradition* 17:2 (Spring 1978): 55-72.

———— "Prayer as Dialogue." In *Reflections of the Rav, Volume One*, edited by Abraham Besdin. World Zionist Organization, 1979.

———— *Festival of Freedom: Essays on Pesach and the Haggadah,* edited by Joel B. Wolowesly and Reuven Ziegler. Jersey City: Ktav, 2006.

———— "Kashrut and Kedushah of the Body and Soul." Cited in "Parashat Shemini 5776, 2016," by David Etengoff. http://www.reparashathashavuah.org/blog-rabbi-david-etengoff-parashat-hashavuah/parashat-shemini-5776-2016kashrut-and-kedushah-of-the-body-and-soul.

———— Citation in Rakeffet-Rotthkoff, Aaron. *The Rav: The World of Rabbi Joseph Soloveitchik, Volume Two* (New Jersey: Ktav, 1999)

———— Citation in Navon, Chaim. *Theological Issues in Sefer Bereishit, Lecture #24 The Akieda*, http://etzion.org.il/en/akeida

Sperber, Daniel. *On the Relationship of Mitzvot between Man and His Neighbor and Man and His Maker*. Jerusalem/New York: Urim Publications, 2014.

Taragin, Moshe. *Dividing One's Time for Torah Study*. http://etzion.org.il/en/dividing-ones-time-torah-study.

Tecumseh. *Works of Tecumseh*. https://www.goodreads.com/author/quotes/8340698. Tecumseh.

Tigay, Jeffery. *The JPS Torah Commentary: Deuteronomy*. Philadelphia/New York: The Jewish Publication Society, 1996.

Weiss, Asher. *Minchat Asher Bereishit*. Jerusalem: Machon Minchat Asher, 2007.

————"Tzitzit and Techelet." http://www.torahbase.org/733/.

———— "Circumventing Mitzvot." http://www.torahbase.org/5774-6/.

Wolbe, Shlomo. *Alei Shur*. Jerusalem: Beit Hamussar, תשמה.

Ziegler, Reuven. *Majesty and Humility: The Thought of Rabbi Joseph B. Soloveitchik*. Jerusalem/New York: Urim Publications, 2012.

Zimmer, Eric. "Men's Headcovering: The Metamorphisis of the Practice," In *Reverence, Righteousness and Rahmanut: Essays in Memory of Dr. Leo Jung,* edited by Rabbi Jacob J. Schachter. Northvale, New Jersey: Jason Aronson, 1992.

The fonts used in this book are from the Arno Koren family.